INDIA: GOVERNMENT AND POLITICS IN A DEVELOPING NATION

INDIA

GOVERNMENT AND POLITICS IN A DEVELOPING NATION

Robert L. Hardgrave, Jr.

The University of Texas at Austin

Harcourt, Brace & World, Inc.

New York / Chicago / San Francisco / Atlanta

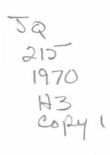
ACKNOWLEDGMENTS For permission to use previously published material grateful acknowledgement is made to the following:

Government and Opposition. For Table 7–3 from Paul R. Brass, "Political Participation, Institutionalization and Stability in India."

Hutchinson Publishing Group Ltd. For Tables 7–1 and 7–2 adapted from W. H. Morris-Jones, *Government and Politics in India.*

Princeton University Press. For Table 6–2 from Stanley A. Kochanek, *The Congress Party in India.* Copyright © 1968 by Princeton University Press. Table p. xxii. For the 1952 figures in Table 7–3 from Myron Weiner, ed., *State Politics in India.* Copyright © 1968 by Princeton University Press. Table 1.13, p. 46. Both selections reprinted by permission of Princeton University Press.

Yale University Press. For Figure 1–1 adapted from Samuel P. Huntington, *Political Order in Changing Societies.* Reprinted by permission of Yale University Press.

MAPS Harbrace

© 1970 by Harcourt, Brace & World, Inc.

ISBN: 0-15-541350-3
Library of Congress Catalog Card Number: 78-110506
Printed in the United States of America

PREFACE

THIS BOOK, COMPLETED DURING THE EVENTS OF 1969 THAT OPENED A new era in Indian politics, seeks to provide an introduction to the problems of political development through the study of a single nation. India, one of the first new states to emerge from colonial rule after the Second World War, has confronted a wide range of problems, and dramatizes, perhaps more than any other developing nation, the crisis posed by the limited capacity of institutions to respond to expanding participation and rapidly increasing demands.

Although the book reflects a particular theoretical perspective, it is not essentially theoretical, either in content or in purpose. It seeks not to argue for a particular theory but to illuminate the problems of political development in the context of a single nation. It is designed to provide a sense of the cultural and historical milieu in which political development takes place and to give a balanced treatment of both structure and process, of both institutions and behavior, in Indian politics. India provides the framework, then, in which problems of political development common to a major portion of the world are explored.

Written primarily for undergraduates, the book is intended to enhance comparative government courses by illustrating the range of variation and the degree of similarity in political life throughout the world. Study of a non-Western nation—and India is the case par excellence—gives students a concrete example of political development and helps broaden their understanding of the growing importance of the non-Western world. In courses on Indian politics the book can be used as the core textbook with a selection of supplemental readings, perhaps concerning policy formation and implementation, that would allow students to analyze the actual operation of the Indian political system through close examination of one problem.

A brief list of valuable readings, most of them easily accessible, follows each chapter. At the end of the book is a research guide to source material dealing with Indian politics.

I wish to express my appreciation to Henry C. Hart of the University of Wisconsin and to James Roach and Tom Jannuzi of the University of Texas, who read the manuscript in its entirety and provided invaluable criticism. Thanks go also to Lloyd and Susanne Rudolph for permission to adapt the research guide they developed for their courses at the University of Chicago. Finally, I am grateful to Duncan Forrester of Madras Christian College and to N. Ram of the *Hindu* for their suggestions on the final draft. For all my appreciation to those who assisted me and stimulated my thought, however, I alone bear the responsibility for what appears here.

ROBERT L. HARDGRAVE, JR.

CONTENTS

LIST OF TABLES AND FIGURES

Tables

Figures

I

THE CHALLENGE OF DEVELOPMENT

IN 1967, THE LONG PERIOD OF CONGRESS DOMINANCE IN INDIA CAME TO an end as the party was swept from office in half the states and secured only a narrow majority at the Center. In November 1969, the Congress itself was torn apart after four months of inner-party conflict. The truncated leadership of the party organization, isolating itself from the will of the majority, expelled Prime Minister Indira Gandhi, daughter of Nehru, from the Congress. In the centenary year of Mahatma Gandhi's birth, two Congress parties fought for the tattered standard of the nationalist movement.

India, the world's largest democracy, with an electorate of 250 million people, passed a threshold, leaving behind the fragile stability of two decades for an indeterminate political future—a future dominated by scarcity and by what Adlai Stevenson once called "the revolution of rising expectations." These expectations, however, have more often than not turned into frustrations. Politically conscious, increasingly participant, India's masses are an awakening force that has yet to find coherence and direction. The image of spiritual, Gandhian India pales before continuous agitation, intermittent rioting, and advocacy of violent revolution. The turbulence of modern India brings into focus processes of change experienced throughout the Third World.

The Process of Political Development

In the study of comparative politics, the developing nations in Africa and Asia have become a critical focus of concern. Traditionally, these "exotic" areas were ignored in the introductory comparative course or, at most, were examined as colonial adjuncts to the nations of Europe. In the years following the Second World War, however, the emergent nations of the Third World became an arena of conflict in the cold war: Their stability and development became the objects of awakened American policy concern and of academic interest. At the same time sensitivity to political behavior and process increased, and the theory and methodology of the other social sciences were brought to bear on problems of comparative politics. The new nations became laboratories for the analysis of social and political change.

Seeking fulfillment of their aspirations after independence, the nationalist élites of the new states have committed themselves to rapid economic growth and social transformation. They aim to bring their countries into the modern world without loss of cultural integrity, to enable them to share what they see as the better life of an expanding technological-scientific world culture. The aspiration after modernity is almost universal: Few leaders are willing to relegate their nations to ethnographic museums—fewer still have the choice.

The Impact of Change

The impact of accelerating change has left few areas of the world unaffected and has increasingly dislocated traditional patterns of behavior. The process of modernization involves change in the structure of society, in its attitudinal framework, and in its capacity to respond effectively to stress imposed upon the system. It involves the shift from a predominantly rural, agricultural society to an increasingly urban, industrial society, characterized by a cash and market economy, occupational differentiation, high literacy, and media access. The parochial world of tradition is penetrated by mass transport and communications facilities. The ascriptive determination of status by birth gives way to achievement orientations. The identity horizon of the individual expands beyond the particularistic loyalties of family, village, and tribe to include increasingly universalistic and secular values. Passive fatalism is supplanted by a feeling of ability to control the physical and social environment. The past is no longer the touchstone of behavior. Authority sanctioned by age, status, or divine sustenance no longer commands unquestioned obedience. These changes are the catalyst of the "participation explosion" of demands by new groups seeking access to the political system. Modern society is a participant society.

Economic and social changes in the process of modernization may be more indicative of the disintegration of traditional society than of the creation of a viable modern society. The process may be highly disruptive, more productive of decay than of development. The essential quality of modernity lies in "an enduring capacity to generate and absorb persistent transformation."[1] The fundamental problem of the political system is to control and direct the process of change, to be its master, not its victim. Political development is "a process by which a political system acquires an increased capacity to sustain successfully and continuously new types of goals and demands and the creation of new types of organizations."[2] This process may involve a common content, but it does not involve a definable "end product" or "final stage." It cannot be measured in terms of socio-economic indicators, nor is the path of change unilinear. Political development is "a process of meeting new goals and demands in a flexible manner."[3]

No society is wholly traditional or wholly modern. The character and direction of change will be the product of a dialectical interaction between "tradition" and "modernity," as each infiltrates and transforms the other.[4] The relationship between tradition and modernity—the degree to which tradition is accommodated in the process of change, the ways it responds to the challenge of modernization—is a critical determinant of stability and development. The bargain struck with the forces of tradition may buy short-term stability at the price of revolution, but a failure to adapt to the context of tradition, to use traditional structures as the vehicles of change, may so undermine stability as to prevent the development of the institutional capacity to fulfill the promise of transformation.

The commitment to modernization in the new nations has given primacy to politics. "Seek ye first the political kingdom," Kwame Nkrumah of Ghana declared, "and all things shall be added unto you."[5] Development, however, involves not merely the will but the capacity

[1] Manfred Halpern, "The Rate and Costs of Political Development," *The Annals* (March 1965), p. 22.
[2] Alfred Diamant, "The Nature of Political Development," in Jason L. Finkle and Richard W. Gable, eds., *Political Development and Social Change* (New York: Wiley, 1966), p. 92.
[3] *Ibid.*
[4] Lloyd I. and Susanne H. Rudolph, *The Modernity of Tradition: Political Development in India* (Chicago: University of Chicago Press, 1967), p. 3.
[5] *Ghana: The Autobiography of Kwame Nkrumah* (Camden, N.J.: Thomas Nelson & Sons, 1957), p. 163.

to change, and the institutional capacity to absorb change may be dis-
proportionately small in comparison to the aspiration after change. The
low level of institutionalization may be seen "in the weakness of the
administration, in the lack of the stability and continuity of basic political symbols and administrative and political frameworks, and also in
the relative weakness and underdevelopment of various autonomous
interest groups."[6] The rising level of political demands, stimulated in
part by the efforts of the élite to secure progress and economic growth,
may so strain the limited capacity of the system that institutionalization
becomes increasingly difficult as participation expands. The process of
modernization may unleash a "revolution of rising frustrations" as the
gap widens between aspiration and achievement. Reform may serve to
foster in the masses aspirations that become the catalyst of revolution.
Regional, linguistic, and cultural minorities may become more self-
conscious, and as primordial identifications are injected into political
life, traditional communities may take on the modern form of tribe and
caste associations or of movements advocating separatism or linguistic
nationalism. Conflict increases as new groups become participant, but if
they lack the minimum consensus necessary for the ordered resolution of
conflict, the political system may be unable to accommodate expanded
participation by means of its institutions. Insofar as the system can respond to newly mobilized groups and to accelerating demands, participation strengthens the system and reinforces its legitimacy. When the
system is unable to absorb new demands, however, participation causes
instability.

The Dynamic Gap Between Participation and Institutionalization

"The primary problem of politics," writes Samuel P. Huntington, "is
the lag in the development of political institutions behind social and
economic change."[7]

> Political modernization involves the extension of political con-
> sciousness to new social groups and the mobilization of these
> groups into politics. Political development involves the creation
> of political institutions sufficiently adaptable, complex, autono-
> mous, and coherent to absorb and order the participation of
> these new groups and to promote social and economic change
> in the society.[8]

[6] S. N. Eisenstadt, "Initial Institutional Patterns of Political Modernization," *Civili-
zations*, Vol. 12 (1962), pp. 461–72, reprinted in Claude E. Welch, Jr., ed.,
Political Modernization (Belmont, Calif.: Wadsworth, 1967), p. 261.
[7] *Political Order in Changing Societies* (New Haven, Conn.: Yale University Press,
1968), p. 5.
[8] *Ibid.*, p. 266.

The stability and development of any political system depends on the relationship between political institutionalization and political participation. As participation expands, the capacity of the political institutions to absorb change must also increase if stability is to be maintained.

If stability becomes the highest value, however, increased institutionalization may serve to create repressive order in which the expansion of participation is limited by the attempt to slow the process of social mobilization. This might be accomplished through the reinforcement of horizontal divisions within the society, slowing the entry of new groups into politics; through limitations on communications, reducing exposure to mass media and access to higher education; and through suppression of competition among political élites, minimizing uncontrolled mobilization of the masses, as factions or parties appeal for new bases of support.[9] A political élite committed to economic growth may stimulate the formation of demands in the process of inducing social change. Development programs may seek to create "felt needs" within the traditional society in order to facilitate innovation, but in an environment of scarcity, resources are limited, and the system will be most responsive to those commanding political capital—wealth, status, votes. Traditional élites may be reinforced to ensure stability and to suppress widening popular involvement. Repressive rule supplants democratic response in the name of order. Stability bought through repressive order, however, rather than through higher levels of institutionalization in response to expanding participation, may be the harbinger of chaos.

Development, defined as increasing institutionalization in response to expanding participation, may require a dynamic gap between the two variables. With participation somewhat beyond the capacity of the institutions to respond, the attempt to close the gap serves as the stimulus to higher levels of institutionalization. The interaction between institutionalization and participation, between order and response, thus involves a staggered process of development, as each reacts to the other. Beyond a critical range, however, an imbalance may be increasingly difficult to correct. Overinstitutionalization is conducive to the establishment of repressive order; participation far beyond institutional capacity may foster unacceptable instability and political decay.

The success of a political system in coping with the challenge of development is dependent upon its capacity to affect horizontal and vertical integration. The task of horizontal integration, of nation-building, is the creation of a new sense of community and common destiny among those who previously may have shared only the oppression of a common colonial master. The people in the polyglot states of Africa and Asia must extend their identity beyond the primordial bonds of tribe, caste, language, and region to embrace a more inclusive national community. Horizontal integration does not require that traditional

[9] *Ibid.*, pp. 234–37.

FIGURE 1–1

THE DEVELOPMENT PROCESS

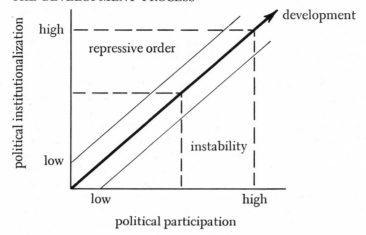

political participation

SOURCE: Adapted from Samuel P. Huntington, *Political Order in Changing Societies* (New Haven, Conn.: Yale University Press, 1968), p. 79.

sources of identity be abandoned, but they must be transcended. Ideology, perhaps combining elements of tradition and modernity, is the instrument for the creation of a new political culture of shared values, of a minimum consensus on fundamental goals and on the institutions of conflict resolution.

Horizontal integration may take place only to the degree that vertical integration is extensive in scope and penetrating in depth. The capacity of the system to generate and absorb change, to respond to demands of expanding participation, requires effective channels of linkage between mass and élite. The institutions of government must command confidence and be regarded as legitimate. They must have the capacity to initiate change and to control its direction and intensity. Channels of access and communication must be available if the system is to respond successfully to change. The political system cannot be simply the dependent variable in a changing world. It must possess the will and capacity to intervene actively in its environment. Through the formal institutions of government, as well as through interest groups and parties, the political system must provide an infrastructure capable of accommodating the rapidly increasing numbers seeking entry. The success of the developmental effort, within the range of available resources, will depend on the ability of these structures to acquire legitimacy and stability and to provide meaningful access and effective response.

What for the West took centuries the new nations seek now to accomplish in decades. The fundamental crises of integration and institutionalization, met sequentially in the West, confront the new nations simultaneously and imperatively.

The Context of Political Development in India

India, among the first of the colonies to emerge from the yoke of imperial rule, gained independence from Britain in 1947. Today it epitomizes both the problems of and the prospects for political development in the non-Western world. With an estimated 525 million people in 1970, India is the world's largest democracy. Its leadership, committed to a fundamental transformation of the society, is confronted by an almost overwhelming cultural diversity, by often intransigent traditions rooted in the village and in religious values, and by poverty bred by scarcity of known resources, ignorance, and staggering population growth.

Jawaharlal Nehru spoke of the "essential unity" of India, of a civilization that was "a world in itself" and gave shape to all things: "Some kind of a dream of unity has occupied the mind of India since the dawn of civilization," he said.[10] But the unity of India was more a quest than a reality. The diversity of India has given richness and variation to its traditions, but diversity has been accompanied by patterns of social and cultural fragmentation, historically rooted in and sanctioned by religion. Almost every known societal division can be found in India: The Indian people are divided by religion, sect, language, caste, dress, and even by the food they eat. These divisions are compounded by the chasm between the rich and poor, between the English-speaking élite and the vernacular mass, between the city and the village.

Urbanization

Some one hundred million people in India live in cities. The rates of urbanization throughout India have not been dramatic, but the largest cities have grown rapidly. Incredibly crowded, lacking in adequate housing, transportation, and sewerage, Indian cities have become almost ungovernable and for some unlivable. But because they offer new economic opportunities, and rich and varied cultural experiences and intellectual stimulation, cities are for most urban dwellers preferable to rural life. And in terms of relative deprivation, even the burdens of the poor in Calcutta, the problem city of the world, may represent an improvement over the marginal subsistence of the village. Nevertheless, with rapid social change, high levels of communication, and a frustrated middle class squeezed by rising prices and a deteriorating standard of living, India's cities suffer a deepening malaise. It is within the cities,

[10] *The Discovery of India* (Garden City, N.Y.: Doubleday, 1959), p. 31.

where the government finds itself unable to respond to accelerating demands, that political unrest is most sharply evident.

Rural Society and Tradition

India, like most of the developing world, is overwhelmingly rural and agricultural. More than 80 percent of India's population lives in some 550,000 villages, most with less than one thousand people. Village life was traditionally narrowly circumscribed, and even today the world of the average villager extends only a few miles beyond his birthplace. Although the villages have now been penetrated by radio, film, and increasing contact with government officials and aspiring politicians, they remain the font of traditional values and orientations. If they are often eulogized as an ideal of harmony and spirituality, even by those who have chosen to leave, traditional villages are nevertheless bastions of parochialism and inequality.

THE CASTE SYSTEM

It is within the villages that the caste system, sanctioned by Hindu tradition, has its most powerful hold. There are more than two thousand castes, or *jati*, in India. Most are confined to relatively small geographical areas within a linguistic region. Marrying only among themselves, the members of each caste share a common lot and occupy by virtue of their birth a defined status and role within village society. Each caste is hierarchically ranked according to the ritual purity of its traditional occupation—whether or not the occupation is still followed. Castes can be distinguished from one another even in the same village by the manner of behavior and speech, the style of dress and ornaments, the food eaten, and the general style of life. The behavior of each caste is restricted. Deviation may bring action from the caste itself through the *panchayat*, the council of caste elders, or it may incur the wrath of the higher castes and bring punitive measures against the aberrant individual or the caste group as a whole.

Although traditionally conflict between castes certainly occurred, caste as a *system* ideally presupposes the interdependent relationship of occupational groups, each functioning according to prescribed patterns of behavior, with the system providing both economic security and a defined status and role. The caste system is what Alan Beals calls "being together separately."[11] "To survive," he says "one requires the cooperation of only a few jati; to enjoy life and do things in the proper manner requires the cooperation of many."[12] Kathleen Gough, however, charac-

[11] *Gopalpur: A South Indian Village* (New York: Holt, Rinehart and Winston, 1963), p. 41.
[12] *Ibid.*

terizes the system as one of "relationships of servitude."[13] A typical village might have from a half-dozen to twenty castes within it. Traditionally, each by its ascriptive status occupied a particular position in relation to the land. In a system of reciprocity and redistribution, each caste provided the landlord with its services, agricultural or artisan, and received in return a portion of the harvest. The relationship of the lower castes to the high-caste landlord was hereditary, but their dependent status carried certain rights. All behavior within the system, however, served to emphasize superordination and subordination, congruent inequalities of power, wealth, and status. Control over land was the critical lever of social control, and today land remains the fundamental resource of political power and the means by which blocs of support may be mobilized.

The ascriptive identity of caste cannot be escaped, even by abandoning the traditional occupation. Although an individual cannot move from one caste to another, within the middle range of castes between the Brahmins and the untouchables there is considerable movement in the local hierarchy, as castes adjust their ritual position to accord with shifting economic status and political power. Such shifts, usually with a lag of several generations, are accompanied by changes in life-style, such as the adoption of vegetarianism in "sanskritized" emulation of higher castes. This movement occurs within the framework of the *varna* system. Classically, castes have been divided into five divisions, the four varna and those beyond the pale of caste. The varna represented the classes of ancient Aryan society. Ranked hierarchically, the first three varnas included the Brahmins, who acted as the priests; the Kshatriyas, who were the rulers and warriors; and the Vaisyas, who were the mercantile classes. The Sudras, the lowest varna, were the common people, the agriculturists and craftsmen. Beyond the embrace of the varna were the outcastes, or untouchables, polluted by their life as scavengers and sweepers and therefore relegated to the lowest rungs of society.

HINDUISM AND THE CONCEPT OF DHARMA

Each man is born into a particular station in life, with its own privileges and obligations, and he must fulfill his own *dharma*, his sacred law or duty. It is better, according to the sacred Hindu text, the Bhagavad Gita, to do one's own duty badly than another's well. The sufferings of man's existence can be explained by his conduct in past lives, and only by fulfilling the dharma peculiar to his position in life can he hope to gain a more favorable rebirth and ultimate salvation. There is a quality of resignation, of passiveness and fatalism, in this religious belief, that has manifested itself in the political attitude of the many Indians who simply accept the government they have as the one they

[13] "Criteria of Caste Ranking in South India," *Man in India*, Vol. 39 (1959), pp. 15–17.

deserve. Expanding communications and political competition have, however, increasingly challenged the traditional order. The vote has brought a new sense of efficacy and power, and a willingness to overturn what was previously accepted simply as written by the gods.

Hinduism, while uniting India in the embrace of the great Sanskritic tradition, also divides the subcontinent. Each cultural-linguistic area has its own "little" tradition and local gods, and it is within the little tradition, rather than in the realm of Brahminical Hinduism, that most villagers live their religious life. The two levels of tradition penetrate each other, however, as the elastic pantheon of Hinduism absorbs the local tradition and is modified by it. Religion at the "higher" level need not be in conflict with the goals of modernization, Gunnar Myrdal argues, but the inertia of popular belief, giving religious sanction to the social and economic *status quo*, remains a major obstacle to social transformation. "Religion has, then, become the emotional container of this whole way of life and work and by its sanction has rendered it rigid and resistant to change."[14]

Poverty

Poverty is the omnipresent reality of Indian life. It is both the greatest impetus and the greatest impediment to economic and social progress. By almost every economic index, India is among the poorest countries in the world. With more than a half-billion people, it has a gross national product of only fifty billion dollars—roughly that of Italy, which has one-tenth its population, and only a little more than half of what the United States *spends* in its annual defense budget.

THE CONDITION OF THE PEOPLE

The average annual income in India is now between eighty and ninety dollars, and most of it goes to provide a meager diet. The average level of nutrition is below minimum standards, but because of the stark social inequalities, averages conceal the even greater poverty of the masses and a nutritional level far below that required to maintain health. The diet, based on a single staple—rice, wheat, or an inferior grain—is monotonous as well. Poor nutrition leads to what Myrdal and others have called hidden hunger—"a general state of weakness that impairs people's labor input and efficiency and decreases their resistence to disease."[15] Indeed, perhaps no more than 10 percent of India's population has sufficient food.

Food is closely related to the general quality of health. There has been

---

[14] Gunnar Myrdal, *Asian Drama: An Inquiry into the Poverty of Nations,* Vol. 1 (New York: Pantheon, 1968), p. 112.
[15] *Ibid.,* Vol. 3, p. 1603.

a dramatic decline in mortality in India as a result of advances in medical technology, but even with the control of epidemic and endemic diseases—malaria, for example, has virtually been eradicated—sanitation and elementary hygiene have improved little. Life expectancy has risen from 20 to 25 years in the early part of the century to its present 46 to 50 years, but even this figure suggests a continuing high rate of infant mortality. India has only 17.6 physicians per 100,000 people (compared to 125 per 100,000 in the United States), and despite the effort to establish a system of rural health centers, most doctors practice in the major urban areas.

Poverty is a syndrome of cumulative and mutually reinforcing deprivations. In addition to low levels of nutrition and low standards of health, India is confronted by mass illiteracy. Education, in its strictly instrumental aspects of attitude change and dissemination of practical knowledge, is vital for progress and development. Despite the rapid expansion of primary education in India, official figures for adult literacy (41 percent for men; 13 percent for women in 1961) are in all likelihood far in excess of reality. About 2 percent of the adult population is literate in English, and literacy figures for the vernacular languages probably include many people who do not have an actual, functional ability to read and write. Illiteracy sustains poverty, although it may reduce consciousness among the poor and render them less likely to be politically restless. Progress in education, a breakthrough in communication, and an incremental improvement in the standard of living, however, have raised the sights of the Indian people and stimulated their aspirations after a better life. The possibilities of satisfying these demands depend on both the will of the government to respond and its capacity to mobilize resources in a context of scarcity.

THE CONDITION OF THE LAND

More than half of India's income comes from the land, but there is little beyond the 325 million acres now under cultivation that can be redeemed for agriculture. The soil, though capable of being rejuvenated by rotation and fertilization, has been depleted by centuries of harvests, and the yield per acre is now among the lowest in the world. Rain is irregular, and the monsoon, which determines the difference between subsistence and famine, is irregular. The uses of irrigation, improved seed grain, and modern agricultural techniques could double India's agricultural output without expanding present acreage, but most of India's peasants, with little access to credit, cannot afford the margin of risk involved in innovation.

In raw materials, India possesses the resources for substantial industrial growth. In the Bengal-Bihar-Orissa triangle, coal, iron ore, and transport facilities provide the base for a major steel industry. Oil deposits have been opened in Assam and Gujarat, and India's rivers offer enormous hydroelectric potential that has only been touched. At the time of independence, India already had an extensive industrial base and one of the largest rail systems in the world. Under the Five-Year Plans, industry and transport have been greatly expanded. In absolute terms, India ranks as a fairly industrialized nation, but in terms relative to its size and population, it is backward. Even with its potential in raw material, India is confronted with a scarcity of exploited resources that severely limits its capacity to invest in developmental efforts. Democratic commitment limits the system's ability to force saving and at the same time places rapidly increasing demands on the capacity of the political system to distribute available resources.

POPULATION GROWTH

Competition for India's limited resources is intense, but there is no claimant greater than population growth. Control of disease in the past fifty years has brought a rapid decline in death rates, the Malthusian equalizer. The annual rate of population growth has increased from about 1.25 percent to 2.5 percent and continues to rise. To reduce birth rates, the Government of India has undertaken the most extensive family-planning program in the world. Billboards, radio, and films proclaim, "A small family is a happy family." To overcome the fatalism of "God's will," propaganda posters announce: "Men! The power to prevent birth is in your hands." The campaigns have yielded impressive results. Five million men have undergone voluntary sterilization; two million women have had intra-uterine devices, or "loops," inserted; one million have taken birth control pills; and a major promotion of condoms is now under way. The statistics pale, however, when matched with the yearly addition of thirteen million people to India's population. At present rates, India's population will reach one billion before the year 2000—and perhaps much sooner.

Population growth has seriously undermined the economic progress made in the past two decades, and unless the population increase is drastically reduced, even an equilibrium of poverty will be impossible to maintain. Expanding population demands 1.5 million additional tons of food grains each year, 2.5 million houses, and 4 million jobs.[16] For all the talk of "green revolution," population pressure deepens India's persistent food crisis.

The Current Dilemma: "The Revolution of Rising Frustrations"

The challenge of population growth demands radical change in the form of a fundamental transformation of society. The inertia of tradi-

[16] *New York Times*, January 19, 1968.

tion can be broken only by creating "felt needs," by stimulating discontent and aspiration after a better life. The leadership of India, committed to goals of modernization, sought to induce social change, and succeeded. But its period of grace was short. The "revolution of rising expectations" has become a "revolution of rising frustrations" as the gap between aspiration and achievement has widened. As demands have increased, as new groups have entered the political system in the expanding participation, the capacity of the government to respond effectively has not kept pace. But beyond capacity, India has often lacked the *will* to initiate and respond to rapid change. Under pressure from sectors of society with a vested interest in preserving the inequalities of the *status quo*, Indian leadership has been emasculated by the paradoxical position in which it finds itself.

> On a general and noncommittal level they freely and almost passionately proclaim the need for radical social and economic change, whereas in planning their policies they tread most warily in order not to disrupt the traditional social order. And when they do legislate radical institutional reforms—for instance in taxation or in regard to property rights in the villages—they permit the laws to contain loopholes of all sorts and even let them remain unenforced.[17]

Without the capacity and the will to respond to increasing demands and to fulfill their own hopes for the transformation of society, India's leaders may now be the victims of the change they once sought to induce. In a process of social mobilization, with the breakdown of traditional society, the expansion of communications and transportation facilities, and heightened political competition, more and more people have become participant and, at the same time, more highly sensitive to the poverty in which they live. How the Government of India responds to this situation is of more than academic interest: It is among the most critical questions in the world.

[17] Myrdal, *Asian Drama*, Vol. 1, p. 117.

RECOMMENDED READING

The Process of Political Development

* Almond, Gabriel, and Powell, G. B. Jr., *Comparative Politics: A Developmental Approach*. Boston: Little, Brown, 1966.
    Advances an approach to political development in terms of political functions and system capabilities.

---

* Available in a paperback edition.

Apter, David, *The Politics of Modernization*. Chicago: University of Chicago Press, 1965.
>   Analysis of modernization in terms of alternative types of political systems, drawing primarily on African field data.

* Black, C. E., *The Dynamics of Modernization*. New York: Harper & Row, 1966.
>   Presents a four-stage model of modernization, with an analysis of patterns of response in wide historical perspective.

Finkle, Jason L., and Gable, Richard W., eds., *Political Development and Social Change*. New York: Wiley, 1966.
>   An extensive collection of readings on the concept of development and various aspects of social change in developing areas.

Geertz, Clifford, ed., *Old Societies and New States*. New York: The Free Press, 1963.
>   A valuable collection of original essays, with a discussion by Geertz of the problems of horizontal integration.

* Huntington, Samuel P., *Political Order in Changing Societies*. New Haven, Conn.: Yale University Press, 1968.
>   An exploration of the problem of political development in terms of the relationship between institutionalization and political participation, with emphasis on the creation of stability and order.

* Pye, Lucian W., *Aspects of Political Development*. Boston: Little, Brown, 1966.
>   Brings together various writings by a specialist in the field of development.

* Welch, Claude E. Jr., ed., *Political Modernization*. Belmont, Calif.: Wadsworth, 1967.
>   A relatively slim but well-selected collection of readings on the problem of political development.

The Context of Political Development in India

* Beals, Alan, *Gopalpur: A South Indian Village*. New York: Holt, Rinehart and Winston, 1963.
>   A concise and well-written study of a Mysore village.

Kapp, K. William, *Hindu Culture, Economic Development, and Economic Planning in India*. Bombay: Asia Publishing House, 1963.
>   The first three chapters deal sensitively with the impact of Hindu society and religion on economic development.

* Lewis, John P., *Quiet Crisis in India*. Garden City, N.Y.: Doubleday, 1964.
>   An examination of economic development in India and of American policy by the former director of the United States Agency for International Development in India.

* Lewis, Oscar, *Village Life in Northern India*. Urbana, Ill.: University of Illinois Press, 1958. Also in a Vintage paperback edition.
>   A rich and extensive study of a village near Delhi.

* Available in a paperback edition.

Marriott, McKim, ed., *Village India*. Chicago: University of Chicago Press, 1955.

> Still one of the best collections of essays on rural Indian society, with a particularly important essay by Marriott on "little communities in an indigenous civilization."

* Mason, Philip, ed., *India and Ceylon: Unity and Diversity*. New York: Oxford University Press, 1967.

> A superb collection of essays dealing with five areas of social tension: linguistic and regional division, and differences of tribe, caste, religion, and education.

* Myrdal, Gunnar, *Asian Drama: An Inquiry into the Poverty of Nations*, 3 vols. New York: Pantheon, 1968.

> A vast study of poverty in South Asia by one of the world's most astute economists, encyclopedic in its breadth, depressing in its conclusions. See in particular the specific sections on India.

* Nair, Kusum, *Blossoms in the Dust*. New York: Praeger, 1961.

> A vivid but anecdotal view of the human factors in rural development.

Panikkar, K. M., *Hindu Society at Cross-Roads*, 2nd ed. Bombay: Asia Publishing House, 1961.

> A plea by an Indian intellectual for an open, united, and democratic Hindu society.

Singer, Milton, and Cohn, Bernard S. eds., *Structure and Change in Indian Society*. Chicago: Aldine, 1968.

> A substantial collection of essays reviewing recent empirical studies that outline theoretical and methodological trends in South Asian anthropology.

Wiser, William and Charlotte, *Behind Mud Walls, 1930–1960*. Berkeley: University of California Press, 1965.

> A deeply personal account of life in an Uttar Pradesh village in 1930, with a perspective on the changes that took place over the next thirty years.

* Available in a paperback edition.

II

THE STRUGGLE FOR INDEPENDENCE

WHEN IT GAINED INDEPENDENCE FROM BRITAIN IN 1947, INDIA EMERGED as one of the first "new states." The society of the vast subcontinent is among the oldest in the world, however, varied and complex in its rich heritage. Five thousand years of history have nourished the growth of a great civilization, vitalized through cross-cultural contact and characterized by diversities of culture and race, of caste, religion, and language. In India there are examples of virtually every known type of societal division: six major religions—Hinduism, Islam, Sikhism, Christianity, Buddhism, and Parseeism; two major language families, Aryan and Dravadian, in which there are fourteen official languages and innumerable dialects and tribal tongues; three racial strains, Aryan, Dravidian, and proto-Australoid; and over two thousand castes, hierarchically ranked, endogamous, and occupational.

The great tradition of Hinduism unites the diverse cultural regions, but within its elastic framework are a myriad of sects and local traditions. Indeed, perhaps by more than anything else, traditional India has been characterized by localism, a fragmentation not simply of cultural-linguistic regions but of villages themselves. By no means completely isolated, the cultural world of the villages nevertheless remains narrowly circumscribed.

In the past the villages were little affected by the changes of governmental authority. For the villager, "it did not matter much who ruled in Delhi—Mughal, Maratha, or Englishman. His concern was with his crops, with the next monsoon, and with the annual visitation of the collecting officer."[1]

Even the most sophisticated administrative system, like that of the Moguls, penetrated the village for almost wholly extractive purposes. Indeed, neither the Moguls, the Muslim rulers who came to power in 1526 and reigned for over three hundred years, nor the great Hindu emperors before them extended their sway over the whole of India. India was a concept, not a political entity. Pockets remained beyond the reach of even Asoka, whose empire in the third century B.C. extended from the Hindu Kush to the Bay of Bengal. Islamic authority never established itself in the extreme South; and even as the Moguls attained the height of their power, they were faced by revolts among the Jats, Rajputs, and Sikhs in the North and challenged by the rising power of the Marathas in the West. These internal conflicts were both exploited and exacerbated by the appearance of the European powers in India in the fifteenth century.

The British Rise to Power

The British entered the struggle for a commercial foothold in India through the British East India Company, founded in London in 1600 during the reign of Akbar. Within a few years the company had secured limited trading privileges from the Moguls, and by the end of the century it had established commercial enclaves at Bombay, Madras, and Calcutta. As Mogul power declined in the eighteenth century, the British pushed for more extensive privileges and wider territories. The inability of the Moguls to control increasing disorder led the company, as early as 1687, to instruct its Madras representative "to establish such a politie of civil and military power, and create and secure such a large revenue to secure both . . . as may be the foundation of a large, well grounded, secure English dominion in India for all time to come."[2]

In expanding their hold, the British played one ruler off against another, annexing a widening range of territory. The princely states led a precarious and vulnerable existence. The price of preservation from Indian conquest was the acceptance of British suzerainty. Security of trade ultimately demanded that the powers opposed to the com-

[1] Percival Spear, A History of India, Vol. 2 (Baltimore: Penguin, 1965), p. 43.
[2] Quoted in R. C. Majumdar and others, An Advanced History of India, 2nd ed. (New York: St. Martin's Press, 1951). Part III: Modern India, pp. 638–39.

FIGURE 2–1

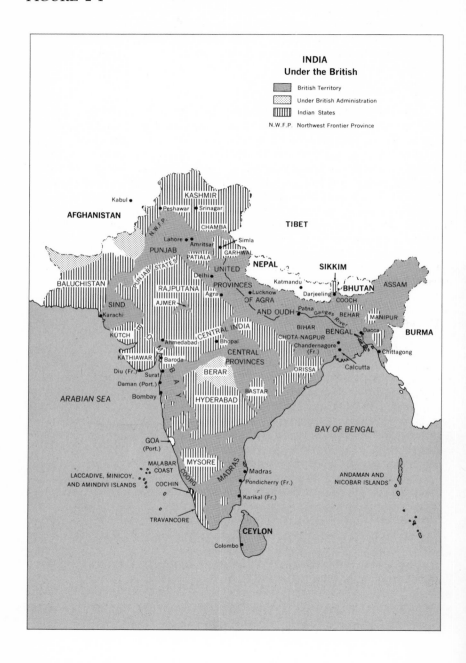

pany be brought under control and that Pax Britannica be extended over the whole subcontinent. By the middle of the nineteenth century, the company had assumed direct control over three-fifths of India, and the remaining areas were held by more than five hundred princely states subject to British control and intervention.

Westernization

As successors to the Mogul empire, the British sought to restore order and to reorganize the revenue system. Conditions were chaotic, and the opportunities for trade were restricted by inland transit duties, a wholly inadequate road system, and the constant dangers of *dacoity*, or gang robbery, which rendered safe travel almost impossible. In the course of pacification, however, the British began the construction of transport facilities—roads, canals, and railroads—opening the interior for the extraction of raw materials and the development of trade.

The British wanted to establish an equitable land and revenue system. In Bengal, revenues had previously been collected by hereditary *zamindars*, who as agents of the Government also held police and magisterial powers. The British mistook the zamindars for landlords and under the Permanent Settlement confirmed them in their jurisdictions, thus creating a new class of wealthy landlords at the expense of the peasants. The mistake was soon evident, and subsequently in Madras the settlement was made directly with the peasant cultivators under the *ryotwari* system.

The British, content in the early years of company rule to let most things continue very much as before, had taken a position of neutrality with regard to the religious and social affairs of their subjects. In the early nineteenth century, however, demands for reform, voiced in England by the Utilitarians and the Evangelicals, were soon felt in India. The Utilitarians, committed to the rule of reason, sought to secure social harmony and justice through the free development of human virtue and common sense, unfettered by superstitution and tradition. The Evangelicals, driven by a personal pietism and public humanitarianism, expressed horror at the abominations of the benighted heathen.[3] Both Utilitarians and Evangelicals found little in India that they liked: Both were ready to condemn and eager to change.

Abusive Hindu customs came under attack, and government action was taken against them. The reforms brought outcries of protest from the orthodox, particularly against the outlawing of *sati*, the self-immolation of a widow on the pyre of her husband. But the measures won the support of many reform-minded Hindus, notably Ram Mohan Roy, "the father of modern India." In general, however, the British sought

[3] Percival Spear, *India, Pakistan, and the West*, 4th ed. (New York: Oxford University Press, 1957), p. 101.

to interfere as little as possible, and reform was largely negative. Not content with such limited response, the Utilitarians and Evangelicals introduced a new concern for education that was to have profound social implications. The Utilitarians advocated "useful knowledge"; the Evangelicals, "moral improvement." The English language was, in the words of Governor General Bentinck, "the key to all improvements."[4] The whole of Hindu literature was seen as less valuable than any shelf of English books. Indeed, Lord Macaulay envisaged in his famous Minute of 1835, "a class of persons, Indian in blood and colour, but English in taste, in opinion and in intellect."

In 1835 English replaced Persian as the official language of government and thereby became the vehicle of advancement and progress. In establishing schools and later universities, the British focused on the English education of the middle classes. The aristocrats for the most part held aloof; the masses, except for missionary concern, were largely ignored. The aspiring Hindu middle classes—particularly those castes with a literary tradition, like the Brahmins—were quick to respond to the advantages of English education. There were those of the *babu* stereotype who sought only a sinecure in the new bureaucracy, but others, like Ram Mohan Roy, were eager for the knowledge of the West —science, medicine, and the values of political liberalism.

The Persistence of Tradition: The Sepoy Mutiny

The rise of the new middle class, which Percival Spear has called "the most significant creation of the British in India,"[5] shifted the balance in the relationship of the various classes in Indian society. The old aristocratic landowning classes were rapidly losing their position of status and power. The changes introduced by the British, both by accident and by design, threatened the old order, and religion particularly was thought to be in danger. Brahmins, who served in large numbers as *sepoys*, or soldiers, in the army, were alarmed by rumors of Christian conversion in their ranks. They feared that they would have to serve overseas and thus break the religious prohibition against leaving India. Muslim resentments were stirred by the annexation of the state of Oudh for alleged misgovernment in 1856, and in an atmosphere of fear, mutiny broke out in 1857 when soldiers discovered that the cartridges of the new Enfield rifles were greased with animal fat of both the cow and the pig, polluting to Hindus and Muslims, respectively. "A consciousness of power," wrote one British official, "had grown up in the army which could only be exorcized by mutiny, and the cry of the cartridge brought the latent spirit of revolt into action."[6]

[4] Quoted in Spear, *India, Pakistan, and the West*, p. 103.
[5] *India, Pakistan, and the West*, p. 110.
[6] Quoted in Majumdar, *Modern India*, p. 775.

In revivalist reaction Muslims rallied to the aged Mogul emperor of Delhi; Hindus, to the heir of the last Maratha *peshwa*, or head minister. Discontent was centered in Oudh, but among those in revolt there was no unity of purpose. The Maratha princes were not eager to see a resurgent peshwa and remained aloof from the mutiny. The Sikhs, though defeated only ten years before by the British, by no means wanted to resurrect Mogul power and thus gave active support to the British in crushing the revolt. The South remained virtually untouched by and uninvolved in the whole affair. Western education brought the Indian middle classes prospects for the enjoyment of status and privilege in a new order, and they pledged their loyalty and active support to the British. "So far from being the first war for independence or a national revolt in the modern sense, the Mutiny was a final convulsion of the old order goaded to desperation by the incessant pricks of modernity."[7]

The mutiny was, as Nehru later wrote, "essentially a feudal rising," and although it had directly affected only a limited area, "it had shaken up the whole of India."[8] The East India Company was abolished, and in 1858 the Crown assumed direct control over British India. The revolt, with all its savagery, marked a fundamental change in British attitude and in the relationship between the Indians and the English. The English became deeply distrustful of their native wards, particularly of the Muslims, who were believed to have been strongly committed to the mutiny. The manner of the British response to the mutiny reflected changes, conditions and attitudes that by 1857 were already well under way. The rise of popular imperial sentiments in England would soon have brought continued company rule into jeopardy had not the mutiny brought matters to a head.[9]

British Reaction and Awakening Indian Nationalism

The British were now determined to be in closer touch with established classes of traditional authority who could keep the masses under control.[10] They rewarded princes for their loyalty during the revolt and guaranteed their territories. They secured landlords in their tenure on conditions of "loyalty and good service." Thus the relics of the past, the vested interests of conservatism, were tied to the British presence in India. At the same time the British exercised new caution in westernization. Their new policy reflected both a desire to placate the conserva-

[7] Spear, *India, Pakistan, and the West*, p. 116.
[8] Jawaharlal Nehru, *The Discovery of India* (Garden City, N.Y.: Doubleday, 1959), pp. 239–40.
[9] Francis G. Hutchins, *The Illusion of Permanence* (Princeton, N.J.: Princeton University Press, 1967), p. 86.
[10] Spear, *A History of India*, Vol. 2, p. 144.

tive upper classes and a certain disappointment and pessimism over Indians' inability to change. "Public works rather than public morals or western values was the guiding star of the post-Mutiny reformer."[11] India was assumed to be changeless, perhaps irredeemable, and it was to be "the white man's burden" to bring enlightened rule to those incapable of governing themselves.

The British sought to reinforce traditional institutions, to minimize social change, and to soften the impact of the West. Their policy "went hand in hand with a new and avowedly imperial sentiment which glorified the British Raj and consigned the Indian people to a position of permanent racial inferiority."[12] While the British looked for support to the moribund traditional ruling classes, the rajas and zamindars, they virtually ignored the rising westernized middle class—the clerks and subordinate officials, the teachers and lawyers. "The fissure between the British and the new India began at this point."[13]

This new Indian class was characterized by a unity of sentiment, but at the same time, this unity was undercut by the growth of regional identity and of self-awareness and assertiveness among different communities, particularly in religion. The West had a double impact on India: It introduced Western liberal thought, but it also prompted the recovery of what was valuable in tradition. The Indian response to the West came in the forms of reform and revivalism. The movement for reform sought to reconcile tradition with modernity, to eliminate those elements of tradition repugnant to reason and liberal values and to reaffirm those that were compatible with them. Revivalism, in contrast, sought to regain the past through a traditionalistic reaction against the West, and while often involving radical reform, it was nurtured by the nostalgia for an idealized "golden age."

Reform and revival represented a quest for national self-respect and drew deeply upon both those who damned and those who praised Indian tradition and society. While often acutely self-critical, reformers and revivalists reacted sharply to the criticism of the Evangelicals, who saw only benighted heathen and a society of superstition and dark ignorance. They were unwilling to accept the latent, and often manifest, racism that relegated the Indian to a position of inferiority and described him, in Kipling's words, as "half devil and half child." In defense of Indian civilization, both reformers and revivalists drew upon the Orientalists, the European scholars who like Sir William Jones and Max Müller revealed the richness of Indian antiquity and the wisdom of the Sanskritic tradition.

Ram Mohan Roy paved the way for a century of social reform with

---

[11] *Ibid.*
[12] Thomas R. Metcalf, *The Aftermath of Revolt* (Princeton, N.J.: Princeton University Press, 1964), p. 324.
[13] Spear, *A History of India*, Vol. 2, p. 153.

the establishment of the Brahmo Samaj, or Divine Society, in 1830. The society, directed toward the literate middle classes, gained a small intellectual following, but under renewed leadership in the 1860's, it became increasingly vigorous in its advocacy of monotheism and social reform. Branches were established throughout India, but only in Bengal and in Maharashtra, where it sparked the Prarthana Samaj, did it meet with significant success. The Prarthana Samaj became the center of social reform in western India under the leadership of M. G. Ranade. Believing revival impossible, Ranade sought to preserve tradition through reform. The Arya Samaj, founded in Bombay in 1875 by a Gujarati Brahmin, Swami Dayananda, took a more aggressive and revivalist stance. The Arya Samaj sought to lead India "back to Vedas," the earliest Hindu scriptures, in an effort to recover and restore the Aryan past. Like Roy and Ranade, Dayananda believed in one god and denounced the evils of post-Vedic Hinduism—idolatry, child marriage, and the restrictions of caste—but he also rejected Western knowledge, claiming that the scientific truths of modern thought were all to be found in the Vedas, if seen with enlightened eyes. The Arya Samaj reacted strongly to the influences of Islam and Christianity, and its proselytic fundamentalism contributed to the rise of enmity toward the Muslim community, particularly in the Punjab and in the United Provinces, where the society found its greatest success.

The conflict between Hindus and Muslims engendered by the activities of the Arya Samaj served only to underscore the alienation of the Muslim community in India. The collapse of Mogul rule brought confusion and doubt to the Muslims. Clinging to traditions of the past and to memories of their former glory, the Muslims remained unresponsive to the changes around them. Since they regarded English as "the highway to infidelity,"[14] they failed to take advantage of English education and were soon displaced in the civil services by the rising Hindu middle class. As the resentment of the Muslim community turned suspicion and hostility upon them, the Muslim reformer and educator Sayyid Khan sought to convince the British of Muslim loyalty and to bring the community into cooperation with British authorities. At the same time, he warned of the dangers of Hindu domination under democratic rule. Hindu rule would fall more heavily upon Muslims than the neutral authority of the British raj.

Growing Political Consciousness

The rise of the new Indian middle class and the movements for reform, while regionally based and accentuating divisions within Indian society, nevertheless served as a catalyst for the development of a na-

14 *Ibid.*, pp. 223–24.

tional self-consciousness. Upon Bengali and Marathi regionalism, the new class grafted an all-India nationalism. "Mother India had become a necessity and so she was created."[15] The obstacles to the growth of Indian nationalism were many and difficult to overcome—the divisions between British India and the various princely states, the divisions between the linguistic regions, and the divisions of religion and caste within the society. The new middle class transcended these divisions, in part, through their unity of mind and speech. Their knowledge of English, commitment to liberal values, and pride in Indian civilization were the foundation for a common all-India view. Reforms served to offer the promise of a better future, and increasing opportunities were opening in the government services for educated Indians. At the same time, however, the British in India often acted without regard to Indian opinion. Indians were virtually excluded from the higher offices of the civil service, and the arrogant stance of imperialist responsibility cut deeply into Indian self-respect. That the behavior of the British in India contrasted so starkly with the values of English liberalism in which the Indian middle class had been steeped served to deepen their national consciousness.

In 1876 Surendranath Banerjea, dismissed—on insufficient grounds— from the Indian Civil Service, founded the Indian Association of Calcutta, which provided the groundwork for an all-India movement for the redress of wrongs and the protection of rights. "Indianization" of the Indian Civil Service was a central issue. The I.C.S. had become the "steel frame" of British administration, and membership carried prestige and status. The Charter Act of 1833, introducing a system of competitive examinations for the service, provided that no Indian "shall by reason only of his religion, place of birth, descent, colour or any of them be disabled from holding any office or employment under the Company."[16] This was reaffirmed in the Queen's Proclamation and in the Indian Civil Service Act of 1861.

There was, however, an obvious reluctance to admit Indians. The examinations were held only in London, and the examination itself virtually required study in England. As an increasing number of Indians successfully surmounted these barriers, admission was rendered more difficult when in 1878 the maximum age for application was reduced from twenty-two to nineteen.[17] The occasion served as an opportunity for Banerjea to organize a national protest. "The underlying conception,

[15] *Ibid.*, p. 166. See also Charles H. Heimsath, *Indian Nationalism and Hindu Social Reform* (Princeton, N.J.: Princeton University Press, 1964), pp. 135–36.
[16] Quoted in Majumdar, *Modern India*, p. 889.
[17] The Indianization of the I.C.S. was negligible in the early years. In 1913, eighty years after the Charter Act, the proportion of Indians in the services was only 5 percent. By 1921, it was 13 percent, but by the time of independence, 48 percent was Indian. Naresh Chandra Roy, *The Civil Service in India* (Calcutta: Mukhopadhyay, 1958), p. 154.

and the true aim and purpose of the Civil Service Agitation," he wrote, "was the awakening of a spirit of unity and solidarity among the people of India."[18] The agitation demonstrated that "whatever might be our differences in respect of race and language, or social and religious institutions, the people of India could combine and unite for the attainment of their common political ends."[19]

It was the Ilbert bill, however, which provided the catalyst for the development of an all-India organization. The bill, introduced in 1883, was intended to remove distinctions between Indian and European judges, thus revoking the exemption of Englishmen in India from trial by native judges. The nonofficial English community in Calcutta exploded in an outburst of racial feeling. They formed a defense association and collected funds to support their agitation against the legislation.[20] The furor led the Government to withdraw the bill. The success of the agitation against the bill left the new Indian middle class with a sense of humiliation, but the effectiveness of organization as a political instrument had been impressed upon them.

THE CREATION OF THE CONGRESS

In response, Banerjea founded the Indian National Conference in 1883. In that same year a retired English civil servant, A. O. Hume, addressed an open letter to the graduates of Calcutta University, urging the organization of an association for the political regeneration of India —what, as he later said, might form "the germ of a Native Parliament."[21] The first meeting of the Indian National Congress, attended by seventy-two delegates, was held in Bombay in 1885. Soon thereafter Banerjea merged his own association with the Congress.

The Congress affirmed its loyalty to the Queen, and with the dignity and moderation of a debating society, it sought by resolutions made at its annual meetings to rouse the British conscience to certain inequities of British rule and to the justice of Indian claims for greater representation in the civil services and in the legislative councils at the Center and in the provinces. The Indian liberals who dominated the Congress from 1885 to 1905 had an almost unlimited faith in British democracy. "England is our political guide," Banerjea declared. "It is not severance that we look forward to—but unification, permanent embodiment as an integral part of that great Empire that has given the rest of the world the models of free institutions."[22] Even Dadabhai Naoroji, who formulated the "drain theory" of India's exploitation by British eco-

---

[18] Quoted in Majumdar, *Modern India*, p. 890.
[19] *Ibid.*
[20] See Metcalf, *The Aftermath of Revolt*, p. 309.
[21] Quoted in Majumdar, *Modern India*, p. 893.
[22] Quoted in A. R. Desai, *Social Background of Indian Nationalism* (Bombay: Popular Book Depot, 1959), pp. 296–97.

nomic imperialism, remained "loyal to the backbone" and was the first Indian elected to the British House of Commons.[23]

In these early years the Government regarded the Congress favorably as a "safety valve" for revolutionary discontent, but remained unresponsive to its polite resolutions and humble petitions. Indeed, Hume was led to remark that "the National Congress had endeavoured to instruct the Government, but the Government had refused to be instructed."[24] As Congress liberals sought to bring somewhat greater pressure on the Government, the raj expressed its official disapproval of the policy and methods of the association. The Viceroy denounced the Congress as reflecting only the interests of the educated middle class, who constituted but a rootless, "microscopic minority" that could hardly be taken as representative of Indian opinion. The British conceived themselves to be the servants of truly representative Indian interests. The "real" India was not to be found among the effete babus of the city, but in the timeless villages, citadels of rugged peasant virtue.[25]

With growing disillusionment, the Congress assumed a stance of constitutional opposition to the Government, but such leaders as G. K. Gokhale retained faith in the "integrity and beneficence of that which was best in the British tradition."[26] Gokhale, friend and disciple of Ranade, was deeply committed to liberal reform and toward that end had founded the Servants of India Society in 1905. In that same year, as its dominant leader, Gokhale was elected president of the Indian National Congress.

THE RIFT BETWEEN MODERATES AND EXTREMISTS

Within Congress ranks, however, a militant Extremist wing grew impatient with the gradualism of the Moderates. The demand for administrative reform was replaced by the call for *swaraj*, or self-rule. Extremist support was centered in the Punjab, Bengal, and Maharashtra, where the militants drew inspiration not from the ideals of English liberalism but from India's past. Reform appealed to the cultivated intellects of the English-educated middle classes, but only the passion of revivalism could capture the imagination of the masses and provide the foundation for wider participation. Aurobindo Ghose in Bengal infused the movement with a "neo-Vedantic" mysticism, and in western India, Bal Gangadhar Tilak evoked the memory of Shivaji, founder of the Maratha kingdom, and of his struggle against the Muslim invaders. Tilak recalled the days of Maratha and Hindu glory and, not without concern among Muslims, sought to stir a revival of Hindu religious con-

[23] Desai, *Social Background*, p. 297.
[24] Quoted in Majumdar, *Modern India*, p. 894.
[25] See Hutchins, *The Illusion of Permanence*, pp. 156–57.
[26] Stanley Wolpert, *Tilak and Gokhale* (Berkeley: University of California Press, 1962), p. 299.

sciousness to serve his political ends. Tilak castigated the Moderates for what he regarded as their cultural capitulation to the West. Struggle, not reform, was the keynote of his message: "Swaraj is my birthright and I will have it."[27] In examining the role of Tilak, "the Father of Indian Unrest," Stanley Wolpert has written,

> His dream was not an India made in its foreign master's image, but one restored to the glory of its own true self. The quicker the British left, the happier he and his land would be. There could be no salvation for India in the self-deception of constitutional cooperation. Better to rely on the yoga of boycott.[28]

In 1905 Bengal was divided into two provinces; East Bengal comprised what is today East Pakistan. The partition gave impetus to the boycott of British goods and advanced the *swadeshi* movement for the use of indigenous products. The partition, designed solely with regard for administrative efficiency, completely ignored the renascent Bengali consciousness. A storm of protest, under the leadership of Surendranath Banerjea and such eminent Bengalis as Rabindranath Tagore, brought widespread popular opposition to the British raj. Boycott offered the possibility of mass participation. The emotion vented in agitation was accompanied by terrorism and, in the name of the demonic goddess Kali, assassination.

The Bengal partition brought a new urgency to the aspirations of Indian nationalists, and at their meeting in 1906 the Congress resolved to support the demand for swaraj. Gokhale and the Moderates envisioned responsible government within the British Empire—a position wholly unacceptable to the Extremists. The following year, the Congress meeting at Surat broke up in an uproar as the Extremists walked out, leaving the Moderates in control of the organization. Tilak, now in a political wilderness, was drawn increasingly toward the advocacy of violence in "political warfare" against the British. The Government enacted increasingly repressive measures to bring the wave of terrorism under control, and Tilak was arrested. Released after six years, he pledged his support and loyalty to the Congress. It was Tilak, however, given the title *Lokamanya,* or Honored by the People, who more than any of the early Congress leaders had sought to reach the masses, to transform the nationalist cause into a popular movement.

The Limited British Response

The Moderate position within the Congress was strengthened by the Morley-Minto Reforms of 1909 and the rescision of the Bengal partition. Since shortly after the assumption of direct rule by the Crown,

[27] *Ibid.,* p. 191.
[28] *Ibid.,* p. 304.

there had been some degree of Indian representation in government, but as Morris-Jones argues, "whether or not the British Empire was won in a fit of absent-mindedness, such a mood seems to have had a good deal to do with the establishment of parliamentary institutions in India. . . ."[29] Under the Indian Councils Act of 1861, three Indians were appointed to the advisory Legislative Council at the Center as nonofficial members. Not until 1891, however, partly to placate the Congress, did the Government increase the number of members in the Central and provincial legislative councils and concede the principle of election, at least indirectly. The Morley-Minto Reforms, drafted in consultation with Gokhale and other Indian leaders, expanded the legislative councils, thereby increasing Indian representation, introduced direct election of nonofficials under limited property franchise, and in the provinces provided for nonofficial majorities. Recommendations of the councils, however, could be disallowed at the discretion of the Viceroy or of the provincial governor; thus the councils were to a degree representative, but not responsible. In fact, Morley declared that "if it could be said that this chapter of reforms led directly or indirectly to the establishment of a parliamentary system, I, for one, would have nothing to do with it."[30]

The reforms provided limited institutional access to the new Indian middle class and sought to accommodate a range of moderate demands for representation. The Congress carried little weight, however, in the face of the highly institutionalized structures of the British raj. The repressive powers of the bureaucracy and the army could at any time be used against the few politically active Indians. The Congress had not yet gained the political capital of widespread popular support, of mass participation, that would allow it to challenge the British presence seriously. The Moderates were ready to work within the framework of imperial rule, making limited, though increasing, demands for greater access; the Extremists, lacking broad support and harassed by the Government, had been driven underground. The British lack of more genuine responsiveness to even the limited aspirations of Indian leaders and their readiness to use the power of repressive order to suppress opposition served, however, to awaken the political consciousness of the growing middle classes.

The Morley-Minto Reforms, by their acceptance of Muslim demands for separate electorates, introduced the principle of communal representation. In presenting their case before the Government, the Muslim notables argued that without separate electorates the Muslim community would be submerged in the Hindu majority, which was becoming increasingly participant and vocal in its demands for representation.

[29] W. H. Morris-Jones, *Parliament in India* (London: Longmans, Green, 1957), p. 73.
[30] Quoted in Majumdar, *Modern India*, p. 915.

To advance their position, these notables organized the Muslim League in 1906 at Dacca. The League was the first real attempt by Indian Muslims to utilize an organization to secure a more favorable position. Its membership was middle class and concerned primarily with more jobs, better educational opportunities, and higher social and economic status. More a clique than a movement, it nevertheless reflected the awakening of Muslim political consciousness.[31]

The award of communal representation to the Muslims was attacked by Congress nationalists as an attempt to weaken national unity, as a part of the strategy of divide and rule. The British had found in the Muslim community a useful counterpoise to the growing force of the Congress. By 1916, however, the Congress seemed prepared to accept separate electorates in exchange for the support of the Muslims, who because of the war between Britain and Turkey had been roused to anti-British feeling. The Lucknow Pact, concluded in that year at a joint session of the Congress and the Muslim League, called for the achievement of self-government.

The Lucknow Congress, held a year after Gokhale's death, marked the reemergence of Tilak as Congress leader. In that same year, Tilak founded the Home Rule League, and he was followed soon after by the English theosophist Mrs. Annie Besant, who organized a Home Rule League in Madras. In alliance, Tilak and Besant reasserted the Extremist faction within the Congress, and in 1917, while interned by the British Government, Mrs. Besant was elected president of the Indian National Congress. Moderate leaders soon withdrew to found the Indian Liberal Federation.

The Morley-Minto Reforms, while gradually moving India closer to responsible government, did not fulfill the rising expectations of Indian nationalists. India's involvement in the world war had brought a commitment of loyalty that soon turned to frustration and a diminished awe of imperial power, as the British called for sacrifice in exchange for vague promises of reform "after the war." Indian agitation for change was strengthened by Woodrow Wilson's declaration of the right of all nations to self-determination. As the demands for swaraj intensified with the home rule movement, Edwin Montagu, who had succeeded Morley as Secretary of State for India, announced in 1917 the Government policy "of increasing association of Indians in every branch of the administration and the gradual development of self-governing institutions with a view to the progressive realization of responsible government in India as an integral part of the British Empire."[32]

The first step toward implementing this policy was the enactment of

[31] Wayne A. Wilcox, *Pakistan: The Consolidation of a Nation* (New York: Columbia University Press, 1963), p. 20. See also Khalid B. Sayeed, *Pakistan: The Formative Phase, 1857–1948*, 2nd ed. (New York: Oxford University Press, 1968).
[32] Quoted in Majumdar, *Modern India*, p. 915.

the Montagu-Chelmsford Reforms in 1919. Under the Act, authority was decentralized, with a division of functions between the Center and the provincial governments. At the Center, there was little substantive change. Bicameralism was introduced, with an elected nonofficial majority in the lower house, but the Governor General, responsible to London, retained the overriding powers of certification and veto. In the provinces, however, the reforms introduced *dyarchy*, or dual government, under which the governor retained authority over certain "reserved" subjects—largely in the areas of revenue and law and order— while "transferred" subjects, such as local self-government, education, health, public works, agriculture, and industry, came under the control of ministers responsible to popularly elected legislatures. Council memberships were enlarged, and the principle of communal representation was extended both at the Center and in the provinces.

The Congress Call for Swaraj

For many Congress leaders, the reforms were just a sop. This seemed confirmed by the enactment of the Rowlatt Bills in 1919, extending the emergency powers assumed during the war to permit imprisonment without trial in political cases. In protest against the repressive "black bills," demonstrations and strikes were held throughout the country. Feelings were most intense in those more politically self-conscious regions where revivalism, and later Extremism, had gained a foothold among the masses. In the Punjab, where the situation was particularly tense, the arrest of two Congress leaders sparked a riot. Martial law was proclaimed and a ban on all public meetings was imposed. Defying the ban, an estimated 20,000 people gathered at the central park of Amritsar, Jallianwalla Bagh. Under the command of General Dyer, one hundred and fifty troops suddenly appeared at the entrance and ordered the crowd to disperse. With the military blocking the only entrance, Dyer then gave the order to fire point-blank into the unarmed masses. When the ammunition was exhausted, 379 Indians were dead and some 1200 more wounded. Dyer intended the massacre "to teach the natives a lesson."[33]

At the end of the year the Indian National Congress met at Amritsar in a mood of outrage and shock. The Montagu-Chelmsford Reforms were denounced as "inadequate, unsatisfactory and disappointing," but Tilak, who was to live less than a year, had mellowed, and he urged a policy of "responsive co-operation" with the Government.[34] Indian restraint, however, was pushed beyond the limit of its endurance when

[33] Michael Brecher, *Nehru: A Political Biography* (New York: Oxford University Press, 1959), pp. 63–64.
[34] Desai, *Social Background*, p. 319.

in 1920 the House of Lords gave a vote of appreciation to General Dyer for his services. Mohandas Gandhi, the new Congress leader, proclaimed that "cooperation in any shape or form with this satanic government is sinful."[35]

The Nationalist Movement

Gandhi's Philosophy of Satyagraha and His Role in the Congress

Gandhi was born into a Gujarati Vaishya family in Kathiawar, where his father was the *diwan*, or head minister, of a petty princely state. After completing university studies in Bombay, Gandhi read for the bar at the Inner Temple in London. After two years, still very much an Indian, he returned to India for legal practice. But the young barrister was soon invited to South Africa to plead the case of the Indian community against discriminatory legislation. He planned to stay one year; he remained for twenty.

In South Africa, with the Gita as his "infallible guide of conduct,"[36] he began his experiments with *satyagraha*, or nonviolent resistence, which he translated as "soul force."[37] It was satyagraha that was "to revolutionize Indian politics and to galvanize millions into action against the British Raj."[38] Already known for his South African victory, Gandhi was greeted upon his return to India in 1915 with the title *Mahatma*, or Great Soul. For the next three years, however, he remained a silent observer of the political scene, taking the advice of his political mentor Gokhale to keep "his ears open and his mouth shut" for a time.[39]

During this period Gandhi became increasingly sensitive to the gap between the predominantly urban middle-class Congress and the Indian masses, and shifted his attentions to the villages and the peasants. In 1918, while introducing satyagraha in India, Gandhi courted arrest in support of the indigo plantation workers of Bihar. A year later, when the repressive Rowlatt Bills were introduced, Gandhi organized the Satyagraha Society, pledged to disobey the unjust law as a symbol of passive resistence. To mobilize mass support, he called for a day of fasting and

---

[35] Quoted in Spear, *A History of India*, Vol. 2, p. 191.
[36] Mohandas Gandhi, *An Autobiography, or The Story of My Experiments with Truth* (Ahmedabad: Navajivan Publishing House, 1927), p. 195.
[37] See Joan V. Bondurant, *Conquest of Violence* (Berkeley: University of California Press, 1965).
[38] Brecher, *Nehru*, p. 59.
[39] Quoted in Louis Fischer, *Gandhi: His Life and Message for the World* (New York: New American Library, 1954), p. 53.

hartal, or general strike, in protest against the legislation.[40] The violence that marred the demonstrations led Gandhi to regard satyagraha as premature, as a "Himalayan miscalculation."[41] For others, however, it marked the turning point in the struggle for swaraj.

Gandhi regarded his participation in the 1919 Amritsar meeting as his "real entrance" into Congress politics.[42] Thereafter, he became its guiding force. In seeking to mobilize mass resistence to the Government, Gandhi gained Muslim support through his appeal on the emotionally charged Khilafat issue, denouncing the dismemberment of the Ottoman Empire and the deposition of the Caliph, the religious head of all Muslims. The noncooperation movement was launched with the call for a boycott of the impending elections and the law courts, and for withdrawal from all government schools and colleges. Middle-class Indians, institutionally co-opted by the British raj, were now drawn into new patterns of political participation. Congress members were asked to resign from government office and to renounce all titles. More than thirty thousand Congressmen, including Motilal Nehru and his son Jawaharlal, courted arrest in defiance of "lawless laws" and gained honor through imprisonment. The civil disobedience was accompanied by the outbreak of sporadic strikes, by the rebellion of Muslims in Malabar on the southwestern coast, by no-tax campaigns, and on the visit of the Prince of Wales, by a nation-wide hartal. In February 1922, to the dismay of Congress leaders, Gandhi abruptly called an end to the movement, as he had done before, when mob violence in a small town in Uttar Pradesh left twenty-two policemen dead. Gandhi declared that he would not purchase independence at the price of bloodshed.[43] Within days, he was arrested and tried for sedition.

During the two years that Gandhi was imprisoned, Hindu-Muslim unity was broken by the outbreak of communal rioting. Upon his release in 1924, Gandhi began a twenty-one-day fast for Hindu-Muslim solidarity, but to no avail. Thereafter, the Muslim League, representing the greater portion of the Muslim community, took an increasingly separate path from that of the Congress. The breach seemed irrevocable when the Congress refused in 1928 to accept separate communal electorates as part of the proposed constitutional change.

Within the Congress, the solidarity forged during the noncooperation movement gave way to division on the issue of council entry. The legislative councils, boycotted by the Congress, were growing in importance and prestige under the provincial non-Congress ministries. While

---

[40] Explaining this political tactic in the cultural context of India, Spear notes, "In theory, the soul is too shocked by some abuse to be able to attend to practical affairs for a time." *A History of India,* Vol. 2, p. 191.
[41] Gandhi, *Autobiography,* pp. 346–47.
[42] *Ibid.,* p. 358.
[43] Fischer, *Gandhi,* p. 71.

Gandhi was still in prison, C. R. Das and Motilal Nehru led the Congress in the formation of the Swaraja party to contest the next council elections with the purpose of destroying the reforms from within by "uniform, consistent and continuous obstruction."[44] The very entry of the Congress into the councils, however, increased their prestige and made them all the more difficult to subvert. Many Swarajists were led increasingly to favor a position of "responsive cooperation" with the Government for the achievement of swaraj. The Gandhians, or "no-changers," opposed the Swarajist strategy and, losing their dominance in the Congress for the time, retired to engage in "constructive work." From his *ashram*, a retreat near Ahmedabad, Gandhi worked for the uplift of the untouchables, whom he called *harijans*, or children of God, and with his own hands performed their "defiling" tasks. While the Swarajists debated in the councils, Gandhi led his swadeshi campaign for the use of *khadi*, a homespun cloth. Clothed simply in a loincloth and shawl, he would spin for a half-hour or more each day and urged all Congressmen to do likewise. The spinning wheel, emblazoned in the center of the Congress flag, became the symbol of the society Gandhi sought to achieve—a peasant society, self-governing and self-sufficient. Purity of the soul was requisite to the attainment of swaraj: Only through self-discipline could India prepare herself and make herself worthy of freedom.

In accordance with the provision of the Montagu-Chelmsford Reforms for a parliamentary review after ten years, the Simon Commission was appointed for the recommendation of constitutional changes. The Congress regarded the commission's all-British membership as not in accord with the principle of self-determination and resolved to boycott its proceedings. In 1928 the Congress, the Muslim League, and the Liberal Federation came together in an All-Parties Convention to frame a constitution for an independent India. The report, drafted by Motilal Nehru, called for responsible government and dominion status. The young radicals Jawaharlal Nehru and Subhas Chandra Bose opposed the recommendation for dominion status. With the intervention of Gandhi, the Congress agreed to accept the Nehru Report, but only if the proposed constitution were accepted in its entirety by Parliament before the end of 1929. Failing this, the Congress would launch nonviolent noncooperation in pursuit of independence.

The Governor General, Lord Irwin, announced that "the natural issue of India's Constitutional progress . . . is the attainment of Dominion status" and that toward that end a round-table conference would be held in London to discuss the recommendations of the Simon Commission.[45] In accordance with the pledge, the Congress met in December 1929 at Lahore and there declared complete independence as

[44] Quoted in Majumdar, *Modern India*, p. 986.
[45] Quoted in Majumdar, *Modern India*, p. 920.

its goal. It was resolved to boycott the legislative councils and the Round Table Conference and, under the direction of Gandhi, to begin a program of civil disobedience and nonpayment of taxes. At Lahore, the elder Nehru, with little more than a year to live, passed the chair of the Congress presidency to his son. On December 29 Jawaharlal Nehru hoisted the national flag of India.

The Civil Disobedience Campaign

In launching the campaign of civil disobedience, Gandhi announced his intention to violate the salt tax, a burden on even the poorest peasant and a source of bitter resentment against the raj. He would march from his ashram to the sea, a distance of 241 miles, and there by taking salt from the sea would disobey the law. The dramatic march lasted twenty-four days, and with this act of defiance, mass demonstrations, hartals, and civil disobedience began throughout India. The Government quickly responded with repressive measures. More than one hundred people were killed in police firings, and indiscriminate beatings of men and women were widespread. In less than one year some sixty thousand people were imprisoned.

During the Congress campaign, non-Congress representatives attended the Round Table Conference, but the Viceroy realized that any decisions would be hollow without Congress participation. In 1931 he released Gandhi and began a series of conversations that concluded in the Gandhi-Irwin pact. The Government agreed to withdraw its repressive measures and to release all political prisoners except those guilty of violence. Gandhi called off the civil disobedience campaign and agreed to attend the next round-table conference as a representative of the Congress. The London conference deadlocked on the question of communal electorates, and Gandhi returned "empty-handed" to India. With renewal of Government repression, the Congress reopened the civil disobedience campaign and called for the boycott of British goods. By March 1933 more than 120,000 people had been imprisoned.

At this inopportune moment, the Government announced its constitutional proposals, which included a provision for separte electorates for the untouchables. Believing the untouchables to be an integral part of the Hindu community, Gandhi, in jail, vowed to "fast unto death" against the provision. Gandhi began the fast despite the pleas of all. On the fifth day, as Gandhi's life was believed to hang in the balance, Dr. Ambedkar, leader of the untouchables, gave way and agreed to abandon separate communal electorates, but, to safeguard the interests of the untouchables he demanded that a number of seats be reserved for them within the allotment of seats to the Hindu community.

The fast, while stirring concern for the untouchables, diverted attention from the issue of independence and brought the collapse of the civil disobedience campaign. Radicals within the Congress declared that Gandhi had failed as a political leader and called for a new leadership. In the radical view the nationalist movement under Gandhi had become what was later described as "a peculiar blend of bold advances followed by sudden and capricious halts, challenges succeeded by unwarranted compromises . . . ."[46]

British Accommodation: The Government of India Act of 1935

The British sought to respond to widening political participation and increasingly vocal demands with the Government of India Act of 1935, which adapted the high levels of institutional capability to a changing environment. Abandoning its policy of repression, the Government sought to buy stability through accommodation: Stability was the *raison d'état*. The Act abolished dyarchy and provided for provincial autonomy with responsible government, accountable to a greatly expanded electorate. The franchise continued to carry a property qualification, but by the Act, the electorate was expanded from six million to thirty million, one-sixth of the adult population. The federal arrangement—never actually brought into operation—provided for the integration of princely states with British India. The all-India federation, which provided the model for the federal structure of independent India, was to consist of governor's provinces, chief commissioner's provinces, and those acceding princely states. Legislative power was divided according to detailed lists, distinguishing Central, provincial, and concurrent jurisdiction. Representation in the federal legislature was heavily weighted in favor of the princes, giving a conservative cast to the Center. At the Center, a dyarchical arrangement was introduced by which the Governor General, responsible only to the British Parliament, was invested with a number of discretionary powers and enjoyed "reserved power" over such departments as defense and external affairs. A. B. Keith, in his study of the constitutional history of India, argues that these provisions rendered "the alleged concession of responsibility all but meaningless."[47] Nehru termed the reform act a "slave" constitution—yet many features of the 1935 Act were later incorporated into the Constitution of the Republic of India.

In a very real sense the provincial autonomy granted under the Act was a substantive move toward meeting Congress demands for swaraj. Once again, as in 1922, the Congress resolved to work within the new reforms, and in 1937 it swept the provincial elections for Hindu seats and formed ministries in seven of the eleven provinces. The Muslim League fared poorly among the Muslim electorate and failed to secure majorities in any of the four predominantly Muslim provinces. Mo-

[46] Desai, *Social Background*, pp. 343–44.
[47] Quoted in Brecher, *Nehru*, p. 216.

hammed Ali Jinnah, the westernized leader of the League, offered to form coalition ministries with the Congress in each province, but the Congress refused to recognize the League as representative of India's ninety million Muslims. "There are," Nehru remarked, "only two forces in India today, British imperialism and Indian nationalism as represented by the Congress."[48] History, however, bore out Jinnah's response: "No, there is a third party, the Mussulmans."[49] The Congress was to pay dearly for its imperious attitude: "The opening shots had been fired in the calamitous Congress-League war which was to envelop north India in flames and ultimately result in partition."[50] In 1940 Jinnah declared that the Hindus and Muslims formed two separate nations. The Muslim League now adopted as its goal the creation of a separate and independent Islamic state, Pakistan.

During their term of office, the Congress ministries demonstrated considerable administrative ability and produced a distinguished record of achievements in social reform.[51] Inevitably, with their assumption of office question arose as to the relationship between the ministries and the party. Participation in provincial government was only one aspect of the Congress struggle, and Nehru emphasized the primary responsibility of each ministry to the Congress high command from whom they would take directive. The high command itself was by no means united, but in 1939, with the resignation of Bose after his confrontation with Gandhi, the two main factions, the old guard (Rajendra Prasad and Sardar Vallabhbhai Patel) and the socialists (Nehru), united behind Gandhi's leadership.

Bose formed a new party, the Forward Bloc, and in 1941 appeared in Germany and later in Japan to secure support for the Government of Free India, which he proclaimed in Japanese-occupied Singapore. There Bose, now called *Netaji*, or Leader, organized the Indian National Army.

Renewed Demands for Independence

The tide of war imposed a new strain on the nationalist cause. In 1939 the Vicerory proclaimed India's involvement in the war without consulting Indian leaders. The Congress condemned fascist aggression but declared that India could not associate itself with the war effort unless it was given immediate independence and equality as a free nation. When this demand was ignored, the Congress directed the provincial ministries to resign in protest. In August 1940 Congress again

[48] Quoted in Brecher, *Nehru*, p. 231.
[49] *Ibid.*
[50] Brecher, *Nehru*, p. 231.
[51] For a discussion of the Congress ministries, see Reginald Coupland, *The Constitutional Problem in India* (New York: Oxford University Press, 1944).

offered complete cooperation in the war in exchange for at least a provisional national government. The Viceroy made vague allusions to independence "after the war," but went on to promise the Muslims and other minorities that Britain would not accept any constitutional modification to which they were opposed.

The Muslim League refused to cooperate with the Congress, and after the resignation of the Congress ministries, it proclaimed a "Day of Deliverance" from the "tyranny, oppression and injustice" of Congress rule.[52] The departure of the Congress from provincial government at that critical time left the League in an advantageous position, one that by the end of the war would be virtually irresistible.

With the failure of the Congress offer, Gandhi again assumed leadership and opened a campaign of individual civil disobedience designed to symbolize Congress protest without disrupting the British war effort. Congress moderation was met by severe Government reaction. In 1942, however, as the Japanese advanced through Burma, Sir Stafford Cripps, on mission from London, promised the establishment of a constituent assembly and full dominion status after the war. Nehru and perhaps the majority of the Congress high command were responsive to the offer, but Gandhi, firmly opposed, held the balance. Nehru held out until the last, but finally submitted to Gandhi's persuasion. In August 1942 Gandhi demanded that Britain "quit India" or confront mass civil disobedience. The Government declared Congress illegal, and within hours Gandhi and the Congress leadership were taken into custody. They spent the rest of the war in prison. (C. Rajagopalachari, unable to support the resolution, resigned from the Congress.) The arrests set off a political explosion. Violence erupted throughout India, and by the end of the year, about one hundred thousand people had been arrested and more than one thousand killed in police firings.[53]

The "quit India" movement represented the apogee of the independence struggle in terms of mass involvement, but in a nation of nearly four hundred million people, the relative numbers of participants must have been small indeed. The various noncooperation movements beginning in the 1920's under Gandhi fundamentally changed the character of the Congress, transforming it from an urban middle-class coterie into a movement with an extensive social base reaching into the villages. If by 1942 Congress had enlisted four to five million members and widespread support, other millions, for various reasons of self-interest, remained loyal to British rule, and even greater numbers remained uninvolved or wholly unaware of the dramatic events transpiring around them. The nationalist movement, even in penetrating the villages, had limited impact. Those who were mobilized in the rural areas were far more likely to be the fairly prosperous peasants than the

[52] Quoted in Brecher, *Nehru*, p. 264.
[53] Brecher, *Nehru*, p. 290.

landless laborers. The mobilization of the still largely inert Indian masses to political consciousness and participation would remain the developmental task of India's leaders in the years after independence.

The Achievement of Swaraj

With the release of Gandhi in 1944, negotiations began again, as the Governor General proposed the formation of a national government. Discussions broke down when the Congress refused to recognize the League as the sole representative of the Muslim community. The war years had consolidated Jinnah's strength in the Muslim areas, however, and in the elections held at the beginning of 1946, the League swept the Muslim seats, as did the Congress the general seats. "The two-nations theory of Mr. Jinnah had found political expression."[54]

Prime Minister Atlee now announced the appointment of a Cabinet mission to India "to promote, in conjunction with the leaders of Indian opinion, the early realization of full self-government in India."[55] Confronted with the widening gap between the Congress and the League, the mission sought to preserve a united India and to allay Muslim fears of Hindu domination through the proposal of a loose federation. Without satisfaction, both sides accepted the plan, but the Congress rejected the proposals for an interim government, again over the issue of allotment of seats: The Congress, representing all India, was unwilling to accord the Muslim League its claim to represent all Muslims and therefore to have the right to fill all seats reserved for Muslims in the Cabinet. The Congress announced that it would, nevertheless, participate in the Constituent Assembly to frame the constitution. Jinnah countered by declaring a day of "direct action," unleashing a wave of communal rioting.

In September 1946 Nehru took office as *de facto* Prime Minister of the interim government. Fearing isolation, Jinnah brought the League into the Government, but only to demonstrate that the Hindu and Muslim communities could not work in harmony and that the formation of Pakistan was the only solution.[56] The obstructionist stance of the League brought negotiations to an impasse. At this point, on February 20, 1947, the British Government declared that it intended to quit India no later than June 1948 and that Lord Mountbatten had been appointed Viceroy to arrange for the transfer of power to Indian hands—however prepared to accept it.

Communal rioting again broke out, and the Punjab approached civil war. Gandhi was prepared to see the whole of India burn rather than concede Pakistan. Congress power, however, lay with Nehru and

[54] Spear, *A History of India*, Vol. 2, p. 231.
[55] Quoted in Majumdar, *Modern India*, p. 992.
[56] Brecher, *Nehru*, p. 323.

the more traditional Sardar Vallabhbhai Patel, both of whom by this time had come to accept the inevitability of partition. With their agreement Mountbatten laid out the plan for the transfer of power. The predominantly Muslim provinces would be allowed to form a separate Islamic state and to draw up their own constitution. Bengal and the Punjab, where the two communities were almost equal in numbers, would be divided as defined by a boundary commission. In the Northwest Frontier Province, where a pro-Congress Muslim government had a precarious majority, a referendum would be held. The princely states, released from British paramountcy, would be given the freedom to accede to either India or Pakistan—or, presumably, to declare their independence. Moving with incredible speed, Mountbatten, who was to stay on as the first Governor General of the new India, moved up the calendar of British withdrawal. On August 15, 1947, India became an independent nation. "Long years ago," Nehru declared, "we made a tryst with destiny, and now the time comes when we shall redeem our pledge . . . ."[57]

The Partition and Gandhi's Assassination

The achievement of swaraj was dimmed by the tragedy of partition and the assassination of Gandhi. The partition, in dividing Hindus and Muslims, had shattered Gandhi's dream of a free and united India, but the territorial division left millions of each community on both sides of the border. In the Punjab the boundary award, as anticipated, divided the cohesive and militant Sikh community almost equally between the two states. Here, in mounting hysteria, violence, and atrocity, Muslims fell upon Sikhs and Hindus in the West, and Sikhs and Hindus upon Muslims in the East. Before the end of the year a half-million people had been killed. In the movement of refugees four and one-half million Hindus and Sikhs left West Pakistan for India; six million Muslims moved in the other direction.[58] Rioting broke out in Bengal, but massacre was avoided, in part because of a Bengali consciousness that transcended religious division, but also because of the presence of Gandhi in Calcutta, "a one man boundary force." The costs of human suffering were, nevertheless, enormous: More than one million persons crossed the Bengal border from East Pakistan into India, leaving behind most of their possessions and bringing with them a bitterness that was to infect the communal life of Calcutta for years to come.

The Punjab was brought under control, but as hundreds of thousands of refugees poured into Delhi, the Muslims who either had chosen to remain or else could not leave now faced a bloodbath of revenge. Gandhi sought to reconcile the two communities by his presence, to

[57] Jawaharlal Nehru, *Independence and After* (New York: John Day, 1950), p. 3.
[58] Penderel Moon, *Divide and Quit* (Berkeley: University of California Press, 1962), pp. 268–69.

protect the Muslims and urge them to stay, and to calm the troubled city. On January 13, 1948, Gandhi began a fast, to the death if necessary, to stir "the conscience of all"—Hindu, Muslim, and Sikh. The fast, which lasted five days and brought the Mahatma near death, ended only with the Indian Government's agreement to release Pakistan's share of the assets of British India and with agreement by representatives of all communities, led by Nehru, Prasad, and Azad, to "protect the life, property, and faith" of the Muslims.[59]

Some within the Congress, such as Sardar Patel, did not approve of Gandhi's intervention on behalf of the Muslims. Others, the Hindu militants of the Mahasabha party and the Rashtriya Swayamsevak Sangh, openly denounced Gandhi for allegedly helping the Muslims against the Hindus. A bomb attempt was made on Gandhi's life, and then on January 20, twelve days after he had broken his fast, as he proceeded to his prayer meeting on the lawn of the palatial Birla House, Gandhi was shot by a young Hindu fanatic of the R.S.S. That evening, Nehru announced to the world, "The light has gone out of our lives and there is darkness everywhere . . . ."[60]

Gandhi had served to mobilize widespread support for the Congress struggle for independence, and if he did not hasten its arrival, he nevertheless imbued the movement with moral concern and stirred the conscience of the world. By making the Congress a more representative organization, Gandhi fundamentally changed the character of the nationalist struggle for independence. He broadened the base of the party in his appeal to the masses, but at the same time served to "Indianize" the middle class. His vision of society, however, had turned him from the path of the modernists and their commitment to industrialization and Western parliamentary government, and with independence, he urged Congressmen to leave politics for "constructive work." Gandhi argued that the Congress "as a propaganda vehicle and parliamentary machine [had] outlived its use" and that "it must be kept out of unhealthy competition with political parties."[61] Gandhi's death, mourned by all, brought a national reaction against the Mahasabha and Hindu extremism. It also served to free Nehru from the constraints of Gandhi's vision—but Gandhism had entered the political culture, more a charismatic memory than a revolutionary force, espoused by every shade of opinion and utilized for every purpose.

Formation of the Indian Union

In the wake of partition and Gandhi's death, India faced the problems of consolidation: the integration of the princely states and the framing of a constitution. Approximately two-fifths of the area under

[59] Fischer, *Gandhi*, pp. 253–58.
[60] Brecher, *Nehru*, p. 386.
[61] Quoted in Myron Weiner, *Party Building in a New Nation: The Indian National Congress* (Chicago: University of Chicago Press, 1967), p. 39.

the raj had been made up of these 562 principalities, ranging in size from a few square miles to an area as large as Hyderabad, with seventeen million people. With persuasion and pressure, Sardar Vallabhbhai Patel succeeded by Independence Day, August 15, 1947, in securing the accession of all states with the exception of three—Junagadh, Hyderabad, and Jammu and Kashmir.

Junagadh was a tiny state in Kathiawar with a Hindu population and a Muslim ruler, surrounded by Indian territory. When the state acceded to Pakistan, it was occupied by Indian troops and after a plebiscite, Junagadh joined the Indian Union. Hyderabad, with a Muslim ruler, the Nizam, and a Hindu majority, presented a similar but more complicated situation. The largest of the princely states, Hyderabad, though landlocked in the heart of India, sought independence as a sovereign state and entered a one-year standstill agreement with India while negotiations proceeded. With increasing disorder in Hyderabad and the rising influence of paramilitary Muslim extremists, the Indian Government moved troops into the state in a "police action" to restore law and order. Hyderabad then acceded to the Indian Union.

The state of Jammu and Kashmir, contiguous to both India and Pakistan and acceding to neither, had a Hindu ruler and a predominantly Muslim population. The Muslims were centered in the central valley, the Vale of Kashmir, with the Hindu minority concentrated in the region of Jammu to the south. As invading Pathan tribesmen from Pakistan pushed toward the capital of Srinagar, the Maharaja called upon India for military assistance. India, on the recommendation of Mountbatten, refused to send troops unless Kashmir agreed to accede formally to India. With accession, India announced its intention, once peace was restored, to hold a referendum on the choice of India or Pakistan. Because of near war between the two states over Kashmir in 1948 and the subsequent demarcation of a United Nations cease-fire line, the plebiscite was never held. Since then India, over the protest of Pakistan, has come to regard Kashmir as an integral part of its own territory, arguing that Kashmir legally acceded to India and that the large Muslim population of Kashmir serves as a force for secularity in India and as a protection for the forty million Muslims left in Indian territory after partition.

Once the princely states had acceded to India, the process of integration began. Smaller states were merged with neighboring provinces. Others were consolidated as centrally administered areas. Another class of states, because of their affinity, were consolidated as new federal units; these included Rajasthan, Saurashtra, and Travancore-Cochin. Mysore, Hyderabad, and, in a separate class, the state of Jammu and Kashmir retained their integrity as separate states of the Indian Union. Each new unit developed from the former princely states was to have as its head a *rajpramukh*, elected by the Council of Rulers, which was made up of the former princes. Some princes, such as the Maharaja of Mysore, distinguished themselves in government service and others entered political life, but most of them, provided with special privileges and privy purse allowances, became relics of the past in a democratic state.

The man who guided the integration of states never captured the imagination of the Indian people or the attention of the world, as did both Gandhi and Nehru, but for the period of transition, 1947 to 1950, Sardar Vallabhbhai Patel shared power with Nehru in an uneasy alliance that Brecher has termed the "duumvirate."[62] Temperamentally and ideologically, the two men could hardly have been more unalike. Nehru, reflective and sometimes considered indecisive, was a man of international vision, a committed socialist, secular in approach, of aristocratic Brahmin background and European manner. Patel, of Gujarati peasant stock, plebeian and orthodox, "was a man of iron will, clear about his objectives and resolute in his actions."[63] He was the realist, the machine politician, the defender of capitalism, of Hindu primacy, and of traditionalism. In the duumvirate, created by Gandhi to hold the Congress together and sustained by his memory, Patel, the Deputy Prime Minister, held the critical domestic portfolios, which along with the party organization gave him effective control over domestic affairs. Nehru was responsible for foreign affairs. "In the broadest sense they were equals, with one striking difference. Patel controlled a greater aggregate of power in the short-run, through the party and the key ministries of government, but Nehru commanded the country at large."[64] With the death of Patel in 1950, Nehru assumed full leadership within the Congress, the Government, and the nation.

One of the most important achievements of this period of transition was the constitution. This document, symbol of India's new freedom, embodied the basic principles for which the Congress had long struggled and provided the institutional framework for the political life of modern India. Before the leaders of India lay the tasks of political development, of creating and sustaining an institutional structure designed not simply to maintain order, but to stimulate expanded participation, to provide access to increased demands, and to effect a fundamental transformation of society.

[62] See Brecher, *Nehru*, pp. 389–425.
[63] Brecher, *Nehru*, p. 392.
[64] *Ibid.*, p. 400.

RECOMMENDED READING

* Basham, A. L., *The Wonder That Was India*. New York: Grove Press, 1954.
   A rich portrayal of pre-Muslim Indian civilization, its culture, political life, social structure, art, literature, and religion.

* Available in a paperback edition.

* Brecher, Michael, *Nehru: A Political Biography*. New York: Oxford University Press, 1959.
The best of many Nehru biographies, the book brilliantly utilizes the life of Nehru as the thread which weaves together the dramatic events of the nationalist movement and the first critical years of independence.

Erikson, Erik H., *Gandhi's Truth*. New York: Norton, 1969.
"The Event" of the 1918 Ahmedabad strike is the lens for this psychological and historical study of Gandhi.

* Gandhi, Mohandas, *An Autobiography, or The Story of My Experiments with Truth*. Ahmedabad: Navajivan Publishing House, 1927.
Although dealing only with his early life, the autobiography is a deeply revealing portrait of this highly complex and charismatic leader.

Hutchins, Francis G., *The Illusion of Permanence*. Princeton, N.J.: Princeton University Press, 1967.
An exploration of the changing self-image of the British presence in India and of the development of a fragile imperial confidence.

Menon, V. P., *The Transfer of Power*. Princeton, N.J.: Princeton University Press, 1957.
A detailed and dispassionate account by the man who served as constitutional adviser to the Governor General from 1942 to 1947.

Metcalf, Thomas R., *The Aftermath of Revolt: India, 1857–1870*. Princeton, N.J.: Princeton University Press, 1964.
An analysis of the impact of the mutiny on British imperial policy and on the people of India.

Mosley, Leonard, *The Last Days of the British Raj*. London: Weidenfeld and Nicolson, 1961.
A vivid description of the transfer of power, but with a decidedly jaundiced view of Lord Mountbatten.

* Nehru, Jawaharlal, *The Discovery of India*. Garden City, N.Y.: Doubleday, 1959.
Written during the time of his imprisonment, this history of India reveals Nehru's understanding of its heritage and his perspective on the nationalist struggle.

Seal, Anil, *The Emergence of Indian Nationalism: Competition and Collaboration in the Later Nineteenth Century*. Cambridge: Cambridge University Press, 1968.
An examination of the social roots of the Indian nationalist movement.

* Spear, Percival, *A History of India*, Vol. 2. Baltimore: Penguin, 1965.
An account of modern India, from the coming of the Moguls through the independence movement.

* ————, *India, Pakistan, and the West*, 4th ed. New York: Oxford University Press, 1967.
A brief but useful survey of Indian civilization and history through the time of independence.

* Available in a paperback edition.

III

THE FRAMEWORK OF POLITICS

THE CONSTITUTION OF INDIA IS AMONG THE LONGEST IN THE WORLD, with 395 articles and 8 schedules. It continued the constitutional development that took place under the British, retaining the basic precepts of the Government of India Act of 1935 and taking from it approximately 250 articles, verbatim or with minor changes. The "borrowed" constitution was attacked as "un-Indian" and unsuited to a people inexperienced in democratic self-rule. "Democracy in India is only a top-dressing on an Indian soil which is essentially undemocratic," Dr. B. R. Ambedkar argued; "constitutional morality is not a natural sentiment. It has to be cultivated."[1] The constitution was to be the agent of that cultivation. Democracy was to be achieved through its exercise.

[1] Constituent Assembly debates, quoted in M. V. Pylee, *Constitutional Government in India* (Bombay: Asia Publishing House, 1965), p. 8.

The Constituent Assembly and the Drafting of the Constitution

The task of the Constituent Assembly was to draft a constitution that would provide a framework for democratic government and an institutional structure capable of both sustaining and accelerating change. It was to provide the instrument for stimulating increased participation and for securing the higher levels of institutionalization necessary to accommodate expanding demands.

Under the Cabinet mission's provisions for the transfer of power, the Constituent Assembly was indirectly elected in 1946 by the provincial assemblies. Reflecting the Congress victories in the provincial elections the year before, the Congress commanded an overwhelming majority in the assembly, and Rajendra Prasad was elected president at its opening session. The boycott of the assembly by the Muslim League clouded the first sessions, however, and anticipated the settlement that was to divide India and provide a separate constituent assembly for Pakistan.

When India gained independence, the assembly, functioning under a modified Government of India Act of 1935, became the Provisional Parliament. Its fundamental task, however, remained that of framing the constitution. Dr. Ambedkar chaired the drafting committee and steered the document through nearly a year of debate over its various provisions. Four leaders, Nehru, Patel, Prasad, and the Congress Muslim leader Maulana Abul Kalam Azad, through their commanding grip on the Congress Assembly Party and the assembly's eight committees, constituted a virtual oligarchy within the assembly. Issues were openly debated, but the influence of the Congress leaders was nearly irresistible.[2] Although they themselves were by no means always of one mind, they sought to promote consensus, and in the end, the constitution was adopted by acclamation. On January 26, 1950, Republic Day, the new constitution went into effect.

The preamble of the constitution embodies the substance of Nehru's Resolution on Aims and Objectives and reflects the aspirations of the nationalist movement.

> WE, THE PEOPLE OF INDIA, having solemnly resolved to constitute India into a SOVEREIGN, DEMOCRATIC REPUBLIC and to secure to all its citizens:
>
> JUSTICE, social, economic and political;
>
> LIBERTY of thought, expression, belief, faith and worship;
>
> EQUALITY of status and opportunity; and to promote among them all

[2] Granville Austin, *The Indian Constitution* (New York: Oxford University Press, 1966), p. 22.

FRATERNITY assuring the dignity of the individual and the unity of the Nation;

IN OUR CONSTITUENT ASSEMBLY . . . do HEREBY ADOPT, ENACT AND GIVE TO OURSELVES THIS CONSTITUTION.

The new India was to be a parliamentary democracy, federal, republican, and secular. There were some members of the assembly who pushed for a Gandhian constitution, one that would provide for a decentralized state with the village panchayat as its nucleus. The vast majority, however, were committed from the beginning to a centralized parliamentary government. India had had a lengthy experience with representative institutions, and its leadership had been tutored in the liberal democratic tradition. The foremost task of the new government would be to restore order and unity to the nation. Only through the centralized authority of a modern state, they believed, could India achieve the stability requisite for economic progress. Only through democratic institutions could India begin to fulfill its aspirations after social revolution. The assembly, "with an abundant faith in the common man and the ultimate success of democratic rule,"[3] sought to break down the parochialism of local loyalties through the provision for direct election by adult suffrage.

Changes in the structure of India's government—the establishment of the dyarchy in 1919 and of a federal system in 1935—brought about a devolution of authority, but power remained centralized. To achieve the goals of social change and to overcome the "fissiparous tendencies" of communalism, the pattern of centralized authority was retained in the new constitution. The quest for unity was tempered, however, by demands to accommodate India's diversity. Provincial politicians, substantially represented in the Constituent Assembly, had had a taste of power and were therefore unlikely to yield to a purely unitary constitution. Moreover, there was a fundamental suspicion of the concentration of power that had enabled a handful of Englishmen to hold down a nation of four hundred million people. Most critical was the problem of integrating the princely states under a single constitution. With these considerations, the assembly concluded, "The soundest framework for our constitution is a federation with a strong Centre."[4]

The assembly determined also that India would be a republic, free and independent of the British Crown. After the transfer of power in 1947, India had become a dominion in the British Commonwealth of Nations. The head of state was the Governor General, appointed by the King on advice of the Indian Prime Minister. Lord Mountbatten, the

[3] Alladi Krishnaswami Ayyar in the Constituent Assembly debates, quoted in Austin, *The Indian Constitution*, p. 46.
[4] Second Report of the Union Powers Committee, July 5, 1947, quoted in R. L. Watts, *New Federations: Experiments in the Commonwealth* (New York: Oxford University Press, 1966), p. 18.

last Viceroy, was asked to remain as the first Governor General, and he was succeeded by C. Rajagopalachari, who served until the promulgation of the constitution and the accession of Prasad to the Presidency. As India was to be a republic, the Government sought to retain full membership in the Commonwealth without allegiance to the Crown. The formula was expressed in India's willingness to accept the King as the *symbol* of the free association of the member nations and as such the head of the Commonwealth. The first former British colony to request republic status within the Commonwealth, India served as the example to others seeking a continued relationship with Britain that was compatible with nationalist integrity.

The Constitution of India provides for a secular state. Nehru, the architect of Indian secularism, rejected the demand for a restoration of Hindu raj as he had rejected, but without success, the notion that India was two nations, one Hindu, one Muslim. The creation of a Hindu nation, Bharat, as demanded by the Hindu communalists, would have vindicated the Muslim League and recognized the legitimacy of Pakistan as an Islamic nation. It would, as well, have placed India's religious minorities, particularly the forty million Muslims left after partition, in an unenviable, if not disastrous, position. Under the Constituent Assembly, communal tension had reached a peak and war with Pakistan was imminent. The Hindu right, including Sardar Patel, demanded, on the one hand, retaliatory action against Indian Muslims for expulsion of Hindus from Pakistan, and on the other, a favored position for Hindus in India. The assembly did not succumb to fanaticism, however, and adopted instead impressive guarantees of religious freedom and equal protection of all faiths. But the pressures of Hindu communalism have not subsided, and with the growth of the quasi-communal Jana Sangh party, they have become an even more potent force in Indian political life.

The formal institutions of government established by the constitution provide a framework for political behavior. These institutions, often familiar in form, are frequently unfamiliar in operation. Traditional forms of behavior merge with the modern and adapt with resiliency to a changing environment. "Nothing in India is identifiable," E. M. Forster wrote in *A Passage to India*; "the mere asking of a question causes it to disappear or to merge in something else." If modern political institutions in India are often not what they appear, however, they are not mere façade to cloak a resurgent traditionalism. The structure of a political system is not simply passive and dependent. It not only responds to the environment; it also shapes the environment. In the process of development, the political system through its institutions will determine whether the nation has the capacity to meet the challenges of modernization and to change. The Constitution of India is a blueprint for institutionalization.

Fundamental Rights and Directive Principles
Established in the Constitution

The Indian constitution, as Granville Austin states, is "first and fore-most a social document."[5] The core of its commitment to a funda-mental change in the social order lies in the sections on Fundamental Rights and the Directive Principles of State Policy, "the conscience of the Constitution."[6]

The Fundamental Rights, embodied in Part III of the constitution, guarantee to each citizen basic substantive and procedural protections against the state. These rights, which apply to both the Center and the states, fall into seven categories: (1) the right of equality, (2) the right to freedom, (3) the right against exploitation, (4) the right to freedom of religion, (5) cultural and educational rights, (6) the right to property, and (7) the right to constitutional remedies. The right of equality guarantees equal protection before the law. It provides for equal opportunity in public employment, abolishes untouchability, and prohibits discrimination in the use of public places on the ground of religion, race, caste, sex, or place of birth. The rights of minorities are specifically protected in the provisions for freedom of religion and for the right of minorities to establish and administer their own educational institutions and to conserve a distinct language, script, and culture.

The Fundamental Rights reflect both India's assimilation of Western liberal tradition and its desire for the political freedoms it was denied under colonial rule. At the same time, however, these freedoms are not without their limitations. Under the Emergency Provisions of the constitution (Part XVIII), the President may suspend the right to free-dom and the right to constitutional remedies in situations of national emergency. A national emergency was declared when the Chinese in-vaded in 1962 and was followed by the enactment of the Defense of India Act, which provided for the detention of any person

> whom the authority suspects on grounds appearing to that au-thority to be reasonable, of being of hostile origin, of having acted, acting, being about to act or being likely to act in a manner prejudicial to the defence of India and civil defence, the security of the State, the public safety or interest, the maintenance of public order, India's relations with foreign states, the mainte-nance of peaceful conditions in any part of India or the efficient conduct of military operations.

The emergency was revoked only in 1968, long after the immediate threat of invasion. On occasion, it was used by the Government to

5 *The Indian Constitution*, p. 50.
6 *Ibid.*

justify preventive detention (a legacy of British days) in cases like the language riots in Tamilnadu (formerly Madras State) in 1965 that had little to do with the defense of India. The lifting of the emergency and suspension of the Defense of India Rules brought the release of 770 prisoners, the most prominent of whom was Sheik Mohammed Abdullah, leader of the Kashmiri Muslims, who had been held under house detention without trial. The threat of border disputes with China and Pakistan and in particular the unsettled status of Kashmir, however, prompted Parliament to pass in 1968 the Unlawful Activities Prevention Act, which makes many of the emergency powers under the Defense of India Act statutory law. These include a provision to outlaw any organization or imprison any individual found guilty of disclaiming or questioning Indian sovereignty over any piece of India's territorial claims.

The constitution itself provides for preventive detention, sanctioning the confinement of individuals in order to prevent them from engaging in acts considered injurious to society. It was generally agreed in the Constituent Assembly that the times demanded extraordinary measures but that detention procedures should be strictly controlled.[7] In 1950 the Preventive Detention Act was passed to combat the dangers of communal agitators, urban *goondas*, and dacoits in the countryside. The most immediate justification for the measure was the Communist guerrilla activity in the Telengana region of Hyderabad State. Indeed, in the first year of the Act's operation, six thousand of the ten thousand arrests made were in Telengana. As the Government consolidated its position, the number of detentions declined, and it has stabilized at about two hundred each year.[8] Preventive detention has, on the whole, been used with moderation and restraint. Thus, even with these limitations, "the chapter on Fundamental Rights . . . remains a formidable bulwark of individual liberty, a code of public conduct and a strong and sustaining basis of Indian democracy."[9]

The Directive Principles of State Policy delineate the obligations of the state toward its citizens. Almost a platform of the Congress party, the Directive Principles direct the state "to promote the welfare of the people by securing and promoting as effectively as it may a social order in which justice, social, economic and political, shall inform all the institutions of the national life."[10]

The precepts of the Directive Principles are not justiciable—that is, they are not enforceable by a court, as are the Fundamental Rights. They are designed rather to serve as a guide for the Union Parliament

[7] *Ibid.*, p. 111.
[8] See David H. Bayley, *Preventive Detention in India* (Calcutta: Mukhopadhyay, 1962), pp. 26–53.
[9] Pylee, *Constitutional Government*, p. 325.
[10] Constitution of India, Article 38.

and the state assemblies in framing new legislation. Although T. T. Krishnamachari, later Union Finance Minister, dismissed them as "a veritable dustbin of sentiment,"[11] the Directive Principles incorporated into the constitution the aspirations of a new nation and are, according to Article 37, "fundamental in the governance of the country." In evaluating the impact of the Fundamental Rights and Directive Principles, Austin doubts "if in any other constitution the expression of positive and negative rights has provided so much impetus towards changing and rebuilding society for the common good."[12]

The President and the Vice President

The executive power in India is vested by the constitution in the President, the formal head of state and symbol of the nation. He serves a five-year term and may be reelected. The President is subject to impeachment by Parliament for violation of the constitution.

Rajendra Prasad, who had presided over the Constituent Assembly, was elected by that body in 1950 as the first President of the Republic. Under the provisions of the new constitution, he was reelected in 1952 and again in 1957. Dr. Sarvapalli Radhakrishnan, a former Oxford philosopher who had served as Vice President under Prasad, was elected President in 1962. He was succeeded by his own Vice President, Dr. Zakir Hussain, in 1967. V. V. Giri, Congress labor leader, was elected Vice President. The 1967 presidential election was the first to be seriously contested by the opposition. Hussain, the Congress candidate and the choice of Prime Minister Indira Gandhi, was opposed by former Chief Justice Subha Rao. Hussain, a Muslim and a symbol of India's commitment to secularism, was returned by a substantial majority; his election served to reinforce the precedent of vice-presidential succession to the Presidency. In May, 1969, President Hussain died, and V. V. Giri took over as Acting President until elections could be held. The events that followed divided the Congress and underscored the potentially decisive position of the Indian President. (These events are examined in Chapter VI.)

The constitution specifies a complicated procedure for electing the President that is designed to ensure uniformity among the states as well as parity between the states as a whole and the Union. The electoral college is composed of all elected members of the legislative assemblies in the states and of Parliament. Each elected member of a state assembly is given as many votes as there are multiples of one thousand in the quotient obtained by dividing the population of the state by the total number of elected members of the assembly. In 1969 the total

[11] Constituent Assembly debates, quoted in Austin, *The Indian Constitution*, p. 75.
[12] *The Indian Constitution*, p. 115.

value of all votes assigned to members of the legislative assemblies was 430,847, with a range in the value of each legislator's vote from 7 for Nagaland legislators to 175 for Uttar Pradesh legislators. The value of the parliamentary votes at the Center is derived by dividing the total allotment for the assemblies by the number of elected members in the Lok Sabha and the Rajya Sabha, the two houses of Parliament. Thus, in 1969 the vote of each member of Parliament was worth 576.

Members indicate on their ballots their first and second preferences. If an absolute majority is not obtained by any candidate on the tabulation of first preferences, the second preferences indicated on the ballots of the candidate with the fewest number of votes are then transferred to the remaining candidates. The procedure is repeated until the sufficient majority is obtained. A candidate could conceivably win even though he had fewer first-preference votes than his major opponent.

In the balloting in 1969, minor candidates received scattered support in the states, but the contest was primarily between official Congress candidate Sanjiva Reddy, V. V. Giri, running as an independent with the silent support of the Prime Minister, and C. D. Deshmukh, candidate of the right-wing opposition parties. On the first count, no candidate received the majority vote of 418,118, although Giri led with 401,515, followed by Reddy with 313,548, and Deshmukh with 112,769 votes. With the tabulation of the second-preference votes on the Deshmukh ballots, Giri went over the number of votes needed to win, securing a total of 420,077 to Reddy's 405,427.

The Vice President is elected for a five-year term by members of both houses of Parliament sitting in joint session. Votes are tallied according to the same system of simple majority and alternative preference. The 1969 vice-presidential election was held two weeks after the presidential election. The Congress candidate, G. S. Pathak, Governor of Mysore State, easily won over his three opponents, with 400 of 725 votes cast. The Vice President is the ex officio chairman of the upper house of Parliament, the Rajya Sabha, or Council of States. During his term he may not also serve as a member of Parliament or of a state assembly. His functions are minimal, but in event of the death, resignation, or incapacity of the President, the Vice President assumes the responsibility of the office until a new President is elected. Under these circumstances a presidential election must be held within six months.

Powers of the President

The constitution confers an impressive list of powers on the President, but the Constituent Assembly determined that he should exercise these powers in accordance with the advice of his ministers. "Under the Draft Constitution the President occupies the same position as the King under the English Constitution," Dr. Ambedkar stated. "He is head of the State but not of the Executive. He represents the nation but does not rule the nation."[13] This view reflected a distrust of executive power nurtured by the colonial experience, but the constitutional conventions regulating the relationship between the King and Cabinet in Britain were not easily translated into written form. Although there were no specific provisions in the constitution, Prasad expressed the hope in the Constituent Assembly debates that "the convention under which in England the King acts always on the advice of his Ministers will be established in this country also . . . ."[14] It was Prasad, however, who sought as President to challenge this convention. Within two months after the preliminary draft constitution was published and subsequently throughout his tenure as President, Prasad argued that "there is no provision in the Constitution which in so many words lays down that the President shall be bound to act in accordance with the advice of his ministers."[15] He frequently spoke out on policy matters, such as the reform Hindu Code Bill governing marriage and inheritance, which he vigorously opposed, and would have assumed discretionary powers, but he was persuaded to accept a more limited role and exercise his power in accordance with convention. "For ill or creditable motives, Prasad attempted to read into the Constitution what was never intended to be there. Fortunately he failed. In fact, his efforts may have strengthened the Constitution by establishing the firm precedent that within the Executive the cabinet is all powerful."[16]

Even if the Cabinet is dominant, the President is by no means a mere figurehead, however, for the political situation may provide a vast range of opportunities for presidential action. Both Prasad and Radhakrishnan exercised an independent role and sought on occasion to exert their influence on pending legislation. The undisputed position of the Congress before 1967 precluded the intervention of a strong presidential personality, but in a situation of instability, the President may have wide latitude and his actions may be decisive. The position of the President would be particularly critical if the states returned opposition parties to power and together in the electoral college elected a President over a Congress majority in the central Parliament, a situation foreshadowed by the 1967 elections. With the likely possibility that in 1972 the Congress may lack a majority even in the Lok Sabha, the lower house of Parliament, the potential power of the President becomes all the greater, particularly in the latitude he might exercise in his choice of the Prime Minister. The selection of the President in 1969, on the death

[13] Quoted in Pylee, *Constitutional Government*, pp. 357–58.
[14] *Ibid.*, p. 358.
[15] See Austin, *The Indian Constitution*, pp. 135, 142.
[16] Austin, *The Indian Constitution*, p. 143.

of Hussain, was thus not merely a test of factional strength within the Congress, but a response to an uncertain political future and anticipates an increasingly important presidential role.

The President appoints the Prime Minister and on his advice then appoints other members of the Council of Ministers. Under ordinary conditions, he has no discretion: His choice is the leader of the majority party in the Lok Sabha, for the Prime Minister is responsible to the lower house and remains in office only so long as he commands its confidence. If no party holds a clear majority, however, or if the majority party is torn by factional disputes, the President may play a critical role in determining who among the conflicting claimants might form a stable ministry. The Prime Minister holds office at the pleasure of the President. If the Council of Ministers has lost the support of Parliament by defeat on a major issue or by vote of no confidence, the Prime Minister must resign, but he may advise the President to dissolve the Lok Sabha and call new elections. While the President may accept such advice at his discretion, parliamentary convention would suggest that he do so only after surveying the possibilities for the formation of a new Government by the opposition. If formation of a new Government seems doubtful, he would then dissolve the lower house and call elections. The defeated ministry would then be invited to continue as a caretaker government until a new ministry could be formed. The President by his oath of office must act "to preserve, protect and defend the Constitution." Presumably he is not bound by the advice of his ministers to take action he believes to be unconstitutional. The presidential position is by no means clear, but his actions will inevitably be determined by his sensitivity and response to the political climate.

As intended by the Constituent Assembly, the convention that presidential power shall be exercised on the advice of the Council of Ministers has in the years of Congress dominance become well established. On the advice of the Prime Minister, the President appoints the governors of the states, the justices of the Supreme Court and the state high courts, and members of various special commissions. He appoints the Attorney General, his legal advisor, and the Comptroller and Auditor General of India, who as guardian of the public purse sees that both Union and state expenditures are in accord with legislative appropriation. The President is the commander-in-chief of the armed forces and has the power of pardon. He calls Parliament into session and may dissolve the lower house. Every bill passed by Parliament must be presented to him for assent, and except in the case of a money bill, he may withhold assent or return the bill for reconsideration. Parliament can override his veto simply by passing the bill again in both houses.

Under Article 123 of the constitution, the President may promulgate ordinances when Parliament is not in session if he is satisfied that circumstances exist that demand immediate action. A presidential ordinance has the same force and effect as an Act of Parliament, but the ordinance must be laid before Parliament within six weeks after it reconvenes. More extraordinary powers are given to the President in provision for three types of emergency: a threat to security by war or external aggression or by internal disturbance, a breakdown in the constitutional government of a state, and a threat to financial stability. Under proclamation of a war emergency, such as that invoked in 1962, the federal provisions of the constitution may be suspended and the area affected brought under direct Central control. Such proclamations must be laid before Parliament for approval within two months.

The President may declare a constitutional emergency in a state if, on receipt of a report from the governor, a situation has arisen in which the government of the state cannot be carried on in accordance with the constitution. The President may then (1) assume any or all of the state functions to himself or may vest these functions in the governor, (2) declare that the powers of the state assembly shall be exercised by Parliament, and (3) make other provisions necessary to fulfill the objectives of the proclamation, including the suspension in part or whole of any constitutional body or authority in the state except the judiciary. The proclamation must be approved by Parliament; ordinarily it expires after six months, but it may be extended periodically by Parliament for a maximum overall period of three years.[17] President's Rule in the years of Congress dominance was invoked sparingly. Its most dramatic use came in the 1959 supersession of the Communist government in Kerala, when the Center intervened in what it called a breakdown of law and order. In the months immediately following the 1967 elections, however, unstable coalitions in the North toppled one after the other, and within two years the Center had intervened in six states, initiating tremendous controversy over the specific events of each case and the wider problem of the Center-state relationship.

Fear has been expressed that the emergency provisions might provide the foundation for a police state or a presidential dictatorship, or at the least, might act as instrument for the destruction of the federal system outlined in the constitution. Alan Gledhill was led in 1951 to conjure a Weimarian nightmare in which the President assumes dictatorial powers.[18] The check on executive authority is the Parliament, however, and thus far it has not abrogated its responsibility. "If the Federal Executive in India becomes autocratic," Granville Austin has written, "it will be because Parliament and the body politic have defaulted in their responsibility and have acquiesced in their own downfall, not because the intent of the Constitution has been 'constitutionally' circumvented."[19]

[17] See Pylee, *Constitutional Government*, pp. 636–55.
[18] *The Republic of India* (London: Stevens & Sons, 1951), p. 108.
[19] *The Indian Constitution*, p. 140.

Parliament

The Parliament of India as defined by the constitution consists of the President and the two houses, the Lok Sabha, the lower house, and the Rajya Sabha, the upper house. The fact that the President is a part of Parliament stresses the interdependence, rather than separation, of the Executive and Legislative in the parliamentary system.

The Lok Sabha

The constitution as amended by the Fourteenth Amendment in 1962 limits the membership of the Lok Sabha, or House of the People, to 525. Of these, 25 seats are reserved for representatives of the Union territories to be chosen as specified by Parliament. In addition, the President may nominate not more than two representatives of the Anglo-Indian community if none have been elected to the house. The remaining seats are allocated among the states on the basis of population, and members are directly elected on the basis of adult suffrage. Each state is divided into territorial constituencies that are roughly equal in population.

The normal life of the Lok Sabha is five years, but in accord with parliamentary tradition, it may be dissolved earlier by the President. Under a proclamation of emergency, the President may extend the life of the house for one year at a time, but not beyond six months after suspension of the emergency rules. The constitution specifies that the house must meet at least twice a year, with no more than six months between sessions. In practice, it has held an average of three sessions each year. The business of Parliament is transacted primarily in English or Hindi, but provision is made for the use of other Indian languages when necessary. While most members have been able to speak either English or Hindi, some have been determined to speak in their mother tongue. A few have had no other choice.

The Speaker, elected by the house from among its own members, presides over the Lok Sabha without political consideration. He is expected to stand above partisan conflict and is entitled to vote only in a tie. His powers are extensive, however, and his influence may be considerable. He is responsible for the maintenance of order and the conduct of business in the house. Twelve parliamentary committees carry the burden of most of the routine business in the Lok Sabha. Some, such as the Rules Committee and the Business Advisory Committee, are primarily concerned with organization and procedure. Others, however, act as watchdogs over the Executive. Specific committees scrutinize the budget and governmental economy, government appropriations and expenditures, the exercise of delegated power, and the implementation of ministerial assurances and promises. With regard to the financial committees, W. H. Morris-Jones writes that "this type of committee, inspired as it is by the idea not simply of economy nor even of efficiency alone but also of acting as a check against an oppressive or arbitrary executive, achieves a special significance as a substitute for a real Opposition."[20]

The Lok Sabha may conduct business only with a quorum of fifty, but with low levels of attendance, even this small number is often not easily obtained. The first hour of the parliamentary day is devoted to questions that bring the Government to the dock of public scrutiny. At this time a minister responds to the questions that have been submitted in advance by members and faces supplementary questions from the floor that demand his skill and quick judgment. As in Britain, the question hour supplies information to Parliament, but more significantly, it is an instrument of control over the Prime Minister and the Cabinet. The questions may highlight Government activity in a variety of areas, but they also serve to ensure that the Cabinet will remain responsive to the opinion of the legislative majority and sensitive to the criticism of the opposition. In the hands of the opposition, questions may seriously embarrass the Government, revealing inefficiency, incompetence, or scandal. Revelations of this kind have forced the resignation of such important ministers as T. T. Krishnamachari in 1958 and K. D. Malaviya in 1963.[21] The question period illustrates the educative role of a parliament in a democratic society.[22]

The ultimate control of the Lok Sabha over the Executive lies in its power of censure, the motion of no confidence that can bring down the Government. The motion may be introduced only with the support of fifty members, and until 1967, because of Parliament's splintered opposition, it was brought on only one occasion, in 1963. It did not carry.

The Lok Sabha was often criticized as Nehru's *durbar*, or princely court; but even though the Congress has had overwhelming dominance, the opposition has been respected, and Parliament has often been the arena of significant debate that the Cabinet has not ignored. While not genuinely a deliberative, policy-making body, Parliament has occasionally played an important role in modifying legislation submitted to it for ratification. Although Parliament has assumed a more important role since Nehru's death, it still remains under the shadow of the Prime Minister. However, the Lok Sabha debates are closely followed in the daily press, and through the pressure of this publicity, Parliament has been able to keep the Prime Minister sensitive and responsive to its opinion.

[20] *Parliament in India* (London: Longmans, Green, 1957), p. 308.
[21] Various "remarkable resignations" are discussed by R. J. Venkateswaran, *Cabinet Government in India* (London: George Allen & Unwin, 1967), pp. 73–93.
[22] See Morris-Jones, *Parliament in India*, pp. 219–26.

For a group or party to be considered an "official" party, it must have at least fifty members in the house. From the time of independence, opposition at the Center has been weak and heterogeneous, and in no Parliament has any party other than the Congress attained sufficient strength to meet the requirements for official recognition. Nevertheless, members of the opposition have been consulted on the arrangement of business in the house, represented on various committees, and recognized by the Speaker in the course of debate. The fragmentation and weakness of the opposition in the face of Congress dominance, its lack of experience and leadership, have tended, on the one hand, to make opposition criticism unrealistic and often irresponsible, and on the other, to predispose the Government to scorn of the opposition and unresponsiveness toward it.[23]

There is perhaps an inevitable tension between the Government and the members of Parliament, both in the opposition and the majority. It is after all the Cabinet that is the decision-making body of the political system, and a distrust of government lingers from the days of the nationalist movement. "This distrust is further aggravated by the lack of mutual respect between politicians and civil servants. This, too, is a relic of the past when the civil service was an arm of that foreign administration which put in prison a large number of those who are now the leading politicians."[24] When a member becomes a minister, he is seen as having gone over to the other side and is viewed with a mixture of envy and antagonism.

The Rajya Sabha

The Rajya Sabha, or Council of States, consists of a maximum of 250 members, of whom 12 are nominated by the President for their "special knowledge or practical experience" in literature, science, art, and social service. The allocation of the remaining seats among the states corresponds to their population, except that smaller states are given a somewhat larger share than their numbers alone would command. The representatives of each state are elected by the members of the state legislative assembly for a term of six years. The Rajya Sabha is not subject to dissolution, and the terms are staggered, as in the United States Senate, so that one-third of the members stand for election every two years.

In the debates of the Constituent Assembly, some argued that second chambers were undemocratic bastions of vested interest and acted as "clogs in the wheels of progress." Others upheld the chamber as "an essential element of federal constitutions," declaring that it introduced

---

[23] *Ibid.*, pp. 153–54.
[24] *Ibid.*, p. 152.

"an element of sobriety and second thought" into the democratic process. In any case, as Morris-Jones wrote in his study of the Indian Parliament, "Whatever uncertainty there may have been on the purpose of an Upper House, there was at no stage any doubt that the House of the People would be the more powerful."[25] The Government rests on the confidence of the popular assembly. The Council of Ministers is responsible only to the Lok Sabha, and while the Rajya Sabha has the right to be fully informed of the Government's activities, it is not empowered to raise a motion of censure.

The Legislative Process

Private members' bills are considered in an allotted period once a week, but it is the primary responsibility of the Government to draft legislation and introduce bills into Parliament. Any bill other than a money bill may be introduced in either house. Most bills originate in the Lok Sabha, however, and proceed through three readings, as in the British Parliament. The bill is introduced in the first reading, usually by title only and without debate. It may then be referred to a select committee of the house, appointed specifically for consideration of the bill, or in the case of bills of particular importance or complexity, to a joint committee of both houses. After the bill has been reported from the committee and accepted for consideration by the house, the second reading takes place; each clause is debated and voted on. Amendments may be moved at this stage. The third and final reading of the bill is the motion that the bill be passed. After passage, the bill is transmitted to the Rajya Sabha, where it follows the same procedure.

Differences between the bill as passed by the two houses may be resolved by sending the bill back and forth for reconsideration. If agreement is not reached, the President calls for a joint sitting of Parliament, and the disputed provision is decided on by a simple majority vote.[26] When the bill has passed both houses, it is sent to the President for his assent. He may return the bill to Parliament for reconsideration, but if it is passed again, the President may not withhold his assent.

Bills for taxing and spending, money bills, may be introduced only in the Lok Sabha. If amended or rejected by the Rajya Sabha, such a bill need merely be repassed by the lower house and sent to the President. There are certain powers relating to the position of the states, however, that are conferred upon the Rajya Sabha alone. It may, for example, declare by a two-thirds vote that Parliament should for a period up to one year make laws on the matters reserved by the constitution to the states. In most legislative matters, including constitutional amendments,

[25] *Parliament in India*, p. 90.
[26] This occurred only once, in 1961.

the Rajya Sabha exercises the same power as the Lok Sabha. The two houses are similar not only in power but also in composition, and as Morris-Jones noted more than ten years ago, the Rajya Sabha "has, not surprisingly, failed to evolve a distinct role for itself."[27] It has provided neither the expertise for technical revision nor the atmosphere for more leisurely and considered debate. Indeed, the duplication and rivalry between the two houses has been criticized as "a most wasteful exercise of political energies [that] can only serve to lower Parliament as a whole in public esteem."[28]

Although the Supreme Court may hold an Act of Parliament unconstitutional, the Parliament may amend the constitution with relative ease. The Indian constitution combines both rigidity and flexibility in its amending process. The greater portion of the constitution may be amended by a majority of the total membership of each house and by at least two-thirds of those present and voting. Some parts, however, may be amended by a simple majority of each house, the vote required to pass ordinary legislation. For example, the Parliament may by ordinary legislative procedure, create, reorganize, or abolish the constituent states and territories of the Union, if the President after consultation with the state assemblies so recommends. Other provisions, such as those dealing with the legislative powers of the Union and the states, may be amended only with a two-thirds majority in Parliament and ratification by not less than one-half of the states. Up to 1969, there have been twenty-one amendments to the constitution.

Members of Parliament

The members of Parliament are poorly paid, and like the M.P.'s of England, they lack the perquisites considered essential in the United States—office, staff, and clerical assistance. There is in Indian political life an ethos of self-sacrifice, but the difficulties that the members have often had to contend with hardly facilitate efficiency and expertise.

Many of the men who have served as members of Parliament, in the opposition parties as well as in the Congress, were prominent leaders of the nationalist movement and had served in the legislative bodies both in the states and at the Center. Even in the first parliament, however, returned by the 1951–52 elections, more than half the members had never before served in a legislative body. An increasing number have been drawn into political life only in the years since independence, and these frequently have been without previous parliamentary experience.

Professionals, particularly lawyers, have predominated in Parliament, but among the members are some of rather humble origin and little

[27] *Parliament in India*, p. 257.
[28] *Ibid.*, p. 262.

education. The percentage of lawyers has declined from 35 percent in the first Lok Sabha to 30 in the second, 24.5 in the third, and 17.5 in the fourth. At the same time, landed agrarian interests have increased. The percentage of M.P.'s giving agriculture as their main occupation has increased from 22.4 percent in the first Lok Sabha to 31.1 percent in the fourth. They now constitute the largest occupational group in Parliament.[29]

With each election, there has been a decline in the number of M.P.'s who command English and in their average level of education. This decline in the level of education reflects increasing democratization as the representatives become more nearly like those they represent. On the whole, Parliament still continues to draw men of exceptional quality, although in recent years, as the state has become an increasingly important political arena, many of the more politically able and ambitious men have been attracted to the state assemblies rather than to the Lok Sabha. As a result, many M.P.'s find themselves in a dependent position. Unlike members of the legislative assemblies they often lack a base of local power from which to bargain, and are therefore likely to owe their seats to the chief ministers of their states. Indeed, it was through the parliamentary delegations that the chief ministers, or heads of government in the states, exercised such a decisive role in the succession of Indira Gandhi to the Prime Ministership in 1966.

The Prime Minister and the Council of Ministers

Three Prime Ministers, Jawaharlal Nehru (1947–64), Lal Bahadur Shastri (1964–66), and Indira Gandhi (1966–), have served India. The constitution provides for the appointment of the Prime Minister by the President, but because the ministers are responsible to the Lok Sabha, it is assumed that he will choose the leader of the majority party in that house or, if there is no clear majority, a member who can command the confidence of a sufficient coalition.

The Prime Minister selects his ministers, who are then appointed by the President. They are not only responsible to Parliament, but are part of it. A minister must be a member of either the Lok Sabha or the Rajya Sabha. To draw on ministerial talent outside Parliament, however, the constitution permits the appointment of a nonmember if within a maximum of six months he becomes a member of Parliament, either by nomination or through a by-election for an open seat. Although a minister is entitled to vote only in the house of which he is a member, he may participate in the proceedings of both the Lok Sabha and the Rajya Sabha to answer questions or pilot a bill through passage.

[29] Ratna Dutta, "The Party Representative in the Fourth Lok Sabha," *Economic and Political Weekly*, annual number (January 1969), p. 179.

The Prime Minister is the connecting link between the Ministry and the President as well as between the Ministry and Parliament. He is, in Nehru's words, "the linchpin of Government."[30] The extensive powers vested in the President are in fact exercised by the Prime Minister, and it is he who, with his ministers, controls and coordinates the departments of government and determines policy through the submission of a program for parliamentary action. So long as he commands the majority in the Lok Sabha, his Government is secure, but if he is defeated on any major issue, or if a no-confidence motion is passed, he must by the conventions of cabinet government submit his resignation. Convention in Britain has established that the Prime Minister shall be a member of the popularly elected lower house. It was presumed that the convention would be retained in India, and the selection of Indira Gandhi, a member of the Rajya Sabha, as Prime Minister was criticized as an unhealthy precedent. She subsequently was returned from a Lok Sabha constituency.

The Council of Ministers includes Cabinet ministers, ordinary ministers (called ministers of state), and deputy ministers, who act as ministerial lieutenants, a position similar to the parliamentary secretaries in Britain. The ministers in theory are collectively responsible for all decisions of the Government, and no minister may publicly dissent from its policy. In fact, however, the Ministry does not meet as a body, and while every minister is expected to accept collective responsibility, the principle has not served to protect ministers from bearing individual responsibility for policy decisions. When heavy criticism has been leveled against a particular minister, he has frequently been dropped—as was Krishna Menon in the wake of the Chinese invasion—and the Ministry has thereby been vindicated. Rajni Kothari has written that "the collective responsibility of a council of ministers that never meets, has more the character of a coalition than a unified team, is divided into several layers of hierarchy, and allocates functions on a basis of drift and stopgap arrangements, can neither be collective nor responsible."[31]

The Cabinet

The Cabinet is not mentioned in the constitution, but usage has equated its functions with those assigned to the Council of Ministers under the constitution. The Cabinet, the inner body of the council, is composed of the principal ministers who, while holding important portfolios, are responsible generally for Government administration and policy. The Cabinet has four major functions: to approve all proposals for the legislative enactment of Government policy, to recommend all

---

[30] Quoted in Michael Brecher, *Nehru: A Political Biography* (New York: Oxford University Press, 1959), p. 459.
[31] "Administrative Institutions of Government," *Economic Weekly* (May 27, 1961), p. 823.

major appointments, to settle interdepartmental disputes, and to co-ordinate the various activities of the Government and oversee the execution of its policies.[32]

The Cabinet must be small enough not to become unwieldy, but its size, which has ranged between twelve and eighteen, has more often been the result of political considerations than of decision-making efficiency. The composition of the Cabinet reflects a concern for a degree of regional balance and for the representation of important communities—Muslims, Sikhs, and untouchables. The Prime Minister's choice of his Cabinet is further constrained by the necessity to include those members of Parliament, across the political spectrum, who have distinguished themselves in party work and who command a position of factional strength. In the Cabinet, as in the larger Council of Ministers, the distribution of the major portfolios and ranking is determined largely by the political weight of each claimant. Each member of the Cabinet is formally ranked. "Ranking of members of the Cabinet is not only uniquely Indian," Michael Brecher notes; "it appears to be based on a composite of the incumbent's political importance in the party and seniority, as intuitively perceived by the Prime Minister. . . . Yet formal status is not a measure of influence or involvement in the decision process."[33] As a "coalition," the Cabinet, which at times has included such polarities as Morarji Desai on the right and V. K. Krishna Menon on the left, has been disparate in character and frequently indecisive.

Only members are entitled to attend the weekly meetings of the Cabinet, but ministers of state, chief ministers, and technical experts may be invited to attend discussions of subjects with which they have special concern. Votes are rarely taken in the Cabinet; decisions usually are reached after discussion by a sense of the meeting. Only major issues are referred to the Cabinet, and frequently even these, such as the preparation of the budget, are decided by the appropriate minister in consultation with the Prime Minister. Most matters are resolved within the separate ministries and departments, and the work of the Cabinet itself is handled largely by committee.

The Cabinet committees, organized by the Prime Minister to co-ordinate the functions of the various ministries, have been largely dominated by the same few ministers. As Prime Minister, Nehru himself was chairman of nine of the ten committees, and the Home Minister was a member of all committees and was chairman of the tenth. The Finance Minister was a member of seven. "Appointments to these committees have been made more on personal considerations than on considerations of bringing only the ministers concerned together in relevant

[32] Pylee, *Constitutional Government*, p. 377.
[33] *Nehru's Mantle: The Politics of Succession in India* (New York: Praeger, 1966), pp. 112–13.

committees."[34] The Emergency Committee of the Cabinet, set up in 1962 and composed of six senior ministers including the Prime Minister, came in Nehru's last years to assume the role of an inner cabinet and took over many of the decision-making responsibilities of the whole Cabinet. As Prime Minister, Nehru exercised a preeminent role: His dominance of the Cabinet was overwhelming.

Under Shastri, the Emergency Committee declined in relative importance. The Cabinet's primacy was restored in domestic affairs, as each minister was given a greater role of initiative and discretion. If under Nehru decisions had frequently been imposed from above, decisions under Shastri reflected more of a genuine consensus. The quest for consensus reflected as well the new balance of power between the Union and the states. What Brecher has termed the "Grand Council of the Republic" is an informal body that came into being during the Shastri succession, made up of those who command decisive influence within the Congress—in the party and in the Government, at the Center and in the states. Brecher describes its operation as a "crisis committee," activated intermittently to deal with any major issue affecting the nation as a whole. It is "the collective substitute for Nehru's charisma: What he could virtually decree for himself . . . now requires their group consensus."[35] The charisma of Nehru as a personality, however, has come to reside, in part, in the office of the Prime Minister, giving added strength and legitimacy to the most critical position in the Indian political system.

The Cabinet and its committees are assisted by the Central Secretariat, headed by the Cabinet Secretary, a senior member of the administrative service. In 1964, to ease the burdens of transition, Shastri set up a second secretariat, analogous to the White House staff, headed by L. K. Jha, a senior member of the Indian Civil Service. While the main function of the secretariat was described by Jha as the preparation "of important speeches, statements and letters," the office carried "the seed of influence," and recalling the days of the "steel frame" under the British raj, demonstrated "the re-emergence of the Civil Service as a powerful pressure group on policy."[36]

In order to consolidate the nation in the first years of independence, 1947 to 1952, and in response to the fact that the Provisional Parliament had not been directly elected, Nehru brought into his first Ministry five non-Congressmen. Among them was Dr. Ambedkar, who had been a vigorous critic of Gandhi and the Congress, particularly in their policy toward untouchables. It was during this period also that Nehru shared power in the "duumvirate" with Sardar Patel. The post of Deputy

[34] Asok Chanda, *Indian Administration* (London: George Allen & Unwin, 1958), p. 91.

[35] Brecher, *Nehru's Mantle*, pp. 123–24.

[36] *Ibid.*, pp. 115–20.

Prime Minister had been created for Patel, and after his death in 1950 the post was not revived until Morarji Desai assumed that office under Prime Minister Indira Gandhi, serving until his resignation in 1969. Mrs. Gandhi's Cabinet contains, as Shastri's did, many of the ministers who served Nehru. Indeed, despite the death of many Congress stalwarts, ministerial resignations and the continued reshuffling of portfolios, there has been a remarkable continuity in Cabinet membership.

The ministries and departments, organized within the Central Secretariat, have expanded since independence in both number and scope. Each is responsible for the execution of Government policy in a particular area and is headed by a minister accountable for all that passes within his sphere of administration. A minister may be in charge of one or more ministries, some of which are then divided into departments. The ministry or department has as its permanent head a senior civil servant, the secretary, who acts as the principal adviser to the minister in matters of policy and administration and who is responsible to the minister for efficient and economical administration.[37]

The Public Services

During the struggle for swaraj, the Indian Civil Service was condemned as an instrument of imperialism and exploitation, its Indian members as traitorous agents of a "satanic government." At the time of independence Sardar Patel rose to defend the service. "Remove them," he said, "and I see nothing but a picture of chaos all over the country."[38] Nehru, who had once denounced the I.C.S. for its "spirit of authoritarianism," declared, "the old distinctions and differences are gone. . . . In the difficult days ahead our Service and experts have a vital role to play and we invite them to do so as comrades in the service of India."[39] Those who had once governed were to become servants. The instrument for law and order was to become the agent of change and development.

The structure of the public services, the "steel frame" of the British raj, was left largely intact. The services are characterized by "open entry based on academic achievement; elaborate training arrangements; permanency of tenure; responsible, generalist posts at central, provincial, and district levels reserved for members of the elite cadre alone; a regular, graduated scale of pay with pension and other benefits; and a system of promotion and frequent transfers based predominantly on seniority

---

[37] Chanda, *Indian Administration*, p. 140.
[38] Quoted in Pylee, *Constitutional Government*, p. 701.
[39] Jawaharlal Nehru, *Independence and After* (New York: John Day, 1950), p. 9.

and partly on merit."[40] The services are divided into three categories: • state services, central services, and all-India services. Each state has its own administrative service, headed in most cases by the chief secretary to the government, and a variety of technical, secretariat, and local government services. The central government services, numbering more than twenty, include the Indian Foreign Service, the Central Secretariat Service, the Postal Service, and the Indian Revenue Service. Each has its own recruitment procedure, rules, and pay scales. There are also separate technical and specialist services. The constitution specifies two all-India services, the Indian Administrative Service and the Indian Police Service, but additional all-India services can be created by Parliament, provided there is approval by two-thirds of the Rajya Sabha.

With concern for national integration, the States Reorganization Commission recommended in 1955 the creation of three new all-India services—engineering, health and medical, and forestry. The states have generally opposed the creation of new all-India services, however. They have argued that the higher pay for all-India officers would impose a financial strain, but in fact, the states resist sharing control over the services with the central government. They also fear that local candidates may fail in an all-India competition and that the posts will be filled by candidates from outside the state.[41] Certain states have indeed had a disproportionate number of direct recruits to the Indian Administrative Service. Tamilnadu, for example, with its high standard of English, has supplied nearly a quarter of the recruits.[42]

The Indian Administrative Service

At the time of independence the Indian Civil Service was 52 percent British in membership, but few chose to continue their service under the new government. With the departure of the British and the loss of Muslim officers at partition, the I.C.S. cadre was reduced from nearly 1500 to 451. These officers retained their prestigious I.C.S. designation and were integrated into the new Indian Administrative Service.[43] Most of the initial appointments to the I.A.S. were made on an emergency basis without the usual examination, but the entrance examination was soon resumed. By 1964 the I.A.S. had a strength of 1,974 officers, representing

---

[40] David C. Potter, "Bureaucratic Change in India," in Ralph Braibanti, ed., *Asian Bureaucratic Systems Emergent from the British Imperial Tradition* (Durham, N.C.: Duke University Press, 1966), p. 142. See also Hugh Tinker, "Structure of the British Imperial Heritage," in Braibanti, *Asian Bureaucratic Systems*, pp. 23–86.

[41] Chanda, *Indian Administration*, pp. 102–04.

[42] Potter, "Bureaucratic Change in India," p. 153.

[43] By 1966, 162 of the old I.C.S. officers, the élite of the élite, were left. The last will retire about 1980.

the élite cadre of the bureaucracy—.002 percent of the approximately nine million government employees in India.[44]

The I.A.S. is composed of seventeen cadres, one for each state, and recruits are permanently allocated to a particular state by the Center. To promote national integration and to secure freedom from local influence, one-half of the I.A.S. cadre in each state must come from other states. Seventy percent of the I.A.S. officers serve the state governments and are under their administrative jurisdiction. There is no Central cadre for the I.A.S.: Senior posts are filled by officers on deputation from the states who rotate, at least theoretically, between their states and the Center. In practice, the Center and the states are engaged in a "tug-of-war" to keep the best men.[45] At both levels, I.A.S. officers occupy the highest positions in the bureaucracy. In recent years, however, the states have drawn more heavily on the state services to fill top administrative posts.

The Union Public Service Commission, an independent advisory body appointed by the President, is responsible for all matters relating to recruitment, appointment, transfers, and promotions, and its advice is generally decisive.[46] The commission also concerns itself with disciplinary matters affecting members of the services and functions to protect the services and the merit system from political interference. Its relations with the Government are coordinated by the Ministry of Home Affairs, but in its day-to-day work the commission deals directly with the various ministries and departments through its own secretariat.[47]

The process of recruitment and training serves to reinforce the élitist character of the I.A.S. Approximately 25 percent of the yearly recruitment of less than one hundred are promoted from the state services, but the remainder is directly recruited through competitive examination. Competition is limited to college graduates between the ages of twenty-one and twenty-four. (The age limit is twenty-nine for members of scheduled castes and tribes, those who because of their backward or depressed status are listed in government schedules for special protection or benefits.) Promising prestige, high pay, and security, the I.A.S. has continued to attract India's brightest youth. In 1960–61, for example, more than five thousand (half of those who applied) took the combined examination for the 345 posts to be filled in the I.A.S., the Indian Police Service, and élite Central Services.[48]

Studies of the social background of direct recruits reveal that most

[44] Potter, "Bureaucratic Change in India," p. 144.
[45] W. H. Morris-Jones, The Government and Politics of India (London: Hutchinson, 1966), p. 125.
[46] M. A. Muttalib, Union Public Service Commission (New Delhi: Indian Institute of Public Administration, 1967), p. 181.
[47] Indian Institute of Public Administration, The Organization of the Government of India (Bombay: Asia Publishing House, 1958), p. 367.
[48] Muttalib, Union Public Service Commission, p. 136.

have come from high-income families—a significant factor in educational opportunity. Ninety percent are Hindu and nearly 45 percent are the sons of government officials.[49] The service, however, is no longer as homogeneous as the exclusive and internally cohesive I.C.S. under the British raj. It is increasingly "a looser organization holding a more disparate collection of civil servants with different backgrounds and experience."[50] A leveling process has changed the character of its composition. Of the seventy-two recruits undergoing training in 1960, twenty-seven were from high-income families; twenty-eight from middle-income families; and seventeen from low-income families. There has been a dramatic increase as well in the representation of scheduled castes and tribes. In 1962, 26.2 percent of the year's direct recruits were harijans.[51]

The I.A.S. examination reflects the generalist orientation of the service: English and general knowledge examinations and an essay that tests logic and expression are required. In addition, candidates may be tested on a wide range of nonadministrative subjects. Scores are considered in combination with a screening interview, but a candidate can no longer fail on "personality" alone. Recruits, on probation, receive a year of training at the service academy at Mussoori, where they take a foundation course that provides a basic background on the constitutional, economic, and social framework of modern India, broad principles of public administration, and the ethics of the profession. On completion of the course recruits must pass a written examination and qualifying tests in Hindi and the language of the state to which they will be allotted. A riding test lingers as a relic of the past.[52]

After completing their training period, the recruits are assigned to one of the state cadres for one or two years to receive training in the field. The state program is organized to provide on-the-job training at every administrative level in a wide range of practical problems.[53] In the British "tradition of the amateur," the I.A.S. officer is a jack-of-all-trades, rotated between the district and the state secretariats, between the state and the Center. At each level, the demand for specialized training is far greater than in the days of the British raj. The chief task of administration is no longer simply the maintenance of order, but the transformation of a traditional society. To overcome the rigidities of the parallel services, pools have been established to meet the demand for expertise. To handle economic matters, the Central Administrative Pool

[49] R. K. Trivedi and D. N. Rao, "Regular Recruits to the I.A.S.—A Study," *Journal of the National Academy of Administration*, Vol. 5 (1960), pp. 50–80.

[50] Potter, "Bureaucratic Change in India," p. 156.

[51] *Ibid.*, p. 153.

[52] After a year as a probationer, Subhas Chandra Bose failed his riding test and was rejected by the I.C.S. Tinker, "Structure of the British Imperial Heritage," p. 64.

[53] See S. P. Jagota, "Training of Public Servants in India," in Braibanti, *Asian Bureaucratic Systems*, pp. 83–84.

was established to draw men from the I.A.S., the central services, and the top class of state services. Some qualified men have been directly recruited from business and academic life. A similar pool was formed for the management of state industries.[54]

Bureaucracy

"The well-ordered bureaucracy left by the British," Morris-Jones has written, "has not yet been replaced by an equally well-ordered one more fitted to the needs of the new planning and welfare state."[55] The élite I.A.S. has nurtured an *esprit de corps* that has perhaps strengthened it against political interference, but it has cultivated what is often seen as a stance of arrogance. The separate services, with their wide disparity in pay scales, have become rigid and self-conscious "classes" and have stimulated jealousies and resentment. Paul Appleby, in his influential report on public administration in India, argued that "there is too much and too constant consciousness of rank, class, title and service membership, too little consciousness of membership in 'the' public service, and too little consciousness turning on particular job responsibilities."[56]

The mistrust of the bureaucracy that characterized the period of the nationalist movement has been perpetuated in the public mind by the rigidities of the system, impersonal treatment, the preoccupation with form and procedures, and the unwillingness of lower officials to accept responsibility. The image of the officialdom has opened "a chasm between the administration and the general public."[57] The achievement of development goals, however, depends on the growth of mutual attitudes of support and responsiveness between citizens and administrators. The results of various surveys, although inconclusive, suggest that increasing contact between a citizen and an official tends to mobilize the citizen's support *if* he believes the official responsive. If the official is unresponsive, more likely the case than not, increased contact can serve to widen the gap between aspiration and achievement, causing criticism, cynicism, and hostility.[58] Expanding participation has brought larger numbers of people into contact with the bureaucracy. If it is to cope successfully with the increasing demands made upon it, the bureaucracy must attain higher levels of institutionalization. An increased specialization of function, with structural differentiation, a decline of the tradition of the amateur, and an opening of the ranks of the services to a

[54] Morris-Jones, *The Government and Politics of India*, pp. 127–28.
[55] *Ibid.*, p. 130.
[56] *Public Administration in India: Report of a Survey* (New Delhi: Government of India, Cabinet Secretariat, 1953), p. 11.
[57] Kothari, "Administrative Institutions of Government," p. 825.
[58] See Samuel J. Eldersveld and others, *The Citizen and the Administrator in a Developing Democracy* (Chicago: Scott, Foresman, 1968), pp. 133–34.

broader social base have all served to enhance the capacity of the bureaucracy to meet the problems posed by expanded participation. The bureaucracy remains essentially an instrument of order rather than of democratic responsiveness, however. It has not yet successfully adapted to the new political environment, and since it has lost much of its prestige and once legendary efficiency, some have argued that the "steel frame" has become a cheap alloy.

The structure of an administration is an important determinant of its capabilities. At the lower rungs of the bureaucracy, formalism has served to stifle bureaucratic initiative and imagination. Procedure involves what Appleby has called "the hierarchial movement of paper."[59] Unwilling to accept responsibility even for minor decisions, petty bureaucrats refer the files, neatly tied in red tape, to a higher level. Responsibility is diluted in delay and inaction. "Red tape becomes a technique of self-preservation," writes Kothari, "and reverence for traditional forms is matched only by attachment to strict routine and an unwholesome preoccupation with questions of accountability."[60] Appleby argues that it is not a question of too much hierarchy, but rather that there is an irregular hierarchy, disjointed and impeding effective communication.[61] Administrative structure is not truly pyramidal, for authority is overly concentrated at the top. The permanent secretary to a state or central government department or ministry is accountable to a minister who holds that portfolio. He may exercise considerable influence over the formation of policy through his advice; but more frequently, the minister intervenes in the administrative process to make *particular* decisions rather than general policy and, when criticized, shifts responsibility to the civil servants. In an atmosphere of distrust, the civil servant may seek to separate policy and administration, sabotaging the former for the protection of the latter.[62]

A relationship of mutual respect between the politician and the bureaucrat is critical. The civil servant must be neither arrogant nor slavish, but in a democratic system, he is subject ultimately to nonbureaucratic control. In the years since Nehru's death, and particularly since the instability following the 1967 elections, the administration has assumed increasing importance. If the pattern of unstable coalitions now manifested in the states is projected to the Center in the 1972 elections, the bureaucracy must be capable of providing the continuity of government, just as in France during the *immobilisme* of the Fourth Republic the bureaucracy sustained the basic pattern of order.

In the states, with the rise and fall of weak coalition governments, the bureaucracy has managed to prevent major disruption. But to pass the

---

59 *Public Administration*, p. 18.
60 "Administrative Institutions of Government," p. 824.
61 *Public Administration*, p. 28.
62 Morris-Jones, *The Government and Politics of India*, p. 133.

responsibility of governmental decision-making to administrators is likely to yield an order increasingly separated from the people, unaccountable to them, and unresponsive to their demands. Indeed, since 1964 the sphere of administrative decision-making in India has been extended. As a result, what under Nehru was a political decision may now be bureaucratic, to a degree insulating the issue from the domain of public conflict.

One major element in the effective operation—and in the public image —of bureaucracy is corruption. While most people continue to see government service as prestigious, their confidence in it is low. Public servants are described as ineffectual, self-seeking, and dishonest. In a survey of residents of Delhi State, almost 60 percent felt that at least half the government officials were corrupt.[63] Corruption is greatly exaggerated in India, perhaps because economically frustrated individuals seek a scapegoat in official misbehavior, but A. D. Gorwala argues that "the psychological atmosphere produced by the persistent and unfavourable comment is itself the cause of further moral deterioration, for people will begin to adapt their methods, even for securing a legitimate right, to what they believe to be the tendency of men in power and office."[64]

In India, as in any country in which the power of a public servant far exceeds his income, corruption is a major problem. The scope of corruption is greater at points where substantive decisions are made in such matters as tax assessment and collection, licensing, and contracts. "Speed money" to expedite papers and files, even when nothing unlawful is involved, is perhaps the most common form.[65] The Government has engaged in a vigorous anticorruption drive, and in 1962 alone it received more than twenty thousand complaints. Less easily substantiated are the reports of corruption at the highest levels of government. Stories circulate in the bazaars of ministers who grow rich in office and favor their family and caste fellows. Kairon, former Chief Minister of the Punjab, was forced from office by the Nehru government on the charge of having "brought the State of Punjab to the verge of ruin by his systematic maladministration, the unabashed use of his official position and power to derive pecuniary gains for himself, the members of his family and relatives."[66]

The public may decry corruption, but traditional attitudes often condone it, and fatalism may make many accept it as inevitable. Nepotism is officially condemned, but in traditional terms it may be viewed as loyalty. For Lalaji, the traditional businessman and father of a high

[63] Eldersveld, *The Citizen and the Administrator*, pp. 29–30.
[64] *Report on Public Administration* (New Delhi: Government of India, Planning Commission, 1953), p. 13.
[65] John B. Monteiro, *Corruption: Control of Maladministration* (Bombay: Manaktalas, 1966), pp. 28–38.
[66] *Report of the Commission of Inquiry* (Das Report), Government of India publication, June 11, 1964, p. 27.

civil servant in Ruth Jhabvala's novel *The Nature of Passion*, influence and favor are a little thing. When he asks his son Chandra for an official favor, he expects it as filial obligation. "How dare he suggest such a thing," demands Kanta, Chandra's wife. "He does not understand," Chandra replies.

> What is there to understand! It is only a question of right and wrong. Everyone can understand what is right and wrong. You are a gazetted Government officer; you are in a position of trust; you are highly respected by many people; when you walk along a corridor, all the peons salute and the clerks and typists pretend to be working hard. Also you have a social position to keep up. How dare he ask you?
>
>   .   .   .
>
> He has different morals. We do not understand him and he does not understand us.[67]

Planning

The bureaucracy is the instrument by which policy is implemented, but the formation of policy is no assurance of its fulfillment. The gap between policy and implementation is nowhere clearer than in the broad area of the economy. The Congress, in its 1955 session at Avadi, committed itself in pursuance of the Directive Principles of the constitution to "the establishment of a socialistic pattern of society." For Nehru, this meant "a society in which there is social cohesion without classes, equality of opportunity, and the possibility for everyone to have a good life."[68] Nehru remained "brilliantly vague," and the commitment to socialism was considerably diluted in response to the conservative base of Congress political support. The commitment to socialism reflected a symbolic emancipation from the "capitalistic-imperialist" past and involved fundamentally a pragmatic approach to democratic planning and a readiness to utilize political power to guide and control the economic and social development of the nation.

This commitment had been clearly evident in the establishment of the Planning Commission in 1950. The commission, an extraconstitutional advisory body under the chairmanship of the Prime Minister, was empowered to draw up plans for the effective and balanced use of the country's resources and to establish priorities within the development program. The composition of the commission, nominated by Nehru, gave it the quasi-political image of a "super-cabinet," but one

---

[67] Ruth Jhabvala, *The Nature of Passion* (New York: Norton, 1956), pp. 153–54.
[68] Quoted in Norman D. Palmer, *The Indian Political System* (Boston: Houghton Mifflin, 1961), p. 161.

removed from accountability to Parliament. The power and centrality of the Planning Commission reflected Nehru's involvement in it, but with Nehru's decline and death, the commission found its political capital sharply reduced. While still important, the Planning Commission has today a more strictly advisory, technocratic role.

In 1951, at the beginning of the First Five-Year Plan, India had a per capita annual income of only fifty-three dollars. Over 80 percent of the population was rural, yet only 48 percent of the national income was produced in the rural sector. There were major shortages of food and raw materials; industrial production was below capacity; urban unemployment was high and what has been called concealed rural underemployment[69] still higher; inflation was beginning to accelerate; and a population increase estimated to be five million annually cut deeply into any economic progress. The First Five-Year Plan drew together a variety of specific programs for coordinated investment, with a major emphasis on agriculture. Owing to good monsoons and sufficient reserves of foreign exchange, the modest targets of the plan were fulfilled. During the plan years, 1951–56, national income rose 18 percent, with population growth only 6 percent, as then estimated.

Buoyed by the success of the plan, the commission drafted a plan for the years 1956–61. It sought

(a)   a sizable increase in national income so as to raise the standard of living in the country;
(b)   rapid industrialization, with particular emphasis on the development of basic and heavy industries;
(c)   a large expansion of employment opportunities; and
(d)   reduction of inequalities in income and wealth and a more even distribution of economic power.

Rapid industrialization was the core of the new plan. Far bolder than the first, the Second Five-Year Plan doubled investment expenditure to a public outlay of more than ten billion dollars. Private enterprise was expected to invest an additional five billion dollars. India's ability to mobilize and direct its own saving and investment potential was limited, however, and its hard currency reserves were rapidly declining. Within months it was clear that India had planned beyond its capacity.[70] Deficits were met with massive foreign aid, but even with midway adjustments, the plan was only 70 percent successful. The problem of foreign exchange has always been critical for India. In order to buy the products necessary for its development effort, it must do so with

[69] The concept of underemployment is controversial and heavily value-laden, for it carries with it a cultural bias as to what full employment *ought* to be.
[70] Benjamin Higgins, *Economic Development*, rev. ed. (New York: Norton, 1968), p. 668.

currencies backed by gold, "hard" currencies accepted as the medium of international trade. With an unfavorable balance of payments, importing more than it exports, India has had to make up the difference through grants-in-aid and through a staggering burden of loans, the interest on which absorbs a major portion of its yearly hard currency receipts, sustaining a vicious circle of economic dependency.

The Third Plan (1961–66) involved an even greater investment, but the emphasis and priorities of the second remained basically unchanged. The plan sought an increase of 30 percent in agricultural production, of 70 percent in industrial output, and an overall 30 percent increase in national income. The Chinese invasion quickly shattered hopes of fulfilling the plan. Development funds were channeled into defense; foreign exchange reserves were exhausted in the procurement of new weaponry; imports ran 50 percent above exports; and inflation brought spiraling prices. The Indo-Pakistan war in 1965 brought further economic dislocation, and India's ability to recover its losses was seriously weakened by the extended interruption of the flow of American aid. This again underscored the vulnerability of the Indian economy in its dependence on foreign support—a fact lost on neither the Government nor the opposition.

The cutoff in American aid, in response to the war, came in the midst of the worst drought of the century. The production of food grain fell nearly 19 percent in one year, and the shortage affected the entire economy. Food prices took a sharp rise, and the Government, to curb runaway inflation, tightened credit and cut government spending. Reductions in investment, coupled with the loss of aid, brought an industrial slowdown and expanding urban unemployment.[71] In 1966 the rupee was devalued in response to pressure from the World Bank, but the devaluation failed to rally the economy from recession. Exports were not stimulated as expected, and the salaried urban middle class was caught in a tightening economic squeeze. The massive American wheat loan under Public Law 480 may have concealed the crisis in Indian agriculture, but the 1965–67 drought brought renewed emphasis on agricultural programs. Plans were formulated for stimulating production, for increased production and use of fertilizer, for the introduction of high-yield varieties in wheat and rice, and for an expanded irrigation program.[72]

During the period of the first three plans, India failed to fulfill its projected targets of growth, but the record of attainment is impressive, even if punctuated by drought, war, and recession. There was an overall growth of nearly 4 percent per year, well below the plan target, but

[71] Max Millikan, "Economic Development: Performance and Prospects," *Foreign Affairs*, Vol. 46 (April 1968), pp. 541–42.
[72] *Ibid.*, p. 542.

substantially above the 1 percent growth rate in the first half of the century. Per capita income grew by about 2 percent annually.[73] In spite of difficulties, agricultural production grew by 3 percent a year, and food-grain production increased by some 50 percent during the three plan periods. Industrial performance was even more impressive, with an increase of 150 percent in production. Coal production doubled; steel production increased fourfold; electric power, sixfold; and consumer goods made substantial, if less dramatic, growth progress.[74] The availability of a rich variety of consumer goods, all made in India, contrasts sharply with the scarcities of even a decade ago.

In education, transportation, and communications, the period from 1951 to 1966 witnessed dramatic changes, as even the most isolated villages were penetrated—thus stimulating aspirations in the people after a better life and frustration at their inability to achieve it. The breakthrough in communications has brought to the Indian masses a new awareness of poverty and a sensitivity to the widening gap that separates them from the rich. The lot of most Indians has improved in absolute terms in the years since independence, but the gains have not been equally distributed. Despite the slogans of socialism, government policy itself has often served to subsidize the fundamental inequities of the society. In urban areas, employment opportunities have increased, to the benefit of both managerial and working classes. The lower middle classes, particularly salaried government employees, have gained little, however, and have seen rising prices push them deeper into poverty. George Rosen warns that the threat of political unrest from this group "is probably increased by the relative deterioration of its economic position in comparison with that of both the upper income groups and the factory workers in private industry."[75] Urban unrest is compounded by the widespread increase in unemployment, particularly among the educated.[76]

In rural areas the largest estates have been reduced by a degree of land reform, but more to the benefit of prosperous peasants than of the landless. Indeed, reforms have led to widespread eviction of tenants and to highly insecure seasonal employment for agricultural laborers. The poor, with no credit and with little margin for risk, are often unable to take advantage of new opportunities when available—and scarcity, perhaps more often than not, denies them even the opportunity. The dominant agricultural castes, on the other hand, "have gained economically by access to credit, fertilizers, seeds, and implements, they have gained politically by control of a major source of influence and patron-

[73] *Ibid.*, p. 532.
[74] *Ibid.*, p. 535.
[75] *Democracy and Economic Change in India*, new ed. (Berkeley: University of California Press, 1967), p. 190.
[76] *Ibid.*, pp. 155–56, 195.

age, and they have gained socially by an improvement in their status as a result of their positions in the new institutions."[77]

At the end of the Third Plan the Planning Commission declared a two-year "plan holiday." One-year plans were considered, but in 1969 the Fourth Five-Year Plan, far less elaborate and ambitious than those that preceded it, began to take shape under the direction of a considerably less powerful Planning Commission. The emerging strategy emphasizes agricultural development, with balanced industrial support, and concentration in those sectors and among those individuals where development prospects are brightest—among the rich peasants who are thus sustained in their dominance. According to the Fourth Plan, "the concern for achieving the desired increase in production in the short run often necessitates the concentration of effort in areas and on classes of people who already have the capacity to respond to growth opportunities."[78] By emphasizing growth *qua* growth as opposed to growth as long-range development, India has opted for production without social change, a policy that implicitly recognizes a growing gap between the "haves" and the "have nots." The disparities of the "green revolution" underscore the tension between economic justice and a narrow production orientation. Many of the old dreams of the independence movement have been sacrificed in what Tom Jannuzi has called "the retreat from commitment."[79] Short-term growth and political stability, moreover, may have been bought at the cost of long-term economic disruption and revolution.

The Supreme Court and the Judicial System

The Supreme Court of India stands at the apex of a single integrated judicial system. Although India is a federation, the centralized judiciary was regarded as "essential to maintain the unity of the country."[80] The Court has original and exclusive jurisdiction in disputes between the Union government and one or more states and in disputes between two or more states. It has appellate jurisdiction in any case, civil or criminal, that involves, by its own certification, a substantial question of law in the meaning and intent of the constitution. The Supreme Court is the interpreter and guardian of the constitution, the supreme law of the land. The Court is considerably less visible than its American coun-

[77] *Ibid.*, p. 145.
[78] Fourth Five-Year Plan, 1969–74, Draft (New Delhi: Government of India, Planning Commission, 1969), p. 9.
[79] "The Retreat from Commitment," *Janata*, Republic Day issue (January 1969), p. 27.
[80] Dr. B. R. Ambedkar in the Contituent Assembly debates, quoted in Austin, *The Indian Constitution*, p. 185.

terpart and has yet to exercise a formative role in shaping Indian political life. Unlike Britain, however, where no court may hold an Act of Parliament invalid, all legislation passed in India by the Center or the states must be in conformity with the constitution, and the constitutionality of any enactment is determined under the power of judicial review by the Supreme Court.

The scope of judicial review in India is not as wide as in the United States. The detail of the constitution gives the Court less latitude in interpretation, and the emergency provisions have severely reduced the Court's review powers in the area of personal liberty. Through its power of judicial review, however, the Court exercises control over both legislative and executive acts. The Court first invoked its power of supremacy in 1950 when it held a section of the Preventive Detention Act invalid and unconstitutional. The Court has since held various Center and state acts invalid, either in whole or part.[81] Its decisions with regard to the protection of the Fundamental Rights, Articles 12 through 35, have been a source of particular controversy, leading Nehru to refer to the Court as the "third House of Parliament." When the Court invalidated the Zamindari Abolition Act on the basis of the equal protection clause of the constitution, Parliament enacted the first constitutional amendment, denying the Supreme Court power to declare government acquisition of property invalid on the ground that it abridges any of the Fundamental Rights. Two subsequent amendments, the fourteenth and the seventeenth, were required to free land-reform legislation from the Court's jurisdiction. Then in 1967 the Supreme Court ruled that the Fundamental Rights cannot be abrogated or abridged by Parliament—even by constitutional amendment.[82] The controversy is not yet settled.

The Supreme Court consists of the Chief Justice and thirteen associate justices (the constitution originally specified a total of eight judges, but this was increased in 1960 to fourteen). Each judge is appointed by the President after consultation with the judges of the Supreme Court and the high courts of the states, as deemed necessary. Consultation with the Chief Justice is obligatory. The judges hold office until retirement at age sixty-five, as specified in the constitution, and may be removed only by Parliament on grounds of "proved misbehaviour or incapacity." The appointments to the Supreme Court must be made on the basis of judicial distinction. Appointments are usually made from the benches of the high courts of the states.

The judges of the high courts are appointed by the President, usually from lower benches, after consultation with the Chief Justices of the Supreme Court and the state high court and with the governor of the

[81] Pylee, *Constitutional Government*, pp. 495–504; Austin, *The Indian Constitution*, pp. 173–75.
[82] G. C. V. Subba Rao, "Fundamental Rights in India Versus Power to Amend the Constitution," *Texas International Law Forum*, Vol. 4 (Summer 1968), pp. 291–339.

state. The number of high court judges varies from thirty-three in the Allahabad High Court (the high court for the state of Uttar Pradesh) to three in the Assam High Court.[83] The jurisdiction of the high courts is not detailed in the constitution, but it is provided that they retain their general appellate jurisdiction as established during British rule. In addition, the high courts have original jurisdiction on revenue matters, superintend all courts within the state, and have the power to issue writs or orders for the enforcement of the Fundamental Rights guaranteed under the constitution. Below the high courts are the district and subordinate courts, similar in structure throughout the country.

The Indian judiciary is a career service. Candidates for the State Judicial Service stand in competitive examination after at least three years' experience before the bar. Successful candidates are then given special training before their appointment to the service.[84] Indian appellate courts are staffed not only from the career service but also, like the American judiciary, from practicing lawyers. The lower courts are staffed by career judges alone.

The "official" law of India may seem alien to most villagers, but they are increasingly ready to work within its framework. The modern judiciary, established by the British as a rule of law—universal, impersonal, and impartial—is today accepted as legitimate throughout India. While the modern legal system has largely displaced that of tradition, traditional society has not passively allowed itself to be regulated: It has used the modern system for its own ends. Traditional groups now find expression in litigation, but as Marc Galanter notes, "all contact with the legal system involves the translation of traditional interests and concerns into 'modern' terms in order to get legal effectiveness."[85] In a sense, he argues, "the new system is Indian: it is a unique system, peculiarly articulated to many of the interests and problems of modern India; and it is a new kind of unifying network through which various aspects of the civilization may find new expression."[86]

The Responsive Capacity of India's Governmental Framework

The institutions of government, established by the constitution on the framework of the British raj, have taken root in the Indian soil. Although transplanted, they are today no longer regarded as foreign imports; they have gained legitimacy and widespread acceptance by political parties across the ideological spectrum. Their meaning and op-

[83] Pylee, *Constitutional Government*, p. 560.
[84] *Ibid.*, pp. 562–63.
[85] "Hindu Law and the Development of the Modern Indian Legal System," unpublished paper presented at the annual meeting of the American Political Science Association, Chicago, September 9–12, 1964, p. 86.
[86] *Ibid.*, p. 88.

eration have been adapted to the Indian environment, and they are
still taking form. The judiciary, developed under British tutelage, is at
its highest levels considerably less important and less visible than in the
United States. It is highly respected, but as yet it has made little impact on the character of the political system. The lower courts, weighted
with a backlog of litigation, are a widely recognized, and perhaps all-too-
often employed, instrument of conflict resolution. The bureaucracy, in
search of a new democratic role, has yet to find a clear identity and remains fundamentally an instrument of repressive order. It has lost
much of its former efficiency in the face of an increased load of demands, and perhaps also some of its quality, with a concomitant loss of
respect. Occupants of the Presidency, while yet to face the test of coalition instability at the Center, have established conventions limiting the
exercise of the post's potential constitutional power. The office commands national respect as symbol of the state. Parliament, particularly
since the death of Nehru, has assumed greater importance. Although its
debates rarely affect the character of legislation, they are closely covered
in India's press, and the Prime Minister and the Cabinet are increasingly sensitive to Parliament's opinions. The impact of Parliament as an
educative institution has been limited largely to the élite political culture. For villagers and many urbanites alike, it is a distant institution
little affecting their everyday lives. For them, the state legislative assemblies are of far greater importance. The Prime Minister, however,
commands a powerful position. The charisma of Jawaharlal Nehru,
Prime Minister in the nation's formative years, has become identified
with the office itself. It is the symbolic repository of India's power and
international prestige. While affected by the personal imprint of the
great leader, the office has transcended personality, and through the
successions, from Nehru to Shastri to Indira Gandhi, the Prime Ministership has proved the most important position in the Indian government.

The political system has been resilient in the face of rapid change and
increasing demands, and as it has met each crisis, it has attained, in a
process of institutionalization, greater capacity to meet future challenge.
It is perhaps a fragile capacity, however, for India is only now beginning to experience expanding political participation. The dismemberment of the Congress in fratricidal struggle and the threat of instability
at the Center may strain the system beyond endurance. On gaining
independence, India inherited a highly institutionalized imperial re-
gime. Relatively low levels of participation and demands provided
India with a period of grace during which the institutions of repressive
order were adapted to new democratic functions. But India has, if not
fallen from grace, at least outrun its institutional advantage. The revolution of rising expectations now places continuous challenge upon these
institutions to respond. It may well be, however, that the success of
India's response will be determined not at the Center but in the states,

through the development of state and local governmental bodies and of interest groups and political parties capable of ordering the newly participant society.

RECOMMENDED READING

Appleby, Paul, *Public Administration in India: Report of a Survey*. New Delhi: Government of India, Cabinet Secretariat, 1953.
> An analysis of bureaucratic weakness in Indian administration.

Bayley, David H., *The Police and Political Development in India*. Princeton, N.J.: Princeton University Press, 1969.
> A study of the role police play in shaping and maintaining the Indian political system.

Chanda, Asok, *Indian Administration*. London: George Allen & Unwin, 1958.
> A critical examination of the Indian administrative structure and the executive branch of government by the former Comptroller and Auditor General of India.

Austin, Granville, *The Indian Constitution*. New York: Oxford University Press, 1966.
> An extremely well-written history of the Indian Constituent Assembly and analysis of the constitution it created.

Braibanti, Ralph, ed., *Asian Bureaucratic Systems Emergent from the British Imperial Tradition*. Durham, N.C.: Duke University Press, 1966.
> A collection of essays dealing with various aspects of the history and structure of the government services in India.

Brecher, Michael, *Nehru's Mantle: The Politics of Succession in India*. New York: Praeger, 1966.
> A detailed account of the events surrounding the successions after the deaths of Nehru and Shastri.

Morris-Jones, W. H., *Parliament in India*. London: Longmans, Green, 1957.
> An extensive study of the Indian Parliament, now dated but still of great use in understanding the character and operation of this institution.

Pylee, M. V., *Constitutional Government in India*, rev. ed. Bombay: Asia Publishing House, 1965.
> A detailed analysis of the constitution and the formal structures of Indian government.

* Smith, Donald E., *India as a Secular State*. Princeton, N.J.: Princeton University Press, 1963.
> A major study of secular government policy and its relationship to various aspects of Hindu religion and society, with a discussion of the particular problems posed by Hindu communalism.

Venkateswaran, R. J., *Cabinet Government in India*. London: George Allen & Unwin, 1967.
> An examination of Cabinet operations under Nehru, Shastri, and Indira Gandhi.

* Available in a paperback edition.

IV

FEDERALISM AND THE STATES

THE FEDERAL STRUCTURE IN INDIA IS CHARACTERIZED FORMALLY BY A bias in favor of the Center—a bias that has been the subject of controversy since the system's inception. Kenneth Wheare has described the system as "quasi-federal,"[1] and Asok Chanda, former Comptroller and Auditor General of India, has stated flatly that "India is not a federal state. In the final analysis," he says, "it is a unitary state in concept and operation . . . ."[2]

The Relationship Between the Center and the States

The unitary emphasis in the constitution, inherited from the Government of India Act of 1935, is to be found in the division of powers and in the various articles specifying the relationship between the Center and the states. The division of powers is laid down in the Seventh

[1] *Federal Government* (New York: Oxford University Press, 1951), p. 28.
[2] *Federalism in India* (London: George Allen & Unwin, 1965), p. 124.

Schedule of the constitution in three lists exhausting "all the ordinary activities of government." The Union List gives the Center exclusive authority to act in matters of national importance and includes among its ninety-seven items defense, foreign affairs, currency, banking duties, and income taxation. The State List, with sixty-six items, covers public order and police, welfare, health, education, local government, industry, agriculture, and land revenue. The Concurrent List contains forty-seven items over which the Center and the states share authority. The most important are civil and criminal law and social and economic planning. The residuary power lies with the Union, and in any conflict between Union and state, Union law prevails.

The paramount position of the Center is underscored by the power of Parliament to create new states, to alter the boundaries of existing states, and even to abolish a state by ordinary legislative procedure, without recourse to constitutional amendment. Under a proclamation of emergency, Parliament is empowered "to make laws for the whole or any part of the territory of India with respect to any of the matters enumerated in the State List."[3] The President, if advised by his representative in the state, the governor, that "the government of the State cannot be carried on in accordance with the provisions of this Constitution," may by proclamation assume all executive functions to himself and declare the powers of the state assembly to be under the authority of Parliament.[4] In an emergency the Government of India in fact takes on a unitary form.

The constitution provides that the Union may give such directions to a state government as may be necessary "to ensure compliance with laws made by Parliament."[5] If a state fails to comply with such directions, the President may invoke his emergency power to supersede the state government. In addition, the Rajya Sabha may by a two-thirds vote resolve that it is "necessary or expedient" that Parliament make laws for a temporary period with respect to any matter on the State List.[6] The Rajya Sabha invoked this power on only one occasion. However, since state representation in the Rajya Sabha is unequal, larger states have the power to transfer a subject from state to Union jurisdiction if opposition parties should gain control of some of the smaller states.[7] A variety of other articles also reveal the constitutional imbalance between the Union and states: the amending process, the single judicial system, the all-India services, the single election commission, and the provision for reservation of certain state bills for presidential assent. The distribution of revenue resources is especially critical in determining the nature

[3] Constitution of India, Article 250.
[4] Ibid., Article 356.
[5] Ibid., Article 256.
[6] Ibid., Article 249.
[7] Chanda, Federalism in India, p. 90.

of the states' relationship to the Center. The Union's tax resources as specified in the constitution are considerably greater than those of the states. Revenues collected by the Center are allocated in part to the states, on the basis of recommendations by the Finance Commission (an independent agency appointed by the President); thus the states are open to Union intervention. The states are further dependent on the Center for grants-in-aid.

For all its unitary character, however, the Center is heavily dependent on the states for the implementation of its policies. The leaders in the states, sensitive to the base of their political support, have often remained adamantly independent, as, for example, in their refusal to levy taxes on agricultural income as the Center has recommended. Indeed, Paul Appleby has argued that "no other large and important government . . . is so dependent as India on theoretically subordinate but actually rather distinct units responsible to a different political control, for so much of the administration of what are recognized as national programs of great importance to the nation."[8] Furthermore, for all its potential, the Center has used its power to intervene in state affairs sparingly. This has led many scholars to stress "cooperative federalism," an interdependence of the Center and the states. India has been characterized by a dual process of centralization and decentralization—centralization in response to the exigencies of national planning, and decentralization as a result of the Center's dependence on the states for administration, the increased solidarity of linguistic states, and the emergence of a new, regionally based state leadership.

The federal relationship is "a bargaining process between central and state leaders, one in which experiment, cooperation, persuasion and conciliation could describe both generally accepted norms and the usual procedural patterns of intergovernmental relations."[9] In a situation of limited resources each state seeks to maximize its advantage, stressing its needs and its potential. "Whereas the emphasis in the Constitution is on demarcation," says W. H. Morris-Jones, "that of practical relations is on co-operative bargaining."[10] In this bargaining process, the role of the Congress party has been critical. It has been widely held that the dominance of the Congress before 1967, when it controlled both the Center and the states, brought the state governments under effective Central control through the exercise of party discipline. However, on the basis of an examination of West Bengal-Center relations, Marcus F. Franda argues that the state Congress party organization may serve to impede Central control: Party cohesion within the state and the ability of the party to mobilize the populace

[8] *Public Administration in India: Report of a Survey* (New Delhi: Government of India, Cabinet Secretariat, 1953), p. 21.
[9] Marcus F. Franda, *West Bengal and the Federalizing Process in India* (Princeton, N.J.: Princeton University Press, 1968), p. 179.
[10] *The Government and Politics of India* (London: Hutchinson, 1966), p. 143.

for political action are major sources of state autonomy.[11] In West Bengal before 1967, the threat of the leftist opposition, supported by a volatile middle class, increased the state government's dependence on the Union for support in maintaining order. But at the same time, the Bengal Congress used the "extenuating circumstances" of the situation to maintain its independence from central party discipline. Because of the threat posed by the left, the national leadership was more willing to allow a wide range of discretion in policy and behavior by the state party organization.[12] Competing for development resources, the former Congress government in Tamilnadu used the threat of rising Tamil nationalist power to extract greater allocations from the Center. Ironically, the Center may find it easier to deal with non-Congress chief ministers than with the Congress bosses who have considerable influence on Congress policy at the Union level. The emergence of regional parties in the states, such as the Dravida Munnetra Kazhagam in Tamilnadu, may substantially reduce Congress power, but unlike an all-India opposition, these parties pose no individual threat to the Congress at the Center. The federal relationship may indeed witness the emergence of a pattern of alliance between the Congress, in control at the Center, and a variety of regional parties at the state level. The D.M.K., while vehemently opposed to the Congress within Tamilnadu, has cooperated closely with the Congress in New Delhi.

The instability that followed the 1967 elections brought increased Central intervention, but if instability facilitates Union dominance, the capacity of the Center to intervene effectively may well be declining. With the Congress split in 1969, the stability of the Center itself was no longer secure. The states, both Congress and non-Congress, have exercised increased autonomy since States Reorganization in 1956. Their political weight, as seen in the role of the states in the successions, for example, is substantial. The emergence of a new state leadership, more politically sensitive to traditional bases of support, has served to strengthen state party organization. With a regionally based machine, such as that in Bengal and Tamilnadu, the Congress derives its electoral success from local, not national, sources. It may be, however, that the local base of party effectiveness makes the party more highly vulnerable to displacement by regional opposition parties, as happened in both Bengal and Tamilnadu in 1967. The federal system serves, nevertheless, to quarantine state crises, for the local character of political conflict may have little effect on the stability of a neighboring state.[13] The states are the arena of the most dramatic increases in political participation, the focus of rising demands, and the critical testing ground of political development in India.

[11] *West Bengal and the Federalizing Process*, pp. 201–24.
[12] *Ibid.*, p. 190.
[13] Myron Weiner, *Party Building in a New Nation: The Indian National Congress* (Chicago: University of Chicago Press, 1967), p. 117.

States Reorganization

With the accession of the princely states in 1947, the process of integration began. The components of the new Union were divided into four categories, depending on both their makeup and relationship with the Center. Some, former governor's provinces and princely states alike, retained their boundaries. Others, however, were formed from the union of various contiguous states. A number of the smaller territories remained under Central administration.

The twenty-seven states of the Indian Union were heterogeneous linguistically and, except for their common link with the past, culturally. From the 1920's, and as late as 1945, the Congress party had called for the formation of linguistic provinces. The provincial branches of the party itself had been reorganized in 1921 on a linguistic basis, with units established for what are today the states of Andhra, Kerala, and Maharashtra. With independence, the Dar Commission was appointed to advise the Constituent Assembly in its deliberations on demands for linguistic states. The commission's report, submitted at the end of 1948, warned that linguistically homogeneous provinces would have a "subnational bias," threatening national unity, and that, in any case, each state would have minorities. The report was received with general disappointment. The issue had become critical, and the Congress appointed Jawaharlal Nehru, Vallabhbhai Patel, and the party president, Pattabhi Sitaramayya, "to examine the question in the light of the decisions taken by the Congress in the past and the requirements of the existing situation."[14] The "JVP" Committee, fundamentally concerned with the problem of national unity, reaffirmed the position of the Dar Commission. "It would unmistakably retard the process of consolidation [and] let loose, while we are still in a formative stage, forces of disruption and disintegration . . . ."[15] It conceded, however, that a strong case might be made for the formation of Andhra from the Telugu-speaking region of Madras, and that, if public sentiment was "insistent and overwhelming," this and other cases might be given further consideration. "This was the opening wedge for the bitter struggle over States Reorganization which was to dominate Indian politics from 1953 to 1956."[16]

The demand for a separate state of Andhra had deep roots among the Telugu people. It had won the agreement of the Madras government

---

[14] Quoted in Joan V. Bondurant, *Regionalism Versus Provincialism: A Study in Problems of Indian National Unity* (Indian Press Digests—Monograph Series, No. 4; Berkeley: University of California Press, 1958), p. 29.

[15] *Ibid.*

[16] Michael Brecher, *Nehru: A Political Biography* (New York: Oxford University Press, 1959), p. 481.

FIGURE 4–1

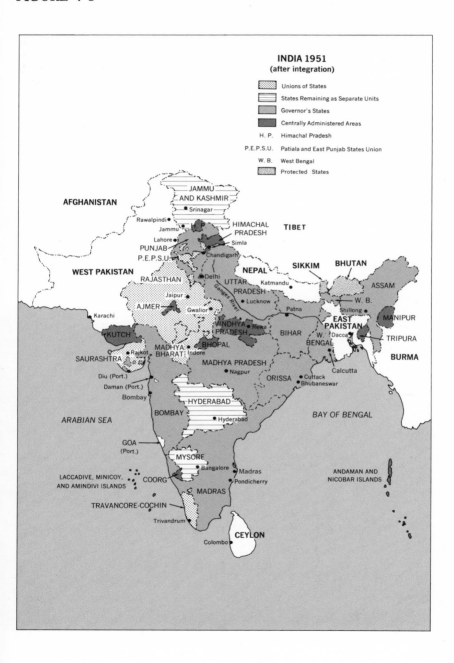

and obtained the support of the Tamilnad Congress Committee, but only after a fast-unto-death by one of the leaders of the Andhra movement did the Center finally respond. In 1953 the state of Andhra was created. Nehru argued against the "foolish and tribal attitudes" of provincialism. The states, he said, were only for administrative purposes —but the demand had been recognized, and other linguistic groups would now have nothing less.

The States Reorganization Commission, appointed by Nehru to examine the question, sought a "balanced approach" between regional sentiment and national interest. The commission, in its 1955 report, rejected the theory of "one language one state," but recognized "linguistic homogeneity as an important factor conducive to administrative convenience and efficiency . . . ."[17] The commission recommended that the political divisions of the Union be redrawn generally in accordance with linguistic demands. The States Reorganization Act, as it was finally passed by Parliament in November 1956, provided for fourteen states and six territories. The boundaries of each state were to be drawn so that they would conform with the region of a dominant language. Following the recommendations of the commission, however, Bombay and the Punjab, two of the most sensitive areas, were not reorganized on a linguistic basis. The demands for separate tribal states, including Jharkhand and Nagaland, were also bypassed.

The commission opposed the division of Bombay into Marathi and Gujarati states largely because of the critical question of Bombay City. Marathi-speakers constituted its largest language group, but the city was dominated by Gujarati wealth. In the Marathi-speaking districts of Bombay State, widespread rioting broke out, and eighty people were killed in police firings. Under pressure, the Center offered, then withdrew, a proposal that the state be divided but that the city of Bombay be administered as a separate state. During this period of indecision and vacillation on the part of Nehru and the Congress high command, the rioting spread to Gujarat. Bombay politics polarized linguistically: Two broadly based language front organizations, the Samyukta Maharashtra Samiti and the Mahagujarat Janata Parishad were formed. In the 1957 elections, the Congress majority in Bombay was seriously threatened. Agitation continued, and in 1960 the Congress gave way to the demand for reorganization. Gujarat and Maharashtra were constituted as separate linguistic states, with the city of Bombay included as part of Maharashtra.

The demand for the creation of Jharkhand out of the Chota-Nagpur region of southern Bihar and the contiguous tribal districts of Orissa was a product of the increasing self-consciousness of the six million members of the scheduled tribes in the area. The Jharkhand party,

[17] *Report of the States Reorganization Commission* (New Delhi: Government of India, 1955), p. 46.

organized by a wealthy, Oxford-educated Munda tribesman, Jaipal Singh, secured various concessions from the Bihar government, but it did not succeed in its demand for a separate state.[18]

The demand for the creation of Nagaland posed a more serious problem. The Naga tribes in the hills along the Assam-Burma border had never been completely brought under control by the British, and they were eager to assert their independence from the new Indian government.The situation was further complicated by the conversion of many of the Nagas to Christianity by American Baptist missionaries. Their missionary tie gave the Nagas outside leverage. When the Government sought to bring formerly unadministered areas of the Naga hills under its control, the Nagas appealed to the United Nations, protesting what they called an Indian invasion, and the Naga National Council was organized to function as a parallel government with Assam. With money and arms secured by the Naga leader A. Z. Phizo, the rebellion became increasingly serious, and in 1956 the Indian government sent in troops to pacify the area. The Naga People's Convention, representing the more traditional leadership of the Naga tribes, opposed Phizo and proposed a settlement "within the Indian Union." The Nagas were finally released from Assamese administration, and in 1963 the state of Nagaland came into being. Sporadic violence has continued, however, and an exile government operates in London under Phizo. More recently, the Mizo tribe has engaged in guerrilla action in frustration over its failure to gain separation from Assam as a tribal hill state.[19] A separate administration has been established for the Mizo hill areas within the state of Assam, but the solution has not satisfied tribal aspirations. A reorganization of Assam is now being considered.

In the Punjab, the Akali Dal, the paramilitary political party of Sikh nationalism, had long demanded a Sikh state, if not the independent Sikhistan it sought at the time of partition. The demand for a separate state of the Punjab (Punjabi Suba) was voiced not in communal but in linguistic terms. There was no real language problem in the Punjab, however; it was rather a problem of script and, fundamentally, of religion. Punjabi is the mother tongue of Sikhs and Hindus alike, but communal passions had led large sections of the Hindu community to renounce the Punjabi language by naming their mother tongue as Hindi for census tabulation. The languages as spoken are very similar, but Punjabi is distinguished by the use of Gurmukhi, the script of the Sikh holy books. Hindus in the Punjab write in Urdu or in Devanagari script. "The only chance of survival of the Sikhs as a separate community," it

[18] See Myron Weiner, *The Politics of Scarcity* (Chicago: University of Chicago Press, 1962), pp. 41–43.

[19] *Ibid.*, pp. 43–48. See also Marcus F. Franda, "The Naga National Council: Origins of a Separatist Movement," *Economic Weekly* (February 4, 1961), pp. 153–56.

was argued, "is to create a State in which they form a compact group, where the teaching of Gurmukhi and the Sikh religion is compulsory . . . ."[20]

The States Reorganization Commission contended that the formation of a separate Punjabi-speaking state would solve neither the language nor the communal problem, but "far from removing internal tension, which exists between communal and not linguistic and regional groups, it might further exacerbate the existing feelings."[21] In the 1956 reorganization the states of P.E.P.S.U. (Patiala and East Punjab States Union) and the Punjab were merged into a single state; the Sikhs, forming only about one-third of the population, were concentrated in the western districts. Punjabi and Hindi were both official languages. But the Akali Dal, encouraged by the bifurcation of Bombay in 1960, began agitating for Punjabi Suba. Akali volunteers courted arrest and filled the jails, while Sikh leaders Sant Fateh Singh and Master Tara Singh engaged in abortive fasts. Agitation continued, but without response from the Government. Then abruptly in 1966, supposedly as a concession to the valor and suffering of the Sikhs in the Indo-Pakistan war of 1965, but partly in response to the growing demand in the Hindi areas for a separate state of Haryana, the Government announced that the Punjab would be divided into two units, Punjabi Suba and Haryana, corresponding to the regions of language dominance. The Sikhs at last constituted a majority in the Punjab—55 percent of the population. The hill districts of the old Punjab became part of Himachal Pradesh, stimulating a demand there for full statehood. Chandigarh, the modern capital designed by the French architect Le Corbusier, was made a Union territory and joint capital for the two states, served also by a common governor and a common high court. Conflict developed between the states. In January 1970 the Government awarded Chandigarh to the Punjab, compensating Haryana with a fertile piece of land in southwest Punjab. Chandigarh remains a Union territory serving both states until Haryana has built a capital.

India's political map has been modified in the years since States Reorganization, so that the Indian Union is now composed of seventeen states and ten Union territories. (See the map inside the front cover.) The formation of new states cannot be ruled out. The Telengana region of Andhra, the area that was part of old Hyderabad State, is now agitating for separate statehood on the ground that it has been discriminated against by the political leaders from the rich, coastal areas of the state. Leaders of the movement argue that the guarantees given in 1956 to protect Telengana rights and to develop the depressed region have been ignored. Conceding that the safeguards had been violated, Mrs. Gandhi urged that grievances could be corrected without separate

---

[20] Khushwant Singh, A History of the Sikhs, Vol. 2 (Princeton, N.J.: Princeton University Press, 1966), pp. 304–05.
[21] Report of the States Reorganization Commission, p. 146.

TABLE 4-1

STATES AND TERRITORIES OF THE INDIAN UNION

States	Principal Languages
Andhra Pradesh	Telugu
Assam	Assamese and Bengali
Bihar	Hindi
Gujarat	Gujarati
Haryana	Hindi
Jammu and Kashmir	Kashmiri, Dogri, and Urdu
Kerala	Malayalam
Madhya Pradesh	Hindi
Tamilnadu (formerly called Madras)	Tamil
Maharashtra	Marathi
Mysore	Kannada
Nagaland	Naga and English*
Orissa	Oriya
Punjab	Punjabi
Rajasthan	Rajasthani and Hindi
Uttar Pradesh	Hindi
West Bengal	Bengali

Union Territories

Delhi	Himachal Pradesh
Manipur	Tripura
Andaman and Nicobar Islands	Laccadive, Minicoy, and Amindivi Islands
Dadra and Nagar Havili	Goa, Daman, and Diu
Pondicherry	Chandigarh

* English is the language used for administrative purposes as a result of both practical necessity and missionary influence.

statehood, which might spur other separatist movements into action. The issues are not solely economic, however, for the leaders of the agitation are discontented Congress politicians who oppose the faction controlling the Andhra state government. By securing their demand for separate statehood, they would in the process carve out their own political fiefdom, comprising 40 percent of the area and population of the present state. Their appeal found immediate response among the people of Telengana. Demonstrations, strikes, and hartals, which began early in 1969, assumed increasingly violent proportions. By mid-summer more than one hundred persons had been killed in rioting and twenty-five thousand had been arrested. Schools and colleges, centers of the agitation, were closed; curfew was imposed in Hyderabad; and the Indian army was called into force, only deepening bitterness and resentment. The intensity of the movement slowly dissipated, and there were only sporadic outbreaks of violence; but the reorganization of the Andhra ministry left few Telengana militants satisfied.

Separatist feeling in Telengana is strong, and there are similar separate statehood movements throughout India, frequently involving depressed regions. These include the tribal areas of Bihar, the hill districts of Bengal, the eastern districts of Uttar Pradesh, the Saurashtra region of Gujarat, and restless areas in Madhya Pradesh and Maharashtra.

In order to counter divisive tendencies among the linguistic states, the States Reorganization Act established five zonal councils to promote cooperation and coordination of policies. Each council consists of the Union Home Minister, acting as chairman, the chief ministers of the states within the zone, and two other ministers from each state nominated by the governor. The councils have only an advisory capacity, and the results of their activities have been less than impressive. There has been some success in hydroelectric power development, but only the Southern Zonal Council has effectively served to coordinate state economic and social policies, notably in the matter of linguistic minorities.

Reorganization gave the states a political identity congruent with their culture and language. It

> brought State politics closer to the people, and made it easier for traditional leaders and influential regional groups to capture control or, at least, exercise much influence over the use of power. . . . Thus, in a sense, reorganization made State politics more democratic, but less western in style. It meant, for one thing, that State politics would be increasingly conducted in the regional language rather than English; thus power was now open to others than the small English-speaking elite.[22]

States Reorganization provided the framework for expanded participation. It made the people more accessible to political mobilization and, at the same time, provided them with increased institutional access for the articulation of demands.

[22] Duncan B. Forrester, "Electoral Politics and Social Change," *Economic and Political Weekly*, special number (July 1968), p. 1083.

State Government

Each of the states reproduces in miniature the structure and organization of the Union government.

The Governor

In his relationship to the chief minister and the state council of ministers and to the state legislative assembly, the governor holds a constitutional position much like that of the President at the Center. He is appointed by the President for a term of five years, and by convention the state ministry is consulted to assure his acceptability. The governor is usually from another state, free from local political commitments and, presumably, able to view the problems of Union-state relations with detachment and objectivity.[23]

Like the President, the governor holds the formal executive power. Although this power is in fact exercised by the council of ministers, the governor has important discretionary powers that he performs as the agent of the central government. The decision as to what lies within his discretion is solely his own. The governor formally appoints the chief minister. If no clear majority is returned to the state assembly, the governor may exercise his discretion in the selection of a leader who can form a stable ministry, and while the confidence of the assembly is required, the governor's role may be critical.

The 1967 elections highlighted this role and brought the position of the governor into controversy. Five states were without clear majorities after the election, and in other states subsequent liquidity of support, with the defection of members to the opposition in floor-crossings, brought on instability that gave governors considerable room to act. In the states without clear majorities governors had to assess which of the competing coalitions could marshal majority support for a ministry; in the other states they had to determine whether the ministry retained the confidence of the assembly and, if not, whether a new ministry could be formed. If no government can be found, a state may then be brought under President's Rule. The governor, as agent of the Union, then assumes the emergency powers of administration. After the 1967 election the process became a familiar one; virtually all of North India came under President's Rule. The midterm elections held in 1969 seemed only to punctuate the pattern of political instability.

In addition to his emergency powers, the governor also has certain legislative powers, including the power to promulgate ordinances. Every bill passed by the assembly goes to him for assent. Most bills are gov-

[23] M. V. Pylee, *Constitutional Government in India* (Bombay: Asia Publishing House, 1965), p. 513.

ernment sponsored, and his refusal to assent would bring him into conflict with the state ministry, but he is empowered to return any bill except a money bill to the assembly for its reconsideration. If, in his opinion, a bill threatens the position of the high court, he may reserve it for the assent of the President.

The Chief Minister

The chief minister occupies a position in the state comparable to that of the Prime Minister at the Center. He is appointed by the governor, but is responsible with his ministry to the popularly elected legislative assembly. Until 1967 the number of ministers in each state averaged about a dozen. In the process of ministry formation after the 1967 elections, however, the ministries were greatly expanded as additional posts were offered to counter opposition attempts to lure members into defection through the promise of ministerial positions in new governments.

The Legislative Assembly and the Legislative Council

The constitution provides that in each state there shall be a legislative assembly. About half the states also have a second chamber, the legislative council. The assembly is directly elected for a five-year term, with a membership of not more than five hundred or fewer than sixty. In order to maintain uniformity in the population represented, the constituencies are reapportioned with each election in accordance with the census. If the Anglo-Indian community is not represented in the assembly, the constitution empowers the governor to nominate an appropriate number of Anglo-Indians as members.

In those states with a bicameral legislature, the upper house, the legislative council, is selected by a combination of direct election, indirect election, and nomination, with a total membership not more than one-third of the number in the legislative assembly but not fewer than forty. The council is not subject to dissolution, and like the Rajya Sabha, it renews one-third of its membership every two years. Unlike the Rajya Sabha, however, the upper house of the states exercises what in fact is an advisory role alone. At most, it can delay the passage of a bill and has been attacked as a "costly ornamental luxury."[24]

Members of the Legislative Assembly

Members of the state legislative assemblies command positions of increasing importance, for it is the assembly rather than Parliament that

[24] Quoted in Pylee, *Constitutional Government*, p. 531.

is the closest legislative unit to the people. Likewise, assembly elections are viewed within the states as far more critical than parliamentary elections. The social character of the assembly differs considerably from that of Parliament in reflecting generally lower levels of education and westernization. The M.L.A. is highly astute politically, however, and it is through him that the masses make their most effective contact with the élite. Reflecting an increasing parochialization as local bosses, adept in the arenas of traditional village politics, rise to positions of state power, the legislative assemblies are the focal point of modern and traditional political styles. The successful M.L.A. is likely to combine the styles in his role as a political broker. What the voters want in an ideal M.L.A. might well approximate the villagers' ideal described by F. G. Bailey in his study of Orissa:

> Their MLA is not the representative of a party with a policy which commends itself to them, not even a representative who will watch over their interests when policies are being framed, but rather a man who will intervene in the implementation of policy, and in the ordinary day-to-day administration. He is there to divert the benefits in the direction of his constituents, to help individuals to get what they want out of the Administration, and to give them a hand when they get into trouble with officials. This is the meaning which the ordinary villager—and some of their MLAs—attach to the phrase "serving the people."[25]

With each election, the assemblies have become more nearly representative of the people, with members drawn from increasingly varied backgrounds. In Tamilnadu, for example, the first assembly (1952–57) was dominated by a highly educated, westernized, English-speaking élite—middle-class lawyers, landlords, and a variety of hereditary notables.[26] Through the creation of a unilingual Tamil state, States Reorganization increased the number of opportunities for mobilization and participation and encouraged more traditional and less well-educated leaders to enter the government. Knowledge of English was no longer essential. Sufficient education to be an effective intermediary between the government and the people was necessary, but increasingly the M.L.A.'s lacked an adequate education for effective policy-making and came to rely more heavily on the bureaucratic structure. Indeed, the "legislative life" of the M.L.A. is secondary to his role as political broker. "The average MLA comes into his own not on the floor of the Assembly but in helping his constituents to get places in college, permits,

---

[25] *Politics and Social Change: Orissa in* 1959 (Berkeley: University of California Press, 1963), p. 25.
[26] Duncan B. Forrester, "State Legislators in Madras," *Journal of Commonwealth Political Studies*, Vol. 7 (March 1969), p. 37.

licenses, and jobs. It is this kind of work that occupies most of his time, and this that pays the greatest electoral dividends."[27]

The legislative assembly in Tamilnadu, as in the rest of India, has increasingly come under rural dominance. Most M.L.A.'s have strong ties to their constituencies, and it is through the M.L.A.'s that localism has come to dominate state politics.[28] Under the Congress, localism carried with it the dominance of the wealthiest sectors of rural society. Landowners and leaders of the traditionally dominant agricultural castes came into prominence through the political machine. Many of these men had remained aloof during the nationalist movement, and only after independence, both to protect themselves and to take advantage of new opportunities to augment their power, did they enter the political arena. The English-educated veterans of the struggle for independence were thus displaced in the assembly by those who were committed to the defense of vested interests and the politics of the pork barrel. Duncan B. Forrester sees their struggle for the spoils of office as the pathway to their own defeat, for political competition has brought larger numbers into political life, made them politically conscious and sensitive to the power of the vote. In 1967 the Tamilnadu electorate reacted and brought in a new assembly composed of a new generation of state political leaders—in general, better educated, more urbanized, less wealthy, less caste-conscious, and more radical than the bosses they pushed out.[29] Tamilnadu, if anticipating a more general displacement of the network of local bosses throughout India, is not typical. In most states, rural landed interests retain their hold over assembly majorities—both Congress and non-Congress—resisting the emergence of new claimants for the limited resources available. Few states, if any, have developed the institutional and resource capacity to accommodate expanded participation and new and varied demands.

Local Government

The system of local government in India today retains a fundamental continuity with the past. Its hierarchical structure was built by the British on the foundations of Mogul administration and has been refined by independent India to suit the needs of a developing society.

The Local Administrative Hierarchy

The major unit of local administration is the district. There are 342 districts in India, varying in size and population from state to state and

[27] *Ibid.*, p. 39.
[28] *Ibid.*, p. 42.
[29] *Ibid.*, pp. 51–52.

often within a state. The average area of a district, however, is about 3,200 square miles, with a population of 1,300,000.[30]

Under the British, a single district officer, commonly referred to as the collector, was charged with keeping the peace, collecting revenue, and administering justice in each district. With the combined roles of magistrate, collector, and judge, he represented the highest quality of the Indian Civil Service. For most Indian villagers the "Collector Sahib" was in fact *the* government. Subordinate to the collector were the district superintendent of police and the chief engineer. In the latter years of the nineteenth century, specialized departments for education, agriculture, and health were established, their district field representatives coordinated by the collector. Today, following the constitutional directive principle that "the state shall take steps to separate the Judiciary from the Executive in the public services,"[31] most states now have a district judge, in no way subordinate to the collector. The collector continues to be the most important government official in local administration, however. As the government has taken increased initiative in rural development and social welfare, his responsibilities have been greatly enlarged, and he carries an almost overwhelming workload. At the same time, his role has become increasingly ill-defined as both power and responsibility in local government have been decentralized.

The collector is appointed by the state government from the Indian Administrative Service or the State Civil Service. As an agent of the state, the collector is responsible for all government action in the district. His powers are extensive and, to some extent, discretionary.[32] The Bombay Revenue Department Manual specifies, for example, that "nothing can or should pass in the District of which the Collector should not keep himself informed."[33] He must frequently be on tour, accessible to all villagers and responsive to their needs. The daily visitors to his office may include wealthy businessmen, influential politicians, or a delegation of illiterate villagers. They come to seek favor, to register a complaint, or simply to make their presence known.[34]

In the structure of local administration, the district is divided into *taluqs* (or *tehsils*). The taluq, usually comprising from two hundred to six hundred villages, is headed by a *taluqdar*, who is responsible for the supervision of land records and the collection of revenue. The government representative in the village is the *patwari*, "the eyes and ears of the Collector." Although no longer the power today he was in the colonial period, the patwari, or "village accountant," is still "the general

---

[30] *The Changing Role of the District Officer* (New Delhi: Indian Institute of Public Administration, 1961), p. ix.
[31] Constitution of India, Article 50.
[32] David C. Potter, *Government in Rural India* (London: London School of Economics and Political Science, 1964), p. 69.
[33] Quoted in Potter, *Government in Rural India*, p. 68.
[34] Potter, *Government in Rural India*, p. 71.

busybody of government."[35] He is primarily concerned with land records, however, and thus he has a position of power with an opportunity for graft that is often difficult to resist. Traditionally the village is also served by a headman, whose position is hereditary, and by a policeman, really a watchman.

Village Government: Panchayati Raj

In the centuries before British rule, the village communities, while subject to periodic visitation by tax collectors, were left to govern themselves through a council of elders, the traditional *panchayat*, meaning literally "council of five." The panchayats declined under the British raj, however, as a result of improved communications, increased mobility, and a centralized administration that emphasized the individual in society and not the elders of the village. By the mid-nineteenth century the panchayats had ceased to be of real importance.[36] At that point, however, the British sought to revitalize the institutions of local self-government. Lord Ripon declared that it was "our weakness and our calamity" that "we have not been able to give to India the benefits and blessings of free institutions."[37] In pursuance of his Resolution of 1882, elected district boards were established to give representation and practical experience in self-government to the Indian people. The district boards (which were retained for a period after independence) were given responsibility for public works, health, and education. There were also some attempts to revive panchayats on a statutory basis as popularly elected bodies.[38] In villages where the older, unofficial panchayats of elders still existed, these new bodies were frequently constituted as parallel panchayats, giving official recognition to matters that had been decided informally by the traditional leadership.

During the independence movement, the panchayats of ancient times were eulogized as democratic "little republics." Gandhi sought to recapture that ideal in a revitalization of village life, but for many, like Dr. B. R. Ambedkar, the village was "a sink of localism, a den of ignorance, narrow-mindedness, and communalism."[39] According to Nehru, the Congress had "never considered" the Gandhian view of society, "much less adopted it."[40] At the Constituent Assembly, a Gandhian

---

35 E. N. Mangat Rai, *Civil Administration in the Punjab*, Occasional Papers in International Affairs, No. 7 (Cambridge, Mass.: Harvard University Center for International Affairs, 1963), p. 13.

36 Potter, *Government in Rural India*, p. 6.

37 Quoted in Percival Spear, *A History of India*, Vol. 2 (Baltimore: Penguin, 1965), p. 155.

38 Potter, *Government in Rural India*, p. 6.

39 Quoted in P. C. Mathur, "Sociological Dimensions of Panchayati Raj," *Indian Journal of Public Administration*, Vol. 10 (January–March 1964), p. 67.

40 Jawaharlal Nehru, *A Bunch of Old Letters*, p. 509, quoted in Granville Austin, *The Indian Constitution* (New York: Oxford University Press, 1966), p. 39.

constitution was offered, based on the principle of economic and political decentralization. The village panchayat was to be the basic unit in a hierarchy of indirectly elected bodies. A national panchayat at the top was to be responsible for such matters as currency and defense.[41] The assembly did not accept the Gandhian proposal. Stability, unity, and economic progress demanded a more centralized government, but the constitution directed the states "to organize village panchayats and to endow them with such powers and authority as may be necessary to enable them to function as units of self-government."[42] The aim was to foster democratic participation, to involve villagers in the development effort, and to ease the administrative burden on the states.[43] Institutions of local self-government were to be both instruments of economic development and social change and agents of community mobilization. They were intended to stimulate participation and provide channels for meaningful political expression.

During the First Five-Year Plan, the Center emphasized the importance of local authorities in community development, but little was done. The Second Plan called specifically for a "well-organized democratic structure of administration within the district"[44] in order to evoke popular initiative and participation. The Mehta Report recommended that the old district boards be replaced by a three-tiered system of local self-government with each tier linked by indirect election. In 1958 the Government asked each state to evolve a system of *panchayati raj*, suited to its own needs, that followed the broad outlines of the Mehta Report.[45]

Panchayati raj is now in operation throughout India alongside and in coordination with the Community Development Program. Although there is some variation in structure,[46] the first system established, that of Rajasthan, provided a pattern of organization. The panchayat is the basic unit and may represent one or several villages. It is a body of twelve to fifteen members that includes a chairman elected by the entire panchayat electorate, eight to ten members from wards within the panchayat (one elected from each ward), and three or four members co-opted to represent women, scheduled castes and tribes. All the chairmen elected to panchayats within a block area constitute the second tier, the *panchayati samiti*. Additional members are also co-opted to ensure

---

[41] Austin, *The Indian Constitution*, p. 39.
[42] Constitution of India, Article 40.
[43] Austin, *The Indian Constitution*, p. 38.
[44] Planning Commission, Second Five-Year Plan (1956), quoted in Potter, *Government in Rural India*, p. 43.
[45] Potter, *Government in Rural India*, pp. 44–45. For an evaluation of the system, see the special number on panchayati raj of the *Indian Journal of Public Administration*, Vol. 8 (October–December 1962).
[46] Such variations include differences in the collector's degree of involvement in the zila parishad and, in Mysore, the direct election of the panchayati samiti by the people of the block.

representation of special interests and to bring in administrative expertise. The average samiti has forty-two members, of whom eight are
co-opted. A chairman is elected from among the members. Members of
the legislative assembly are associate members of the samitis in their
constituency, and the block development officer acts as chief executive
of the body. The *zila parishad* is the third tier and is congruent with
the districts. Its members include the chairmen of all samitis in the
district; the members of the Rajya Sabha, the Lok Sabha, and the state
legislative assembly elected from the district; and the president of the
Central Co-operative Bank. Additional members may be co-opted, and
the collector, ex officio, attends as a nonvoting member.[47]

As the process of decision-making is brought closer to the people
through panchayati raj, it becomes more susceptible to local pressure.
Patterns of traditional dominance, through caste and land ownership,
may be institutionalized with official sanction, as the economically dependent villagers are pressured or intimidated into supporting the leaders' candidates. This development is particularly serious if it serves to
elevate traditional village leaders to higher levels of power through
indirect election. It has also been feared that the dependence of samiti
and zila parishad leaders on local voters, the result of the decentralization of power, may subject them to pressures from traditional village
leadership to weaken the social content of government policy.[48] Panchayati raj has thus brought an infusion of traditional elements into
Indian political life, but the system has provided a vehicle for the
emergence of a new leadership at the local level. David C. Potter, in
his study of Rajasthan, finds that panchayat members tend to be prosperous landowning agriculturalists or village merchants, comparatively
young, educated, and at least in Rajasthan, "progressive in outlook."
The samiti and parishad chairmen represent a generally higher level of
education and a wider range of political contacts.[49]

Village panchayat elections were originally decided by a show of
hands, a method that provided easy targets for recrimination, but secret
ballots are now used. Competitive elections have politicized the villages.
At the time of the local panchayat elections, campaign flags fly from the
most disheveled huts and all available wall space proclaims the candidacy of the political aspirants. The development resources available
to the panchayats, particularly at the critical samiti level, have made
the elections serious business.

With seeming unawareness of traditional conflict, some political observers have warned that "the traditional balance in the village may be
upset leading to disharmony in the even tenor of rural life."[50] Unedu-

---

[47] Potter, *Government in Rural India*, pp. 48–52.
[48] Mathur, "Sociological Dimensions of Panchayati Raj," p. 61.
[49] *Government in Rural India*, pp. 53–56.
[50] Ram K. Vepa, "Changing Pattern of Panchayat Raj in Andhra Pradesh," *Indian Journal of Public Administration*, Vol. 10 (October–December 1964), p. 700.

cated men may be elected who can be manipulated by the forces of extremism. Electoral competition, they argue, will encourage factionalism and caste conflict. "In fact, the new elective process seems to entrench caste even more rigidly and post-election wrangles are likely to operate on purely caste lines."[51] Competition, however, may serve to make the dominant caste more genuinely responsive to the lower castes, for in panchayat elections, factions must inevitably seek the support of lower castes and harijans.

The Mehta Report contended that "one of the banes of democratic village administration has been the intensification of factions and feuds" and that "the system of electoral contests at the village level has often added to these."[52] The traditional panchayat had reached decisions through a sense of the meeting, continuing discussion until a consensus was reached. This consensus admittedly reflected the interests of the dominant caste, but it represented an ideal of unanimity, not the factious rule of a numerical majority. To stem the growth of conflict at the village level, state governments have sought to encourage consensus politics, and at least one state has offered special awards to panchayats with at least 80 percent of their members unanimously elected.

The Gandhian vision of a "partyless democracy" held by former socialist leader Jayaprakash Narayan is shared by many for the village level, and parties are in fact officially prohibited in panchayat elections. Factions clearly operate, but the lack of party competition reduces the possibility of holding one group accountable and ignores the functions of social conflict. Competition may serve to keep the incumbents responsive to the electorate, for they can always be replaced; it may open new channels of access for participation and leadership; and it may stimulate development as groups vie with one another to expand their bases of support. "The nostalgia for traditional village consensus," Susanne H. Rudolph writes, "is neither morally consistent nor practical if at the same time change in the material and moral order of the village is thought desirable."[53] Village consensus reflected a belief in one right answer, but "what was self-evident to the fathers is becoming one alternative among many to the sons. Prescription minimizes conflict; freedom enhances it."[54]

The system of panchayati raj was created to enhance the institutional capacity of local government for economic development and to expand democratic participation in rural areas. The two were to advance together as participation was channeled into the work of community development. Mobilization was to provide the lifeblood of rural uplift. Participation bred conflict, however, stimulating intense competition

---

[51] *Ibid.*
[52] Quoted in Mathur, "Sociological Dimensions of Panchayati Raj," p. 65.
[53] "Consensus and Conflict in Indian Politics," *World Politics,* Vol. 12 (April 1961), p. 396.
[54] *Ibid.*

for development resources. The possibilities for consensus were undermined as traditional village factions were reinforced or displaced by new factional divisions allied with competing political parties at the constituency, district, and state levels. The democracy of panchayati raj has politicized the Indian village, but expanded participation and a heightened political consciousness have created demands to which the institutions can no longer fully respond. Aspirations and demands outnumber the limited resources available. With new power in their hands but without the means of securing the promise of a better life, the poor and the landless of Indian rural society grow increasingly restless.

Urban Government

India is overwhelmingly rural, but according to the 1961 census, 18 percent of India's population lives in towns and cities of over 10,000 and a sizable portion of these people are concentrated in the major metropolitan areas. There are more than one hundred cities with a population of more than 100,000. Estimates for 1970 give Madras a population of about 2,000,000; Delhi, 2,500,000; Bombay, 4,750,000; and Greater Calcutta, 5,750,000. The larger cities are governed by municipal corporations, composed of a popularly elected council and a president or mayor, elected from within the council. A commissioner, appointed by the state government, is the chief executive, and the state may supersede the municipal corporation if it is deemed incapable of maintaining order and effective government. Smaller towns are governed by municipal committees or boards.[55] City government is responsible for the safety, health, and education of its citizens. It is charged with the maintenance of sanitation facilities, streets and bridges, parks and public facilities— responsibilities that it is increasingly unable to meet effectively.

It is within the city that tradition is most severely challenged by rapid change and a heterogeneity of values and behavior. The cities are the locus of new economic and cultural values, of new social roles and action patterns. The availability of mass communications and the density of urban populations have facilitated the mobilization of city-dwellers for political action. India's cities have been centers of opposition and political unrest. Demonstrations, strikes, and riots have become daily occurrences as demands rise beyond the government's capacity to respond. The city may offer rural migrants a chance for a better life, but for the middle classes, committed to an urban life that can no longer satisfy their basic needs, it nourishes explosive frustrations. Municipal governments, stagnant and lacking in adequate finances, cannot begin to meet the problems before them. The state governments, responsive to the rural base of their support, have been unwilling to assume the

[55] The distinction between "larger" cities and "smaller" towns is not uniform but varies considerably from state to state.

burden of the deepening urban crisis. A high and accelerating level of political participation and a low and static level of institutionalization pose the problem of political development in stark form.

RECOMMENDED READING

Chanda, Asok, *Federalism in India*. London: George Allen & Unwin, 1965.
    An analysis of Union-state relations by a distinguished Indian civil servant.

Franda, Marcus F., *West Bengal and the Federalizing Process in India*. Princeton, N.J.: Princeton University Press, 1968.
    Case studies from West Bengal that serve to illuminate the wider problems of the federal relationship throughout India.

Harrison, Selig S., *India: The Most Dangerous Decades*. Princeton, N.J.: Princeton University Press, 1960.
    Posing the problem of India's continued viability as a nation, the volume examines the stresses imposed by the "fissiparous tendencies" of linguistic regionalism, caste, and political extremism.

Leonard, T. J., "Federalism in India," in William S. Livingon, ed., *Federalism in the Commonwealth: A Bibliographic Commentary*. London: Cassell, 1963, pp. 87–143.
    A lengthy bibliographic essay on modern India; while taking federalism as its focus, it ranges widely and is probably the best and most complete source of its kind on Indian political history.

Menon, V. P., *The Story of the Integration of the Indian States*. Bombay: Orient Longmans, 1956.
    An account of the merging of the princely states with the former provinces of British India into a single nation of India, written by a man who played an instrumental part in the events, Sardar Patel's lieutenant, the I.C.S. Secretary to the newly created Ministry of States.

Potter, David C., *Government in Rural India*. London: London School of Economics and Political Science, 1964.
    A concise description of contemporary district administration.

* Rai, E. N. Mangat, *Civil Administration in the Punjab*. Occasional Papers in International Affairs, No. 7. Cambridge, Mass.: Harvard University Center for International Affairs, 1963.
    An examination of the structure and operation of district administration in an Indian state.

Retzlaff, Ralph H., *Village Government in India*. Bombay: Asia Publishing House, 1962.
    A case study of rural government and the operation of the panchayat in an Uttar Pradesh village.

Weiner, Myron, ed., *State Politics in India*. Princeton, N.J.: Princeton University Press, 1968.
    A comparative study of eight Indian states, with particular concern for patterns of political participation, integration, party systems, and governmental performance.

* Available in a paperback edition.

V

ARENAS OF CONFLICT:
INDIAN INTEREST GROUPS

No political system can satisfy all the demands of all its members all the time. Its response to public pressure is calculated in accordance with the political capital backing various demands—numbers, wealth, prestige. The legitimacy of a particular demand, that is, its congruence with basic values in the society, is also a major factor in political response. More important still is the access afforded demands in general, which is of critical importance in the development of a stable and responsive political system. If resources are limited, demands may far outrun the capacity of the government to respond. Rational economic planning may conflict with the exigencies of democratic response, forcing decision-makers to consider demands as such illegitimate and to argue that the compulsions of a backward society require restriction of political access and democratic competition. Competition, from this view, serves only to stimulate the formation of demands as parties bid for support and thus to raise the level of frustration.

In India there is a basic distrust of politics as a struggle for power, reflecting the traditional view that those who seek power are suspect. "Each man must accept his own *dharma* (duty) and perform his duty well . . . . Authority is acceptable, but to struggle for a position of authority is not."[1] W. H. Morris-Jones has written of a "paradoxical or ambivalent attitude to authority. Authority in India appears to be subject at once to much more abusive criticism and much more effusive adulation than one is accustomed to elsewhere."[2] Leaders, ideally, are to be above politics. Gandhi, for example, was not a formal member of the Congress. Dr. Rammanohar Lohia never joined the Samyukta Socialist party, of which he was leader, and Jayaprakash Narayan renounced party politics altogether to follow in the steps of Vinoba Bhave, "the walking saint," whose *bhoodan*, or land-gift, movement calls for self-sacrifice and "polity without power." Asoka Mehta has argued that "development, in our backward country, depends on the acceptance of equality, austerity and hard work."[3] In his view "a broad based government holding power on a long-term tenure—in effect not in law" would be the ideal replacement for the "frequent changes in government that parliamentary democracy assumes."[4] There is a fundamental tension, however, between modern democratic values and the nostalgia for consensus, whether it is in the name of tradition or rationality. The expectation that politicians are to wear a saintly mantle of self-sacrifice and the realization that they are all too often the victims of human foibles have bred a general cynicism about political life.

The Role of Interest Groups in Indian Political Development

As wider sectors of Indian society have been politicized through the expansion, dispersion, and democratization of power, larger numbers of people have been drawn into the political system. Brash and rustic political bosses have replaced the Western-educated leaders of the nationalist movement. Political life at state and local levels—and increasingly at the national level—is directed by a new leadership, with roots in the villages and sensitivity to factional and caste loyalties. The credentials of the new leadership are instrumental, not sacrificial: Government and party are something to be used.[5]

Although the new entrants into politics may often operate in a traditional mode, the political issues are by no means traditional. There is nothing traditional about demands for more schools, roads, wells, fer-

---

[1] Myron Weiner, "Struggle Against Power: Notes on Indian Political Behavior," in his *Political Change in South Asia* (Calcutta: Mukhopadyay, 1963), p. 156.

[2] *Parliament in India* (London: Longmans, Green, 1957), p. 34.

[3] Quoted in Susanne H. Rudolph, "Consensus and Conflict in Indian Politics," *World Politics*, Vol. 12 (April 1961), p. 395.

[4] *Ibid.*, p. 396.

[5] Myron Weiner, "India's Two Political Cultures," in Lucian Pye and Sidney Verba, eds., *Political Culture and Political Development* (Princeton, N.J.: Princeton University Press, 1965), p. 212.

tilizers, and jobs.[6] Traditional structures and patterns of behavior may be resilient and adaptive to new and changing environments, becoming, for example, channels of interest articulation and instruments of political pressure. The distinction between tradition and modernity blurs as, in dialectical relationship, they "infiltrate and transform each other."[7] In this process, politics has become more meaningful to the mass electorate, potentially more responsive to its demands. However, as politics has become more vernacular, it has been decried by those suspicious of group pressure as pandering to the irrationalities of casteism, communalism, and regionalism and to narrow and special interests. Interest groups, as agents of political demands, are seen as disruptive of order and consensus. The quest for stability, however, may be the precursor of repressive order.

Interest groups in India are a form of linkage and a means of communication between the mass and the élite. They provide channels of access for expanding participation, and their institutionalization is a critical element in the development of a responsive political system, for they are barometers of the political climate by which decision-makers can make and assess policy. "The interest group absorbs the raw demands of its members, collates them, sometimes adulterates them in the interests of the majority, and finally articulates them in a form whereby they may be acted upon at the appropriate place within the society."[8] While the interest group makes demands on society for the benefit of its members, it also serves to restrain them.

Interest groups not only act as agents of interest articulation, but they also increase the political consciousness and participation of their membership—democratic achievements, although they may strain on the responsive capacity of the system. In addition, interest groups may be reservoirs of political leadership; this has been particularly true for trade unions in India. Most important perhaps, interest groups are a vehicle for social integration. Bringing individuals from ascriptive relationships into new and modern associations for the expression of common interests, they may bridge the gap not only between the mass and the élite but between traditional divisions within the society as a whole. Interest groups may thus serve as agents of both vertical and horizontal integration. Even interest groups that have reinforced existing cleavages in Indian society, such as caste associations, have frequently been the catalyst for change, opening the community to increasingly differentiated interests and cross-cutting ties. The problem for India, as for most developing societies, has been in having not too many interest groups but too few.

---

[6] *Ibid.*, p. 241.
[7] Lloyd I. and Susanne H. Rudolph, *The Modernity of Tradition* (Chicago: University of Chicago Press, 1967), p. 3.
[8] Bruce H. Millen, *The Political Role of Labor in Developing Countries* (Washington, D.C.: The Brookings Institution, 1963), p. 40.

In India interest groups have been slow to develop and those that exist are weak. They have been unable to accommodate and channel rapidly expanding participation and the emergence of new groups to political consciousness. Under the British, those individuals and groups commanding traditional sources of power exerted pressure at the local administrative level. Those without power had little access to the administration, and from a position of powerlessness they regarded the Government as an extractive force to be avoided whenever possible. Most mass organizations developed from the activities of the nationalist movement, and even in the years since independence, most interest groups have been connected with political parties, more agents of mobilization than of interest articulation: Opposition parties have utilized various front organizations in mass action to rally popular support and augment party strength, and the Congress has sought to co-opt group support through mass organizations and to harness their potential into development activities.[9] The Congress party itself has been an important link between local groups and state governments, acting as a middleman in applying pressure on the state administrative apparatus; in states where the Congress is in power, the administration has proved sensitive to such pressure.[10] Through the response of the local Congress machine, with its access to administration and patronage, the party has slowed the development of autonomous interest groups. Indeed, Congress party factions have served as agents of particular interests. The party's source of power has come increasingly to be associated with rural landed interests, with those who are in effect political brokers, astute in the manipulation of both traditional and modern political styles. The landless and the poor, so long as they remain invisible, may be eulogized and conveniently ignored.

Most Indians have a low sense of political efficacy. In their opinion, government officials are generally distant, unresponsive, and corrupt. Officials, on the other hand, regard interest-group activity with distrust. Rational policy formation, they argue, should be unaffected by their narrow demands. Consequently, group pressure in India has been directed toward influencing the administration and implementation of policy rather than its formation; its greatest success has been achieved in forestalling certain government actions and in modifying policy rather than in initiating it. It is at the state and local administrative levels that officials have been particularly responsive to such pressure, and it has been the landed interests who have been most adept in applying it: Land-reform legislation may be quietly forgotten as development funds are channeled into the hands most capable of utilizing them, the landed middle peasantry. Those who have nothing are unlikely to reap the benefits of government action, for they lack the resources of immediate

---

[9] Myron Weiner, *The Politics of Scarcity* (Chicago: University of Chicago Press, 1962), p. 218.

[10] *Ibid.*, p. 213.

political capital. In the long run, however, once mobilized, their numbers will be overpowering.

In the name of rationality and the public interest, decision-makers have often turned deaf ears to the demands of interest groups. Because the Government is unresponsive, groups resort to mass demonstrations, hartals, strikes, and civil disobedience to force government action. This in turn only confirms the official image that the groups are irresponsible and that such mass activity is against the national interest. The Government does respond to such action, however; the political capital to which it has proved most sensitive is violence. Various legal measures, such as the Preventive Detention Act and the emergency provisions in the constitution, have been enacted to restrain political activity that threatens public order. The line between activities that do threaten public order and those that do not may be thin, since group politics itself is regarded with suspicion. Gandhian techniques of civil disobedience have been used by disaffected groups against the Congress Government, an unfair and perverted use of satyagraha in the eyes of the Congress; but mass political activity has often been violent. Disorder seems vindicated by success. "Only when public order is endangered by a mass movement is the government willing to make a concession," Myron Weiner writes, "not because they consider the demand legitimate, but because they then recognize the strength of the group making the demand and its capacity for destructiveness. Thus, the Government often alternates between unresponsiveness to the demands of large but peaceful groups and total concession to groups that press their demands violently."[11] The capitulation of the Government to the demands for States Reorganization only in the wake of widespread rioting and, more recently, the reevaluation of official language policy after the agitation in Tamilnadu in 1965 are classic examples of the efficacy of violence. That mass actions have succeeded so frequently has given them a certain legitimacy.

The relationship between order and responsiveness lies at the heart of the development process. In India the solution has too often been a declamation of radical intent followed by conservative inaction, reflecting the power of interests upon which Congress political support has rested. The plea for a "bargaining culture" of pluralism only brings to the surface what is already political reality: The Government will be responsive to those groups with effective political resources. The masses may well be ignored, at least until they become dangerously restless. Stability becomes the highest value.

The creation of an effective infrastructure of democratic linkage between the mass and political élite serves initially to draw the conservative, rural leadership into the political system. Through this process the

[11] *Ibid.*, p. 201.

Congress state machines came to power. When this new base of power emerges, the system must become responsive to the political capital that it commands. Stability is purchased at enormous costs—in a capillary process, penetration that brings traditional leaders to wider prominence inevitably mobilizes the "under mass." In place of unimplemented reform, revolution may be the order of things.

Community Associations

The mantle of Indian civilization covers divisions and conflicts of religion, language, caste, and tribe. The "fissiparous tendencies" of regionalism and communalism have posed a serious threat to the creation of an Indian political community and a viable democratic system. In the name of economic change and social mobilization, India's increasingly participant communities[12] have grown more politically self-conscious, and this self-consciousness has deepened existing cleavages. The Muslim League sought and obtained an Islamic state; the Sikhs, through the Akali Dal, achieved Punjabi Suba; the D.M.K. once had aspirations for Dravidasthan; the tribes of Chota-Nagpur struggle for Jharkhand; the Nagas demand independence. Linguistic movements have sought states reorganization and greater regional autonomy; some, such as Maharashtra's xenophobic Shiv Sena ("Drive out the South Indians") and Tamilnadu's Dravida Kazhagam, have marshalled regional loyalties at the expense of cultural minorities. Caste associations have lobbied for representation in legislative assemblies, for posts in the administrative services, for seats in colleges, and for a greater share of government benefits for social and economic improvement.

Though decried as a reversion to "tribalism," the increasingly prominent role played by community associations in political life, for all the problems it presents, reflects an extension of the particularistic and ascriptive ties of primordial sentiment to wider horizons of identity. The development of primordial sentiment into a cultural nationalism—at the level of the linguistic region or within a religious or caste community—may be regarded with horror by those who see it as the seed of separation or destruction. But it may in fact be an effective vehicle for the transference of loyalty to the larger political community, a channel of linkage between the mass and the élite, between traditional behavior and modern democratic processes.[13]

The caste association, representing the adaptive response of caste to modern social, economic, and political changes, reveals the potential "modernity of tradition." Combining the traditional and the modern,

[12] In India, *community* usually refers to a racial, caste, linguistic, or religious group rather than to a locality, as in the United States.
[13] Robert L. Hardgrave, Jr., *The Dravidian Movement* (Bombay: Popular Prakashan, 1965), p. 6.

the caste association is a voluntary association derived from the ascriptive reservoir of caste. As various caste communities have sought social uplift and economic advancement, they have organized to secure more effective political access. Among the largest and most successful caste associations is that of the Nadar community of Tamilnadu.[14]

The Nadars, in one hundred fifty years of change, have moved from the lower rungs of the ritual hierarchy to a position of status and power. Increasing numbers have abandoned their traditional occupation of tapping toddy palms, and as they have risen in education and wealth, the community has differentiated occupationally and economically. In their efforts to achieve social status commensurate with their rising economic position, members of the caste turned to Sanskritization, the emulation of the life-style of higher castes, creating a new myth of Kshatriya status, seeking the service of Brahmin priests, and adopting more Brahminical customs. Their pretensions ended in ridicule and failure. The Nadars then turned from their high-caste cultural models to the pursuit of secular economic and political goals in the creation of the Nadar Mahajana Sangam, their community association.

Founded in 1910, the caste association became the agent of community integration and mobilization, giving organizational strength to the new consciousness of the caste. The voice of the community in articulating its interests and formulating its demands, the association was the vehicle by which the Nadars entered the political system. The efforts of the Sangam for the uplift of the community accelerated internal differentiation. As salient cultural and economic differences between the Nadar community and other castes diminished, community solidarity also declined. Nadars of a particular educational or socioeconomic position began to find that they had more in common with those of similar background in other castes than they did with their fellow caste members. Whereas the Nadars were once united in political action, their support increasingly dispersed. The diffusion of political support followed economic differentiation, and the Sangam, in order to remain representative of the Nadar community, dropped its partisan role in Tamilnadu politics to pursue its interests through the indirect means characteristic of interest groups rather than the direct means of political associations.

The Nadar Mahajana Sangam played a vital role in the political mobilization of the Nadar community, serving as an agent of community integration and as a vehicle for its entrance into the political system of modern India. The caste association, Lloyd I. and Susanne H. Rudolph have written, "provides the channels of communication and bases of leadership and organization which enable those still submerged in the traditional society and culture to transcend the technical political liter-

---

[14] See Robert L. Hardgrave, Jr., *The Nadars of Tamilnad: The Political Culture of a Community in Change* (Berkeley: University of California Press, 1969).

acy which would otherwise handicap their ability to participate in democratic politics."[15] The meaning of caste itself has changed in the encounter between tradition and modernity. "By creating conditions in which a caste's significance and power is beginning to depend on its numbers rather than its ritual and social status, and by encouraging egalitarian aspirations among its members, the caste association is exerting a liberating influence."[16]

With secular aspirations after a "casteless" society, the Congress leadership, joined by most leaders of the opposition, has viewed the demands of community associations as illegitimate. Although each of the major parties has spawned a variety of affiliated mass organizations —labor, agrarian, youth—to mobilize political support, they have for the most part sought to avoid the appearance of intimate association with any particular community. Close identification between the party and one community might seriously affect the party's ability to aggregate wide support, for in few constituencies, much less an entire district or state, does one community so predominate as to command a majority. But the parties have been ready in practice to secure support wherever and however available and in each election have courted various communities.

Community associations, in a process of political mobilization, both stimulate and structure participation. Weiner has argued that "the greatest protection against the demands of powerful community groups is the multiplication of community and non-community associations."[17] When the number of community associations increases, "the possibility that any single community will dominate a state government is likely to decrease. As more caste and tribal groups, trade unions, and peasant associations emerge, those who wish to win power will have to turn to the interests of communities other than their own."[18]

Many communities have exhibited solidary support for a particular party, but most are divided among themselves politically. When in the 1930's the Nadar Mahajana Sangam had become closely identified with the pro-British Justice party, Congress Nadars formed a rival association. In order to survive as representative of the Nadar community, the Sangam withdrew from partisan political activity. In other communities, as well, identification between the association and a particular party has posed a challenge to the association's viability, as political support within the community is diffused across the political spectrum. The Vanniyakula Kshatriya Sangam, the association of the Vanniyar caste in Tamilnadu, which is represented politically by its own caste parties, the Commonweal and the Tamilnad Toilers, can no longer command com-

---

[15] "The Political Role of India's Caste Associations," *Pacific Affairs*, Vol. 33 (March 1960), pp. 5–6.
[16] *Ibid.*, p. 9. See also Rudolph and Rudolph, *The Modernity of Tradition.*
[17] *The Politics of Scarcity*, p. 72.
[18] *Ibid.*, p. 70.

munity solidarity.[19] The Ezhavas, long identified as the base of support for the Communist party in Kerala, are deeply divided politically, and the caste itself has become an arena for political competition.

Community associations, while representing the solidary organization of the community, are the agent of increasing internal differentiation. As the association secures its goals, the social and economic gaps within the community widen, at the same time dispersing political support. The association thus becomes the agent of it own destruction, for in the process of differentiation individuals are subjected to the cross-cutting ties of a multiplicity of interests and associations. In the process of political development, as the structures of society change under the impact of social mobilization, the old clusters of social, economic, and psychological commitments weaken, and individuals become available for new patterns of socialization and behavior.[20]

Agrarian Groups

Agrarian interests in India have been expressed primarily through landlord and zamindari influence at the local and state levels. The peasants, lacking the effective resources of money and organization, have carried little weight in shaping legislation. Even when policy has been directed to their benefit, it has often been frustrated in its implementation at the local level by landed interests. Each of the major parties has adjunct peasant organizations, but they are designed more to mobilize support than to articulate interest. The All-India Kisan Sabha, founded in 1936 as a federation of state peasant movements, began as a Congress front but quickly came under Communist control. The Congress today has its own peasant organization, but the party has proved ineffective in representing the interests of tenants and landless laborers, for at the local level the Congress is controlled by those who would be most hurt by land-reform legislation.[21] Ceilings on land holdings frequently remain unenforced, for the state governments are unwilling to alienate their base of support among the middle peasants and petty landlords. Peasant agitation has been sporadic and uncoordinated, but in favoring the interests of the landlords the Indian Government may simply be laying the foundations for future peasant unrest.

There have been a number of peasant revolts in India. In this century, the Telangana uprising in Hyderabad State was one of the most dramatic and ill-fated. It began with sporadic outbreaks in 1946; by 1948 the movement, led by the Communist party, claimed to have "liberated"

[19] Rudolph and Rudolph, *The Modernity of Tradition*, pp. 89–90.
[20] Karl Deutsch, "Social Mobilization and Political Development," *American Political Science Review*, Vol. 55 (September 1961), p. 494.
[21] Weiner, *The Politics of Scarcity*, p. 131.

some 2,500 villages[22] by turning out landlords and their agents and establishing communes. Support came primarily from peasants whose land holdings were small, although landless laborers were also involved. In the area under Communist control, during the period of the movement's greatest strength, 1948–50, rents were suspended, debts were canceled, and land was redistributed among the landless. The Nizam initiated police action against the revolt, and in September 1948 Indian troops took over the state and moved against the Communists in Telangana. The movement was crushed. Its leadership was jailed, and the Communist party was outlawed in the state. The movement was officially called off by a C.P.I. directive in 1951, beginning a new phase in Communist strategy.

During this same period, a similar Communist-led agrarian uprising began in Thanjavur (Tanjore). In this area, the rice-bowl of Tamilnadu, land was concentrated largely in the hands of absentee landlords—rich landowners and middle-class peasants. The land was worked by landless laborers, 80 percent of whom were harijans. The revolt in the 1950's briefly exposed discontent, but in the mid-1960's, the *kisan*, or peasant, movement in Thanjavur took on new life. Strikes and increasing pressure from the movement, under the direction of both the right and the left wings of the Communist party, succeeded in winning improved wages and guarantees from the landowners, but the inequities of the land system have been accentuated by the intensive development efforts in the district. According to a Communist study of living conditions among the landless laborers, the minimal annual expenditure required to maintain a family of four is 1,500 rupees ($200); a laborer is able to find work for only 177 days in a year; and the average annual income for a man and his wife is 780 rupees ($104). The gap between income and expenditure is filled by borrowing or by reducing the family's food requirements.[23]

Beyond Thanjavur, there are other pockets of militant agrarian unrest. The Naxalite revolutionaries have gained a foothold among the tribal people of the Srikakulam hill area in Andhra. In Kerala, the left Communists have mobilized poor peasants and the harijan landless laborers through the kisan sabhas and have gained wide support among poor Muslim peasants in Malabar. Under the United Front government in Kerala, there was a political atmosphere highly beneficial to the kisan movement, particularly in terms of police policy. In West Bengal, members of kisan movements have forcibly occupied some 150,000 acres, with the tacit support of the United Front government. The movement's intensity has been spurred by the competition of the various

22 Victor M. Fic, *Peaceful Transition to Communism in India* (Bombay: Nachiketa, 1969), p. 20.
23 Cited by N. Ram, "Communist-led Kisan Movement in Thanjavur," *Hindu* (Madras), July 12, 1969, p. 6.

wings of the Communist party to gain control of party leadership. It remains, however, largely in the hands of the Marxist group, the left Communists. Where a landlord is known to have evaded the ceiling on land holdings, landless laborers and poor peasants have taken control of his land. Sporadic violence and political murders and the absence of police intervention have caused moderate elements in the United Front government to denounce the breakdown of law and order in the state.

Most peasants and laborers remain silent and unorganized, but an awakened consciousness, intensified by the "new strategy" of the Fourth Plan, has brought restlessness to India's agrarian poor.

Students

If India's peasants are inarticulate and uncoordinated, students are loudly vocal, but they too lack direction and coherence. The nationalist movement gave students an active role in mass agitation, beginning with the noncooperation movement in 1920 and reaching a height with the "quit India" movement in 1942. When the All-Indian Student Federation, founded in 1936, came under Communist domination, the Students' Congress captured student loyalties in the continuing struggle against the British. After independence, however, the Gandhian program of constructive work held little attraction for the politicized student population. The student movement had lost "its sense of militant unity and ideological purpose . . . . The nationalist fervor of the pre-independence period has been replaced by generally unorganized and sporadic agitation usually aimed at specific grievances."[24] Student activism is a reaction to increasing frustrations caused by unresponsive university authorities and an uncertain future.

Even more than in the West, the university degree in India is the passport to a "good job," but as often, it is the route to educated unemployment. With more than one million students registered in some twenty-five hundred colleges in 1966—four times the number of students at independence—there are far more graduates each year than positions available. Rather than suffer the humiliation of taking a position beneath their newly acquired status, many simply join the expanding ranks of the unemployed.

But if India has a plethora of college graduates, there is a paucity of those capable of handling India's most pressing developmental problems. Graduate students in foreign universities frequently never return, becoming statistics of the "brain drain." India itself simply has been unable to train enough administrative, technical, and scientific talent to meet its needs. The largest number of students pour into already overcrowded arts colleges, only to pull their declining standards still

[24] Philip G. Altbach, "Student Politics and Higher Education in India," *Daedalus*, No. 97 (Winter 1968), p. 260.

lower. A rigid administrative structure, a Victorian syllabus, and the dread comprehensive final examinations have made the Indian university an impersonal and dehumanizing experience. Since the vast majority of today's students enter from rural backgrounds, with often only a rudimentary knowledge of English, the continued use of English as the medium of instruction is both a farce and a tragedy. Although colleges are increasingly shifting to the regional vernacular, the chasm between the majority of the students and the privileged few with an English-language lower-school background remains wide. Those who have a command of English take the coveted positions in the I.A.S. or enter medical colleges. Many of the others settle for the dubious distinction of a "B.A. (Failed)," which at least is evidence of their having attended college.

In such an atmosphere, "student indiscipline" has been endemic. Defined loosely, the term includes any activity that interferes with the normal process of education. Weiner distinguishes four types of such activity.[25] (1) "Activities associated with larger political movements in the areas surrounding the school, college, or university." Examples of such activities include the involvement of Calcutta students in the Bengal-Bihar merger dispute and that of Tamil students in linguistic agitation. Students have figured prominently in the language issue throughout India. In Tamilnadu, student opposition to Hindi as the official language was organized by the ad hoc Student Action Committee; in the North, young Hindi supporters launched their agitation through the All-India Students' Organization, which is associated with the Jana Sangh party. (2) "Demands by students upon university authorities." Students have opposed fee increases or have demanded easier entrance requirements to colleges. (3) "Student demands upon non-university authorities on issues of special concern." Tram-fare controversies have attracted student activists, as have increases in the price of cinema tickets; both incidents have triggered rioting. (4) "Sporadic, generally unorganized outbursts by students only vaguely associated with concrete demands." Students in Calcutta threw over the tables at an examination they considered too stiff, initiating a riot that closed the university.

"Indiscipline" has included the Gandhian technique of satyagraha, as well as strikes, destruction of property, physical attacks on university personnel, and even self-immolation. Disturbances have closed Indian universities for weeks at a time; widespread rioting and police firings have occurred. In Orissa a series of student demonstrations in 1964 succeeded in toppling the state government, and in Tamilnadu the anti-Hindi agitation spearheaded by student groups in 1965 resulted in enormous property damage, the death of more than fifty persons, and an agreement to reevaluate the imposition of Hindi on the South.

[25] *The Politics of Scarcity*, pp. 172–73.

The Indian Government has attributed student unrest to "loss of leadership by teachers, growth of economic difficulties, general loss of idealism, absence of social life, a sense of fear and insecurity and unhappy living conditions."[26] Student unrest is increasing yearly. Political parties have tried to exploit it, but few have succeeded. Only the D.M.K. and the Jana Sangh have successfully launched student movements, and students have played important roles in their processions, demonstrations, and electoral efforts.

Trade Unions

Labor unions in India, as in most developing countries, have been highly political. Reflecting the central role of the state in labor relations, union demands for better working conditions and higher wages are directed less frequently toward management than toward the Government. Government tribunals for binding arbitration as well as wide ministerial discretion have made the Government the critical focus of pressure. With both labor and management dependent on Government intervention, collective bargaining is virtually nonexistent, and the Government has come to bear the brunt of all dissatisfaction. Government labor policy has been guided, in general, by an effort to reduce the number of strikes and lockouts: The particular demands of labor or management are subordinated to the goals of national economic development.[27]

During the nationalist movement, many unions were agents of political mobilization; their activities were subordinated to party priorities. After independence the labor movement fragmented, and unions aligned themselves with India's major parties. The All-India Trade Union Congress (A.I.T.U.C.) had fallen under Communist control. A new Congress-oriented federation, the Indian National Trade Union Congress (I.N.T.U.C.), was organized with Government blessings. The Socialists organized the Hind Mazdoor Sabha (H.M.S.), and non-Communist Marxists established the United Trade Union Congress (U.T.U.C.). Today there are some twelve thousand registered unions in India, representing a little more than three million workers. Of these, about twenty-six hundred unions are affiliated with one of the four federations. Members have little loyalty toward the unions, frequently switch affiliation, and often join more than one. A man may join I.N.T.U.C. to take advantage of administrative privileges enjoyed by the Congress federation. At the same time he may align himself with the Communist A.I.T.U.C. in protest against a broad range of social, political, and economic issues.[28]

[26] Indian Ministry of Educaton, *Education in Universities in India, 1951–52*, quoted in Weiner, *The Politics of Scarcity*, p. 171.
[27] Weiner, *The Politics of Scarcity*, pp. 76–77.
[28] Millen, *The Political Role of Labor*, p. 23.

I.N.T.U.C., the largest trade-union federation, closely associated with the Congress, has declared its loyalty first to the party, then to the Government, to the nation, and last of all to the workers.[29] In contrast to other unions, I.N.T.U.C. has taken a position of moderation, believing that "the interests of workers can best be satisfied by national growth, and national growth depends upon strong government and a strong Congress party."[30] In the service of stability and economic growth, the union has become more an agent of discipline than one of interest articulation. Its close ties with Congress and the Government have reduced I.N.T.U.C.'s effectiveness in presenting labor demands, often to the advantage of more militant, less responsible unions. It has been argued in defense of the Congress-I.N.T.U.C. alignment that I.N.T.U.C. has served as a counterweight to conservative elements within the Congress,[31] but the unions have in fact had little influence over Congress policy. In the selection of candidates, for example, the Congress has generally disregarded I.N.T.U.C. recommendations.[32]

The trade unions' lack of autonomy is revealed in their "outside" leadership of middle-class intellectuals and politicians. Weiner attributes the pattern of outside leadership to a variety of possible factors: need for command of English and special legal and administrative skills; early involvement of politicians in union organization to win support for the nationalist struggle; lack of adequate financing; status considerations; and in some industries, linguistic and ethnic gaps between the workers and management or Government.[33] The union may provide a channel for the leader's personal political advancement, for it may be the instrument by which he seeks political ends only indirectly related to labor problems.

Strikes each year take some 700,000 workers off the job. Militancy frequently descends to sabotage or coercion, as in the *gherao*, the physical encirclement of the managerial staff to secure "quick justice."[34] Excessive and wholly unrealistic demands arise in part from low levels of commitment to industrial occupations on the one hand and from millennial aspirations on the other. Trade unions have not been effective agents of interest articulation. "Unions are poorly organized, membership turnover is great, dues-paying is limited to a few and is irregular, and union activities are limited to strikes, demonstrations, and election

[29] Ralph James, "Politics of Trade Unions in India," *Far Eastern Survey*, Vol. 27 (March 1958), p. 43, quoted in Weiner, *The Politics of Scarcity*, p. 78.
[30] Weiner, *The Politics of Scarcity*, pp. 78–79n.
[31] Millen, *The Political Role of Labor*, p. 130.
[32] See Millen, *The Political Role of Labor*, p. 89.
[33] *The Politics of Scarcity*, p. 91. See also Charles A. Myers, *Labor Problems in the Industrialization of India* (Cambridge, Mass.: Harvard University Press, 1958), pp. 76–80.
[34] See Nitish R. De and Suresh Srivastava, "Gheraos in West Bengal," *Economic and Political Weekly*, Vol. 2 (1967), pp. 2015–22, 2062–68, 2099–2104, 2167–76.

work. Only rarely," Weiner writes, "does a union provide services for its members. Rival unionism is rampant, unions are led by outsiders, and control of unions is often in the hands of political parties seeking to use them for their own ends."[35]

Business Groups

India has committed itself to the development of a socialist pattern of society, but if it is officially socialist, it is in practice overwhelmingly private. Like Birla, one of India's wealthiest industrialists, businessmen are all socialists in their fashion. The private sector has been an object of suspicion, reflecting traditional hostility to the business communities. Indeed, most of the modern business and industrial combines are owned by families of the traditional trading communities—Gujarati Vaisyas, Jains, Marwaris, and Parsis. The public image of the business classes, infected by memories of usury, false weights, and quick profits, has not improved with the rumor of undeclared "black money" or with the revelation of scandal. Organized business thus has sought increasingly to identify itself with the public interests of the welfare state, both to improve its image and to avoid Government disfavor.

The Indian business community has found political access primarily through its associations. These include trade and industrial associations, employer associations, and chambers of commerce. Some are regional; some, like the Marwari (now Bharat) Chamber of Commerce in Bengal, represent particular communities. The activities of these various associations are coordinated by three major national federations, the most prominent of which is the Federation of Indian Chambers of Commerce and Industry, representing some forty thousand firms.

Organized business has sought aid from the Government and protection from industry, but has protested regulation, control, and the jungle of licensing procedures. While accepting an expanding public sector, it has remained apprehensive about the nationalization of air transport, life insurance, the Imperial Bank, and, in 1969, the major private banks. The Forum for Free Enterprise, associated with the Swatantra party, has attempted to educate the public to the cause of free enterprise. The forum has attracted limited support, however; most businessmen prefer to cast their lot with the ruling party in order to secure direct channels of access to the Government. In analyzing the techniques and targets of organized business, Weiner emphasizes informal, personal contact as the most frequent means by which businessmen, as individuals and through chambers, have access to administrative officers. This contact is facilitated by traditional ties of family, community, or personal friendship, but most often by the flow of *bakshish*, a non-legal fee for the per-

[35] *The Politics of Scarcity*, p. 93.

formance of administrative duty. It serves, for example, to expedite an application for a permit or license, and "lends to the administrative system discretion and flexibility . . . without which many businessmen would find it difficult to function."[36] Contributions to the Congress party also serve to facilitate political access. The Congress, as the party in power, has frequently extracted "contributions" from businesses dependent on government licenses.

Indian business has been little concerned with public relations or with formal parliamentary lobbying, but businessmen have sought to maintain close contact with influential members of Parliament. Indeed, many M.P.'s and ministers at the Center, as well as state politicians, are closely involved in business interests. Various business houses maintain staffs in New Delhi to act as liaisons between the company and the various governmental agencies. Businessmen participate regularly on a variety of government consultative committees, and the Birlas have commanded a position of such influence as to give them a strong voice in the selection of the Finance Minister. Although business pressure has sought to shape and modify policy formation, this pressure has been exerted more often by individual businessmen than by organized lobbies. Business has given its greatest attention, however, to the administration of policy—particularly in those state governments responsive to its interests.[37]

The Military

In a large part of the developing world, the military has played a prominent role in political life. With coups, both bloodless and violent, few new nations have been free of military intervention. The Indian army has remained remarkably nonpolitical, however. The explanation does not lie in the character of the military, for with essentially the same traditions, organization, and social background, the Pakistani army seized power under General Ayub Khan. The most important causes of military intervention are political and are to be located in the availability of meaningful channels of political access and of institutions for mediating and resolving conflict. If the political system is unable to respond to increasing participation and escalating demands and at the same time maintain order, the military, cohesive and bureaucratized, may step in.

The Indian army, numbering more than a half-million men, has a proud and romantic tradition. But although regimental color and Sandhurst tastes remain, the army today, however modern, has lost much of its former administrative and social status and carries the lingering taint

---

[36] *Ibid.*, p. 121.
[37] *Ibid.*, p. 129.

of association with British imperialism. Morale, although bolstered by the heroism of Indian soldiers in the twenty-two-day war with Pakistan in 1965, has never completely recovered from the humiliation of the Chinese invasion.[38] While Indian defense expenditure declined from 1950 to 1961, then rose rapidly in response to the Chinese threat, it has maintained an overall average of approximately 30 percent of total government expenditures. In India, as elsewhere, however, defense expenditures are often hidden in a variety of budgetary allocations. Military expenditure may thus be considerably larger than official figures indicate. In addition, India has received considerable military assistance from the Soviet Union, and from the United States immediately after the Chinese threat. The defense establishment has gained a powerful position in bidding for scarce resources within the public sector, but as yet the military has not sought greater leverage in political life.

Even if the army were to overcome its tradition of restraint, a coup would require the concerted action of the four regional commands— no easy task. That the President might in a governmental crisis declare a state of emergency and invite military intervention is more plausible. Political democracy in India, Lloyd I. and Susanne H. Rudolph warn, is by no means secure: "The authoritarian character created by the traditional family, the attraction of cultural fundamentalism to the urbanized lower middle classes, and the appeal of order, discipline and efficiency to the professional classes, now marginal features of Indian political life, are susceptible of mobilization by military leadership under the right circumstances."[39]

The Scope of Interest-Group Activity in India

A developed group infrastructure acts not merely to facilitate the articulation of demands and to provide linkage between the mass and the élite. In providing meaningful access to the political decision-makers, it gives order to expanding participation and focuses disparate demands so that they may more readily be acted upon. Indian interest groups, however, have a low level of institutionalization. Viewed with suspicion, their activities are generally seen as illegitimate, and for many people this opinion is confirmed by their recourse to violence in the face of governmental unresponsiveness.

[38] Various memoirs by Indian generals have been released, including B. M. Kaul, *The Untold Story* (Bombay: Allied Publishers, 1967); J. P. Dalvi, *Himalayan Blunder* (Calcutta: Thacker, 1969); and J. N. Chaudhuri, *Arms, Aims, and Aspects* (Bombay: Manaktalas, 1966).

[39] "Generals and Politicians in India," *Pacific Affairs*, Vol. 37 (Spring 1964), p. 7.

Comparatively few of India's newly mobilized political participants are involved in organized interest-group life. Formal memberships, if impressive in absolute terms, are inconsequential in relation to the mass of India's half-billion population. Three million labor-union members, one hundred thousand or so student activists, a handful of formal members in agrarian associations are unlikely to command much political capital, particularly because the organizations lack autonomy from political parties. Even the community associations have only limited membership, primarily from among the urban and educated middle classes. The Nadar Mahajana Sangam has only twenty thousand members from a community of more than one and one-half million. However, these associations and interest groups represent the yet-unorganized millions who with mass communications and party competition for their votes can be stirred to political consciousness. Their group identity is now only beginning to take form. Untouchables, for example, who number some sixty-five million, are just awakening to their potential power as a political bloc, and though geographically dispersed, they are likely to command increasing weight in the electoral calculus.

While these different groups share the wider political culture of India, in varying degrees, each constitutes within itself a sub-culture of common orientations and shared values. Many are highly fragmented; others are cohesive and self-conscious. Linguistic and communal minorities, the Sikhs and Muslims particularly, have highly articulated political cultures. Every individual, however, is a member of a number of political cultures. The various cultures may be seen as a nesting system, the narrowly parochial at the center and the national on the outside. Political mobilization has extended the identity horizon of the Indian masses in widening participation and involvement, but interest groups have been unable to provide the institutional channels of access to structure and order what Weiner has called the "emergent mass political culture."[40] Political parties, notably the Congress, have assumed this critical role.

[40] "India's Two Political Cultures," p. 199.

RECOMMENDED READING

Altbach, Philip, ed., *Turmoil and Transition: Higher Education and Student Politics in India.* New York: Basic Books, 1968.
    An examination by seven social scientists of the problem of student unrest.

* Bondurant, Joan V., *Conquest of Violence.* Berkeley: University of California Press, 1965.
    A sympathetic study of satyagraha and Gandhian political theory.

* Available in a paperback edition.

Carstairs, G. M., *The Twice-Born*. Bloomington: Indiana University Press, 1958.
A study of Hindu personality-formation in Rajasthan.

Chaudhuri, Nirad C., *The Continent of Circe*. London: Chatto & Windus, 1967.
A highly individual interpretation of Hindu personality by a controversial Indian intellectual.

Das Gupta, J., *Language Conflict and National Development*. Berkeley: University of California Press, forthcoming.
A study of group politics and national language policy.

Hardgrave, Robert L., Jr., *The Nadars of Tamilnad: The Political Culture of a Community in Change*. Berkeley: University of California Press, 1969.
An analysis of the relationship between social structure and political behavior within a changing caste community in South India.

Lambert, Richard D., *Workers, Factories, and Social Change in India*. Bombay: Asia Publishing House, 1963.
A discussion of the labor situation and of factory life in Poona.

Myers, Charles A., *Labor Problems in the Industrialization of India*. Cambridge, Mass.: Harvard University Press, 1958.
An examination of the relationship between labor and government, with particular concern for the creation of a labor force with a commitment to an industrial discipline.

Park, Richard L., and Tinker, Irene, eds., *Leadership and Political Institutions in India*. Princeton, N.J.: Princeton University Press, 1960.
A major collection of essays dealing with varied aspects of Indian political life.

Rudolph, Lloyd I. and Susanne H., *The Modernity of Tradition*. Chicago: University of Chicago Press, 1967.
A study of the ways in which tradition and modernity penetrate one another in a dialectical relationship. The dynamic of tradition is explored in the context of caste associations, the personality of Gandhi, and the Indian legal tradition.

Rudolph, Susanne H., "Consensus and Conflict in Indian Politics." *World Politics*, Vol. 12 (April 1961), pp. 385–99.
An insightful analysis of the role of consensus in traditional Indian society and its implications for democratic politics.

Shils, Edward, *The Intellectual Between Tradition and Modernity: The Indian Situation*, Supplement I, *Comparative Studies in Society and History*. The Hague: Mouton, 1961.
An exploration of the varied aspects of the Indian intellectual as a man between two worlds.

* Smith, Donald E., ed., *South Asian Politics and Religion*. Princeton, N.J.: Princeton University Press, 1966.
A collection of essays on the diversity of India's religions and their impact on politics.

* Available in a paperback edition.

Srinivas, M. N., *Caste in Modern India and Other Essays*. Bombay: Asia Publishing House, 1962.
   A penetrating analysis of politics and social change in India.

* Weiner, Myron, "India's Two Political Cultures," in Lucian Pye and Sidney Verba, eds., *Political Culture and Political Development*. Princeton, N.J.: Princeton University Press, 1965.
   A discussion of Indian political life in terms of its élite culture and the emerging mass participant culture.

————, *The Politics of Scarcity*. Chicago: University of Chicago Press, 1962.
   An analysis of group politics in India and the political response to the pressure of demands. One of the best studies yet on Indian politics.

* Available in a paperback edition.

VI

THE PARTY SYSTEM

THE YEAR 1969 OPENED A NEW ERA IN INDIAN POLITICAL LIFE. WITH the formal split in the Congress party, the Government of Indira Gandhi no longer commanded an absolute majority in Parliament. Some sixty Congressmen sat on the benches of the opposition in the Lok Sabha. Although a few Congress rebels from earlier days began to return to the party fold, the survival of the Government now depended on support from members of the opposition.

The Prime Minister weathered her first challenge on the opening day of the winter parliamentary session. On a *de facto* motion of censure for adjournment in the Lok Sabha, a number of independents, waverers from various parties, the D.M.K., and the two Communist parties stood with the Congress Government. Ranged on the other side were the Jana Sangh, Swatantra, the Praja Socialists, the Samyukta Socialists, and the opposition Congress.

The split in the Congress was mirrored in the contradictions and confusion of the parties in opposition, but the prospects for a general polarization in Indian politics are unlikely, for both on the left and on the right there are deep divisions in ideology, temperament, and social base. The Prime Minister, to maintain support and to ready herself for forthcoming elections, will have to implement the Congress economic program effectively. Slogans and rhetoric will no longer suffice. The Government will inevitably be drawn further to the left, both to fulfill its own self-image and to meet the pressure from its new allies among the opposition. The confidence the Prime Minister commands will be strained increasingly, however, as each of the groups sustaining her survival demands a greater role in the Government. At the end of 1969 the Prime Minister, though supported by a substantial majority, was vulnerable to political blackmail, for any one of the elements supporting her could threaten to withdraw and potentially defeat the Government. Mrs. Gandhi can only go so far without losing the base of support within her own party. At a point where the Prime Minister is unable or unwilling to yield to outside pressure, she might then dissolve the Lok Sabha and, in parliamentary mid-term elections, seek a mandate from the people in the form of an absolute majority in her own right. In order to gain control of the Congress organization in the states, or to establish alternative structures where necessary, Mrs. Gandhi is likely to postpone elections as long as possible, perhaps until the general election of 1972. In late 1969 she commanded vast popular support, however, and would be at a tactical advantage in holding parliamentary elections separately from the general elections, since the contests for the state assemblies would challenge the Prime Minister's search for a stable Congress majority at the Center with distracting local issues.

The instability and pattern of defections that have characterized politics at the state level since 1967 might well rise to the top. Political *immobilisme* might, as in the French Fourth Republic, shift the responsibility for government from popularly elected representatives to bureaucratic civil servants. Presidential intervention becomes a serious possibility at the Center and the position of the military becomes more critical. The events of 1969 opened a wide range of possibilities: The changing pattern of the party system will give them shape.

The Congress Party

In India before 1967 and the party split two years later, the critical arena of political competition was the Congress "system" of one-party dominance.[1] This system, which operated effectively in India until the

[1] The party system in India has been characterized in this way by Rajni Kothari, "The Congress 'System' in India," in his *Party Systems and Election Studies,* Occasional Papers of the Center for Developing Societies, No. 1 (Bombay: Allied Publishers, 1967), pp. 1–18; by W. H. Morris-Jones, "Parliament and Dominant Party: Indian Experience," in *Parliamentary Affairs,* Vol. 17 (Summer 1964), pp. 296–307; and by Gopal Krishna, "One Party Dominance—Developments and Trends" in *Party Systems and Electoral Studies,* pp. 19–98.

mid-1960's, was a competitive one, but one in which the single party of consensus occupied a dominant, central position. In this system the dominant Congress party, factionally divided itself, was both sensitive and responsive to the margin of pressure; the opposition did not constitute an alternative to the ruling party but functioned from the periphery in the form of parties of pressure. In such a system, the role of the opposition parties, writes Rajni Kothari,

> is to constantly pressurize, criticize, censure and influence it by influencing opinion and interests inside the margin and, above all, exert a latent threat that if the ruling group strays away too far from the balance of effective public opinion, and if the factional system within it is not mobilized to restore the balance, it will be displaced from power by the opposition groups.[2]

The one-party dominance system has two prominent characteristics. "There is plurality within the dominant party which makes it more representative, provides flexibility, and sustains internal competition. At the same time, it is prepared to absorb groups and movements from outside the party and thus prevent other parties from gaining strength."[3]

The breakdown of the Congress "system" was rooted in its own dynamics—the internal contradictions within the party.

The Factional Character of the Congress

Within the Congress, in the years of dominance, factions interacted in "a continuous process of pressure, adjustment and accommodation" to provide a built-in opposition.[4] The party retained the character of the nationalist movement in seeking to balance and accommodate social and ideological diversity within an all-embracing, representative structure. During the struggle for independence, the Congress party, as the vehicle of the nationalist movement, brought together an eclectic body of individuals and groups in united opposition to the British raj. Claiming sole legitimacy as the nationalist party, the Congress sought to resolve or avoid internal conflict, balance interests, and blur ideological distinctions in its search for consensus.[5] Within its ranks, however, in factions and internal parties, were the roots of opposition. Organized groups emerged from the Congress umbrella as distinct parties, but each left within the Congress an ideologically congruent faction. Thus each of the opposition parties—the Jana Sangh, Swatantra, the Socialists, and the Communists—retained access to the Congress that provided it with an influence disproportionate to its size.

2 "The Congress 'System' in India," p. 3.
3 *Ibid.*, p. 6.
4 Rajni Kothari, "Party System," *Economic Weekly* (June 3, 1961), p. 849.
5 Krishna, "One Party Dominance," p. 26.

The responsiveness of the Congress to these pressures was revealed in the flexibility and contradictions of its programs and practices. The Congress sustained itself by undermining the opposition, taking over their programs, conceding basic issues, and co-opting their leadership. At the national level, the Congress stole the thunder of the Praja Socialist party through its 1955 resolution in support of a socialist pattern of society. In the states, the Congress became the voice of regionalism, as in Kamaraj's appointment of a non-Brahmin ministry in Tamilnadu, in order to undercut the growth of separatism. At the local level, the party relaxed its policy of land reform to win support from the landlords and keep Swatantra at a distance. At the top, the Congress party has repeatedly denounced casteism as a reversion to a tribal mentality, but at the bottom, the Congress, like the Jana Sangh and even the Communists, anchored its organization among the dominant castes.

In consolidating its power after independence, the Congress sought to achieve a national consensus through the accommodation and absorption of dominant social elements that had kept aloof from the nationalist movement. Traditional caste and village leaders, landlords, and businessmen made their way into the Congress.

> In its effort to win, Congress adapts itself to the local power structure. It recruits from among those who have local power and influence . . . . The result is a political system with considerable tension between a government concerned with modernizing the society and economy and a party seeking to adapt itself to the local environment in order to win elections.[6]

With the resources of government power and patronage, the Congress attracted careerists, who sought to gain support by appealing to the parochial loyalties of language, caste, and community. "The composite character of the party was preserved," writes Gopal Krishna, "indeed made more heterogeneous by promiscuous accommodation of divergent elements, whose commitments to the new consensus created around the objectives of economic development, socialism and democracy remained superficial."[7] Paul R. Brass concurs: "The Congress Party has chosen to make adjustments and accommodations, to interact with rather than transform the traditional order. In India, modernization is not a one-way process; political institutions modernize the society while the society traditionalizes institutions."[8]

As the party penetrated society, it was influenced by it. Political mobilization served to stimulate a new consciousness and solidarity. As

---

[6] Myron Weiner, *Party Building in a New Nation* (Chicago: University of Chicago Press, 1967), p. 15.
[7] "One Party Dominance," p. 29.
[8] *Factional Politics in an Indian State: The Congress Party in Uttar Pradesh* (Berkeley: University of California Press, 1966), p. 2.

a channel of communication and integration providing effective vertical linkage, the party drew increasing numbers into political participation. In a capillary effect they infused the party with a new leadership, regional in the base of its support, more traditional in the idiom of its political behavior. Political consciousness was activated faster than the integrative process, however, and as a result group identity was often emphasized at the expense of the national community.[9] As the new electorate, caste-conscious and parochial in orientation, was drawn into a more participant political life, the Congress and the opposition parties sought to win their support through the tactics of the American political machine—patronage, favors, promises, and bargains. As the electorate was politicized, the parties were traditionalized. The parties became "mediating agencies between the largely traditional and politically diffuse electorate and the modern state system with its emphasis on citizenship, purposive direction of public policy and political integration."[10]

Although all parties served to induct the new citizens into the political culture, the Congress, as the dominant party, was the critical channel of linkage between the élite and the mass. Gandhi had attempted to bring the Congress directly to the masses, but it was the development of the party organization, with its roots in tradition, that consolidated the Congress and made politics both comprehensible and meaningful to Indian peasants. In the process, however, the Congress became an advocate of much that it had opposed, encouraging both sectionalism and integration, preaching socialism, and sustaining the *status quo*.[11]

Brass, in his study of the Congress in Uttar Pradesh, describes the internal life of the party in terms of factional conflict. The conflict is not ideological but personal; it is characterized by shifting political coalitions. "Alliances develop and splits and defections occur wholly because of the mutual convenience and temporarily shared power-political interests of the group leaders."[12] The groups are "loose coalitions of local, district faction leaders, tied together at the state level partly by personal bonds of friendship, partly by caste loyalties, and most of all by political interest."[13] Although there seem to be no persistent conflicts, Brass argues, there is in each faction a relatively solid inner core, bound together in personal loyalty to the leader and divided from other factions by deep personal enmities.

Factional conflict is rooted at the district level, and factional systems are largely autonomous, arising out of conditions and personalities peculiar to the district. This served to compartmentalize conflict, to quarantine discontent, and to make discontent more manageable.

[9] Krishna, "One Party Dominance," p. 31.
[10] *Ibid.*, p. 32.
[11] *Ibid.*, p. 33.
[12] Brass, *Factional Politics in an Indian State*, p. 54.
[13] *Ibid.*, p. 55.

Factionalism in the party is closely related to factionalism in the villages, since traditional village factions increasingly seek to ally themselves with a party group. The factional character of the Congress served to accommodate local conflict and to internalize it. If the Congress were unable to tolerate factions, opposition parties would secure the support of one of the two factions in each village—as in certain regions they are now beginning to do. Highly institutionalized, the factional system within the Congress, at least until 1967, was able "to sustain popular support in the midst of intense intra-party conflict."[14]

Although factionalism often leads to paralysis at the level of local government, it may also perform certain integrative functions. The faction, as a vertical structure of power, cuts across caste and class divisions and is based on a combination of other traditional loyalties and individual interests. "All faction leaders seek cross-caste alliances, for it is political power they desire and not merely the advancement of the claims of their own communities."[15] Factional conflict also broadens the base of participation within the party as each faction competes for wider group support. By drawing in new caste and religious groups, for example, factions have politicized them in secular terms.[16]

Factionalism, however, may also lead to a form of *immobilisme*, as each faction holds the other in check. The factional character of the Congress has meant that the chief opposition to the Government has frequently come from within the Congress itself. Conflict between the governmental and organizational wings of the party virtually constituted a two-party system but one hardly designed for coherent and effective policy.[17]

The Organization of the Congress

Under Gandhi the Congress organization, shown in Figure 6–1, was structured as a parallel government, extending down to the village level. Except for the fact that Congress provincial units were organized along linguistic lines, this structure corresponded to administrative boundaries, such as that of the district, not to electoral constituencies. After independence the system was retained, with parallel party and government structure from top to bottom.

There are two types of party membership: primary, requiring the acceptance of Congress objectives and the payment of four annas[18] dues annually, and active, requiring the wearing of khadi, a homespun cloth, abstinence, opposition to untouchability and communalism, participa-

[14] Weiner, *Party Building in a New Nation*, pp. 159–160.
[15] Brass, *Factional Politics in an Indian State*, p. 236.
[16] *Ibid.*, p. 242.
[17] See Kothari, "Party System," pp. 851–52.
[18] The term *anna*, one-sixteenth of a rupee, is still used, although the coin was discontinued with the introduction of decimal *paise*.

FIGURE 6–1

THE FORMAL ORGANIZATIONAL STRUCTURE OF THE CONGRESS

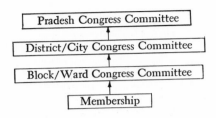

tion in constructive work, and payment of one rupee dues annually. All members within a block (or ward) elect the block (or ward) Congress committee, corresponding to the samiti or development block. The district (or city) Congress committee consists of elected, ex officio, and co-opted members so as to be generally representative of various factions and groups within the party. The pradesh (or provincial) Congress committee is similarly constituted and is the locus of Congress power within each state.[19] The Congress is the only party with a permanent organization in every state. The organizational character of the opposition parties has varied with time and from party to party, but their organization tends to be patterned after that of the Congress.

The Congress organization is coordinated through a pyramidal decision-making structure, shown in Figure 6–2, with the Working Committee and the president at the apex.

The Relationship of the Congress and the Government

Stanley A. Kochanek, in a study of Congress organization, describes the evolution of party-Government relations and the transformation of inner party structure as passing through three stages. The conflict between the two wings of the Congress reached its height and "resolution" in 1969 in the formal party split.

"THE PERIOD OF TRANSITION"

The period of transition, 1945–51, "was marked by conflict between the party and the Government and by disorder and confusion at the executive level of the party organization as the Congress sought to adapt a nationalist movement to a political party."[20] When he resigned as

---

19 For specifics of Congress field organization, see Stanley A. Kochanek, *The Congress Party of India* (Princeton, N.J.: Princeton University Press, 1968), pp. 452–53.

20 Kochanek, *The Congress Party*, p. xxiii.

FIGURE 6–2

THE NATIONAL DECISION-MAKING STRUCTURE OF THE CONGRESS

| President of the Congress |
elected by all the delegates
for a two-year term

| Working Committee |
Congress president and twenty members:
seven elected by the All-India Congress Committee and
thirteen appointed by the president

| All-India Congress Committee |
one-eighth of the delegates of each province
elected by the delegates of that province

| Annual Congress Session |
president, former presidents, and
all delegates
(all members of the pradesh Congress
committees are delegates)

SOURCE: Stanley A. Kochanek, *The Congress Party of India* (Princeton, N.J.: Princeton University Press, 1968), p. xxii.

Congress president to head the interim government, Nehru took the top echelon of the party's leadership with him into the Cabinet. During the independence struggle the high command of the party had strongly asserted the supremacy of the organization, but with swaraj the leadership abandoned the organization for the responsibilities of public office. They had won honor through their activities in the nationalist movement, and office was their reward. The political center of gravity shifted from the party to the Government, but J. B. Kripalani, the new Congress president, insisted that Government decisions be made only in consultation with the Congress president and the Working Committee. Unwilling to oversee the subordination of the party, Kripalani resigned and later left the Congress altogether.

The decisive confrontation came with the election of the conservative P. Tandon as Congress president, which placed the organization in the hands of the right wing of the party. But when the conservatives sought to consolidate their position, the death of Patel deprived them of their major patron and protector. Nehru then assumed a more prominent role in party affairs, and with the first general elections approaching, he sought to wrest control of the organization from the right wing. Threatening to resign from the Working Committee, Nehru forced Tandon to step down in his favor. In 1951 Nehru was elected president, thus bringing the party and Government under the control of a single leader. His emergence as undisputed leader of the Congress "confirmed the pre-eminent role of the Prime Minister and reinforced the boundaries of the office of Congress President, which had been revealed once more as limited strictly to organizational affairs with no special responsibility for policy-making."[21]

Nehru's assumption of the Congress presidency marked the beginning of the period of centralization and convergence, 1951–63. His three-year joint tenure restored harmony between the party and the Government, but at the party's expense. The Government was responsible not to the party but to Parliament and the electorate. To hold the Prime Minister accountable to the party, Nehru argued, would reduce parliamentary democracy to a "mockery"; the party might "broadly affect" policy or "push it in this direction or that," but responsibility for decision-making lay with the Government.[22] In 1954 Nehru turned over the organization to a succession of "captive" party presidents who carried his personal endorsement—U. N. Dhebar, Indira Gandhi, Sanjiva Reddy, and D. Sanjivayya. Their dependence on the Prime Minister precluded any effective challenge to his leadership, and while some independent action was possible—for example, Mrs. Gandhi played an important role in bringing down the Communist ministry in Kerala in 1959—the Congress president was frequently described in this period as "a glorified office boy of the Congress central government headed by the prime minister."[23]

Under Nehru the Working Committee was brought under the dominance of the parliamentary wing, the most powerful chief ministers and important Central Cabinet ministers forming the core of its membership. It

> came to play an important role in providing policy leadership to the party organization, in coordinating party-government relations, and in accommodating the conflicting demands of Congress leaders representing the broadening base of the party. The Working Committee became the sounding board by which the Prime Minister could test the acceptability of new policies as well as an important feedback mechanism by which to assess the reactions of party and state leaders.[24]

[21] *Ibid.*, p. 53.
[22] *Ibid.*, p. 57.
[23] Frank Moraes, *India Today* (New York: Macmillan, 1960), p. 98.
[24] Kochanek, *The Congress Party*, p. 307.

In the period of transition the Working Committee had virtually no control over the state governments, but Nehru sought to use the committee for the direction of state Congress ministries. The Working Committee became the agent of arbitration, conciliation, and mediation in an effort to achieve a new national consensus on the Congress economic program. Divergent factions were drawn under the Congress umbrella through persuasion, reconciliation, and accommodation. In the process, however, as power devolved to leaders at the state level, Dhebar warned of the dangers of bossism, entrenchment, and indiscipline.[25]

While the Congress at the national level was made subordinate to the Government, and political reality receded in the face of a complacent and romantic ideology, the lower levels of the party organization were gradually captured by a new generation of politicians. These men were brokers who, in understanding both traditional society and machine techniques, provided the channels of linkage between the villages and the modern political system. The party organization became the vehicle for their own advancement, the agent of upward mobility for an aspiring new leadership. For some, the movement into the party organization was from an established base of traditional influence within their village or samiti. For others, politics was a vocation. K. Kamaraj Nadar, for example, rose from the bottom of the party organization to secure control of the Tamilnad Congress Committee. In the states the new leadership gained control of the organization, challenged the old order, and took over the government, its power and patronage. Kamaraj, boss of the Congress in Tamilnadu, ousted Rajagopalachari as chief minister. C. B. Gupta in Uttar Pradesh, Chavan in Maharashtra, and Patnaik in Orissa were all organization men who, with the party machinery in their hands, took control of their state governments and came to wield considerable power at the national level.

"THE PERIOD OF DIVERGENCE"

The changes evidenced in the states made their appearance at the national level in 1963 with the introduction of the Kamaraj Plan. This opened what Kochanek has called the period of divergence. Kamaraj proposed "that leading Congressmen who are in Government should voluntarily relinquish their ministerial posts and offer themselves for full-time organizational work."[26] All chief ministers and Central Cabinet ministers submitted their resignations. The decision as to which resignations to accept was left to Nehru. Six chief ministers, including Kamaraj, and six Cabinet ministers were asked to take up organizational work. The Kamaraj Plan was generally regarded as a device to get rid of Morarji Desai, considered conservative and rigid, but its more significant

[25] *Ibid.*, p. 64.
[26] Quoted in Kochanek, *The Congress Party*, pp. 78–79.

consequence was the induction of state party bosses into positions of power at the national level, with Kamaraj at the helm of the organization as new Congress president. The plan "restored" the prestige and power of the central organization, which had been virtually eclipsed under the dominance of Nehru.[27]

The Congress and the Politics of Succession to the Prime Ministership

Following the Kamaraj Plan in 1963, in an effort to deny Desai the Congress presidency and to isolate him further from power, a group of powerful state leaders (Kamaraj, Atulya Ghosh from West Bengal, Sanjiva Reddy from Andhra, S. Nijalingappa from Mysore, and S. K. Patil from Bombay), informally organized as "the Syndicate," united behind Kamaraj as the man most likely to provide stable and effective party leadership. In January 1964, Nehru suffered a stroke. G. L. Nanda and T. T. Krishnamachari, the senior ministers, assumed responsibility for those areas normally handled by the Prime Minister. The question "after Nehru, who?" was now raised more poignantly than ever before. Lal Bahadur Shastri, who had left the Cabinet under the Kamaraj Plan, was now brought back as Minister without Portfolio. With Nehru's blessing and the powerful support of the Syndicate, Shastri occupied a strategic position. Four months later, on May 27, 1964, Nehru was dead. Home Minister Nanda was designated to act as Prime Minister until the Congress Parliamentary Party, composed of all Congress M.P.'s, could elect a successor.

Although Shastri held majority support within the C.P.P., Desai sought to prevent Shastri's election. Maneuvering for a unanimous election, Kamaraj called a meeting of an enlarged Congress Working Committee. The forty-two-member body, which Michael Brecher has called "the Grand Council of the Republic,"[28] included the regular members of the Working Committee, the chief ministers, the leaders of the Congress party in Parliament, senior Cabinet ministers, and invited members such as Krishna Menon. The election was to be held two days later and the Congress president was authorized to "ascertain the consensus of opinion on the question of the choice of Leader of the Congress Party in Parliament and tender his advice accordingly."[29] In the next forty-eight hours, Kamaraj consulted all the chief ministers, the members of the Working Committee, and many members of the C.P.P. Shastri's election was assured, and in response to overwhelming pressure, Morarji Desai agreed to second Shastri's nomination to secure his unani-

---

[27] Kothari, "The Congress 'System' in India," p. 16.
[28] *Nehru's Mantle: The Politics of Succession in India* (New York: Praeger, 1966), p. 61.
[29] Quoted in Kochanek, *The Congress Party*, p. 89.

mous election.[30] An example of party discipline, the Congress effort to avoid a contest reflected a search for consensus that not only is traditional in Indian political culture but was characteristic of the party's struggle against the British when it could not afford an open split in its ranks.

Desai had had the support of a diverse coalition—the traditional right wing, business elements, harijans, and in addition, disaffected leftists led by Krishna Menon. Shastri, on the other hand, was backed by the leaders of the South and the non-Hindi states of Maharashtra and West Bengal; moreover, as a native of Uttar Pradesh he represented the Hindi heartland, despite the fact that the major leaders of this region were for Desai. The Syndicate played the critical role in coalescing the diverse interests behind Shastri and in securing consensus. According to Michael Brecher,

> the outcome was determined by peaceful competition among various interest groups. The decisive factor was the clear majority for Shastri in the three key institutional groups, the Working Committee, the state party machines, and in the CPP, superimposed on the relatively inarticulate but known choice of Shastri by the mass public.[31]

The Syndicate gave political form to that national preference.

The succession served also to reveal the shift in political gravity toward the states. The state party organizations occupied a pivotal position —in the role of the chief ministers in the decisions of "the Grand Council of the Republic" and in their control over blocs of votes within the Congress Parliamentary Party.[32]

In January 1966, less than two years after he had taken office, Shastri died, just hours after having signed a truce with Pakistan at Tashkent. Faced with the second succession, Kamaraj no longer commanded the position of strength from which he had directed the events following Nehru's death. The Syndicate had lost its cohesion: "The politics of unanimity" had given way "to the politics of overt conflict."[33] Kamaraj sought to weld a consensus behind Indira Gandhi by means of massive pressure conveyed indirectly through the chief ministers. The Syndicate had no choice but to go along. Kamaraj had again emerged as "king-maker," but the process had been more difficult. Morarji Desai, against the advice of his colleagues, pressed for an open contest. He would not step down in favor of another as he had done in 1964. In the vote, the first contested election for leadership, Mrs. Gandhi overwhelmed Desai, 355 to 169. The successions revealed the capacity of the Congress to

---

[30] For an analysis of the succession, see Brecher, *Nehru's Mantle.*
[31] *Nehru's Mantle,* p. 88.
[32] *Ibid.,* p. 72.
[33] *Ibid.,* p. 205.

absorb conflict, but at the same time exposed deep division within the party.

The ascendancy of Kamaraj indicated a revitalized party, and his role in engineering the two successions underscored the more prominent position the party sought in the post-Nehru years. The party presidency was certainly enhanced, but "while it is impossible not to recognize that Kamaraj added new stature and authority to the Congress presidency, played an influential role in policy-making, and enjoyed considerable autonomy in organizational affairs, it is also clear that his position was in many ways subordinate to that of the Prime Minister."[34] Indira Gandhi was not going to allow herself to become the puppet of the Syndicate, and her relations with Kamaraj became increasingly cool.

The struggle for succession revealed not merely the power of the party but, even more critically, the pivotal position of the state Congress organizations. The result was a polycentric system of decision-making in which power was dispersed among several competing but overlapping groups: the Working Committee, the chief ministers, the Cabinet, and the Congress party in Parliament. With the national leadership split, the Working Committee could no longer effectively play its mediating role. Dominant factions in the states sought to consolidate their positions. Dissident state factions, "feeling isolated from power within the party because of the inability of the central leadership to intervene to protect them," defected from the party.[35] The dilemma confronting the Congress was basic: "To dominate, Congress must accommodate; yet accommodation encourages incoherence which destroys the capacity to dominate."[36] The more autonomous the Congress party in each state became, with its effectiveness derived from local resources, the more vulnerable it was to displacement by regional opposition parties operating from the same sources of strength.

The defeats sustained by the Congress in the 1967 elections again opened conflict over party leadership and control of the new Government. The Congress was in disarray, with dissension and defections on all sides. The electoral reverses, however, "had generated tremendous pressures for a consensus on the leadership issue in order to avoid a schism in the already weakened party."[37] Kamaraj, despite his own defeat at the polls, achieved a bargain settlement by which Mrs. Gandhi was unanimously reelected Prime Minister, while Desai was appointed Deputy Prime Minister. Reinforcing the consensus, Nijalingappa, Chief Minister of Mysore, was chosen the new Congress president. Mrs.

---

[34] Kochanek, *The Congress Party*, p. 93.

[35] *Ibid.*, p. 315.

[36] W. H. Morris-Jones, "Dominance and Dissent," *Government and Opposition*, Vol. 1 (July–September 1966), p. 460.

[37] Kochanek, *The Congress Party*, p. 412.

Gandhi, freed of the pressures of the old state bosses by their election defeats, emerged with new strength.

Crisis and Split

The 1969 presidential election increased the tension between the Government and the organizational wings of the party to the point of open conflict and initiated the four-month crisis that split the eighty-four-year-old Indian National Congress. Challenging the Syndicate, Indira Gandhi sought to reestablish securely the dominance of the Prime Minister within the party; and looking ahead to the 1972 elections, she sought to obtain her choice of candidates in nomination and to give effective meaning to the Congress commitment to socialism.

The first round of battle took place at the meeting of the All-India Congress Committee at Bangalore in July 1969. To gain the initiative at the Bangalore session, Mrs. Gandhi sent a note of "stray thoughts" to the Working Committee urging a more aggressive stance toward economic policy—nationalization of major commercial banks, effective implementation of land reforms, ceilings on urban income and property, and curbs on industrial monopolies. The Syndicate, lacking ideological cohesiveness, was divided in its reaction. S. K. Patil and Congress president Nijalingappa sided with Morarji Desai in opposition; Kamaraj and Home Minister Y. B. Chavan expressed favor. To avoid a split on the eve of the presidential nomination, Chavan secured a unanimous resolution calling on the central and state governments to implement the Prime Minister's suggestions. The Syndicate, however, in alliance with Desai, sought to retain its hold over the party and to secure the Congress presidential nomination for its own man, Sanjiva Reddy, Speaker of the Lok Sabha, in opposition to Mrs. Gandhi's preference for V. V. Giri, the seventy-four-year-old Acting President.

By custom, the nomination is made by the eight-member Central Parliamentary Board, elected by the A.I.C.C. With no chance for Giri, Mrs. Gandhi, supported by Fakhruddin Ali Ahmed, Industries Development Minister, formally proposed Jagivan Ram, Minister for Food and Agriculture. Reddy's nomination, however, was secure with the support of Nijalingappa, Kamaraj, Patil, and Desai. Chavan threw his lot with the majority. This was not the first time the Parliamentary Board had been divided. In 1950, Nehru had wanted C. Rajagopalachari as the first President, but under pressure from Sardar Patel and Azad, he accepted the party's choice of Prasad. In 1967, the board was evenly divided between Radhakrishnan's continuation as President, supported by Kamaraj, and the selection of Zakir Hussain, who was supported by Mrs. Gandhi. Radhakrishnan's decision not to run ended the deadlock.

When Reddy was nominated by Congress, V. V. Giri entered the presidential contest as an independent. He resigned as Acting President and, in accordance with the constitution, was replaced by the Chief Justice of India, M. Hidayatullah. In a vigorous campaign, Giri drew the support of the Samyukta Socialist party, the D.M.K., the Muslim League, the two wings of the Communist party, and almost all elements of the United Front governments of Kerala and West Bengal. Swatantra, Jana Sangh, and the coalition Bharatiya Kranti Dal of Uttar Pradesh jointly put forward former Finance Minister C. D. Deshmukh as their candidate. The Praja Socialists sat the fence between Giri and Deshmukh.

Within the Congress, as Chavan sought a *rapprochement* between the Prime Minister and the Syndicate, Mrs. Gandhi relieved Morarji Desai of his Finance portfolio, deepening the wedge between the two groups. To save his "self-respect," Desai then resigned as Deputy Prime Minister. Although Mrs Gandhi claimed to have taken the action because of Desai's position on her economic measures, Desai had, if grudgingly, accepted the A.I.C.C. resolution. The Syndicate considered the affair a vendetta, but as sympathy grew for Desai, Mrs. Gandhi retained the initiative. She announced the nationalization of fourteen major commercial banks, at once justifying her earlier action and pushing the Desai controversy into the background. The purpose of nationalization, she announced, was to provide more equitable access to bank credit, particularly for small farmers and artisans. Chavan, Kamaraj, and Atulya Ghosh, previous advocates of bank nationalization when Mrs. Gandhi seemed uninterested, welcomed the decision. The banks, holding some 70 percent of the country's total bank assets, were largely in the hands of a few dominant business families, the Birlas, Tatas, Dalmias, and Jains. Nationalization involved the expenditure of little political capital and reaped widespread support for the Prime Minister. She called the action "only the beginning of a bitter struggle between the common people and the vested interests in the country."[38]

Although she had signed Reddy's nomination papers, Mrs. Gandhi had yet to come out clearly in favor of the party's conservative nominee. Indeed, there was speculation that Reddy would try to use the untested powers of the Presidency against the Prime Minister, if not to unseat her altogether. Whereas Reddy's election at first seemed assured with the Congress holding 52 percent of the votes, increasing rumors of defections to Giri caused considerable unease among Syndicate members. Within one week of the election, party president Nijalingappa issued a whip instructing all Congress M.P.'s and M.L.A.'s to vote for Reddy and requested Mrs. Gandhi to make an immediate statement of support for the Congress nominee. The Prime Minister, leader of the Parliamentary Party, refused to issue a whip for Reddy, and her supporters called for a "free vote" of conscience in the elec-

[38] *Hindu* (Madras), August 5, 1969.

tion. More than half of the Congress M.P.'s indicated their favor for a free vote; some publicly tore up the whip notice. Support for Giri was now in the open.

Fifteen candidates, with three leading contenders, stood for the election, held on August 16. Neither Reddy nor Giri achieved a majority on the first count; the second preferences of the Deshmukh ballots were then tabulated. On the second count, Giri was declared elected. Giri's lead on the first ballot came primarily from the non-Congress states of Tamilnadu, West Bengal, and Kerala. On the second count, it was the second-preference votes of the B.K.D. that gave him the requisite for victory. Violations of the Congress whip—particularly in Andhra and Uttar Pradesh—were considerable. On the first-preference vote, two out of five Congress M.P.'s and one out of four M.L.A.'s supported Giri. Most of the second-preference votes of the Jana Sangh and Swatantra went to Reddy.

Giri's election was greeted with tremendous popular enthusiasm. In the wake of Reddy's defeat, the Syndicate was in disarray. It had been embarrassed and was determined to bring disciplinary action against the Prime Minister. With pressure from those states with narrow Congress majorities, where a split might put them out of office, and with the mediation of Chavan, the Working Committee "closed" the matter with a plea for unity.

The unity resolution only papered over an almost conspiratorial atmosphere on both sides. Moving to give "a more cohesive and purposive direction"[39] to the work of the Council of Ministers, Mrs Gandhi requested the resignation of four junior ministers who were known to support the Syndicate. In heated exchanges with Nijalingappa, Mrs. Gandhi launched a signature campaign among the members of the A.I.C.C. to have a new Congress president elected by the end of the year. The Prime Minister argued that Congress policies could not be fully implemented unless the party organization was fully committed to them. More than four hundred of the seven hundred odd elected members of the A.I.C.C. signed the requisition.

Seeking to cast the inner-party struggle in an ideological mold, Mrs. Gandhi had strengthened her hand immeasurably. "Ideological divergences offered aid and abetment the more they were brought in to conceal ambition; towards the end they began to matter more than anything else."[40] The Syndicate is fundamentally nonideological, but conservative in temper and tied to a base of support among landed and big business interests. Indira Gandhi, if committed to socialism, is no radical, and among her followers are some of highly questionable ideological credentials. The chief ministers, most of whom had aligned with her, had never been particularly eager to implement a socialist

[39] *Hindu* (Madras), October 15, 1969.
[40] Pran Chopra, *Citizen* (New Delhi), August 23, 1969, p. 10.

policy of land reform and risk the alienation of their landed source of money and votes. Their assessment of Congress chances in 1972, however, prompted an inclination to move slightly to the left and a recognition that long-professed Congress policies if left unimplemented would leave Congressmen behind at the polls at the next election.

On October 31, the night before the scheduled meeting of the Working Committee, Nijalingappa announced his decision to drop two of Mrs. Gandhi's supporters from the C.W.C. Fakhruddin Ali Ahmed, a nominated member, was charged with antiparty activities and informed that he no longer enjoyed the confidence of the Congress president. C. Subramaniam, opponent of Kamaraj in Tamilnadu, was told that his membership had "lapsed" with his pressured resignation from the presidency of the Tamilnad Congress Committee. These actions, designed to ensure the Syndicate of a majority in the Working Committee meeting, were met by the Prime Minister and her supporters with boycott and a parallel meeting at her residence. There, with Home Minister Chavan now firmly behind Mrs. Gandhi, they resolved to hold a meeting of the A.I.C.C. at Delhi in late November to elect a new Congress president.

With demonstrators outside, the eleven members out of twenty-one who attended the regular Working Committee meeting at the A.I.C.C. headquarters declared the requisition illegal. They affirmed their commitment to the path of socialism, however vague, and accused the Prime Minister of attempting "to find in the Congress organization a scapegoat for the manifest failures of the administration."[41] Exchanges between the two camps continued with increasing vituperation and pettiness. Nijalingappa, pressed by Kamaraj and Morarji Desai, accused the Prime Minister of intrigue, indiscipline, and corruption and served a "show cause" notice on her to explain why disciplinary action should not be taken against her. Mrs. Gandhi, in turn, requested the resignation of the Railway Minister, Dr. Ram Subhag Singh, a Syndicate supporter. The Congress chief ministers, working to save their own governments, attempted various compromise formulas and even arranged an abortive luncheon between the two combatants.

On November 12, 1969, the Working Committee expelled Indira Gandhi from the Congress and instructed the Congress Parliamentary Party to elect a new leader. The C.P.P., however, has its own constitution, and a motion of no confidence requires a two-thirds majority. When the party met the following day, an overwhelming majority of its members reaffirmed support for the leadership of Mrs. Gandhi. Syndicate supporters in Parliament boycotted the meeting and met informally at Morarji Desai's residence. Meeting again two days later in formal session, 111 Congress M.P.'s elected Desai chairman of the opposition Congress Parliamentary Party. Dr. Ram Subhag Singh was elected

41 *Indian Express* (Madras), November 3, 1969.

leader of the party in the Lok Sabha. The number of opposition Congressmen was sufficient to earn them official recognition (which no opposition party before had ever had), and Dr. Singh emerged as India's first Leader of the Opposition. Against the 60 to 65 Congressmen in opposition in the Lok Sabha, the Prime Minister held the support of more than 200, but her Government no longer commanded an absolute majority. The Congress had split: The verdict would be pronounced at the polls.

The Socialist Parties

The Indian socialist parties are the direct descendants of the Congress Socialist party, founded in 1934 in response to Congress failure to pursue a more revolutionary policy. The Socialists sought to gain control of the Congress, within which they had organized, through a process of gradual displacement of right-wing leaders by the "composite leadership" of the left. They failed to build sufficient numerical strength to challenge Congress leadership, however, and although the Socialists gained a position of influence during the "quit India" movement, their strength was soon dissipated by their resignation from the Congress Working Committee and refusal to participate in the Constituent Assembly or to accept seats in Nehru's Cabinet.[42]

Nehru and an increasingly sympathetic Gandhi wanted to accommodate the Socialist leaders, but the Patel group blocked further Socialist incursions into party leadership, and following Gandhi's death brought a resolution by the All-India Congress Committee outlawing political parties within the Congress. At this point the Socialists, confident of their own strength, withdrew from the Congress. The new Socialist party sought to weld an alliance of the left for "nationalism, socialism, and democracy"; it aimed to challenge the Congress through a program of Gandhian "constructive work," parliamentary activity, and non-violent agitation—"the spade, the vote, and prison."[43]

The 1951 elections dealt the Socialists a severe blow. Although the party gained a little more than 10 percent of the vote in the parliamentary elections, it secured only 12 seats out of 489 in the Lok Sabha —making it only the third strongest party, after the Communists with 16 seats. They had grossly overestimated their own strength and had failed to foresee the splintering of opposition strength among the various parties and independent candidates.[44] In order to salvage their

---

[42] Thomas A. Rusch, "Dynamics of Socialist Leadership in India," in Richard L. Park and Irene Tinker, eds., *Leadership and Political Institutions in India* (Princeton, N.J.: Princeton University Press, 1959), p. 191.

[43] *Ibid.*, pp. 200–01.

[44] *Ibid.*, p. 202.

position, the Socialists negotiated a merger with the similarly disillusioned Kisan Mazdoor Praja party, a collection of Congress dissidents led by Archarya J. B. Kripalani. The K.M.P.P., which had withdrawn from the Congress on the eve of the election, was Gandhian in orientation. Its strength lay primarily in the eastern and southern states, complementing the concentration of Socialist representation in the North and West. The two parties minimized the differences between them by weakening the Socialist platform, and in 1952 formed the Praja Socialist party. It was soon joined by a section of the Forward Bloc, a West Bengal party devoted to the political memory of Subhas Chandra Bose.

The Praja Socialist Party

The Praja Socialist party was an uneasy but pragmatic mixture of various ideological positions. The Congress Socialists had reflected three divergent but overlapping tendencies—Marxism, democratic socialism, and Gandhism. Over the years, however, their socialism took on an increasingly Indian character. Emphasis on Gandhian notions of decentralization, nonviolence, constructive work, and the land-gift movement "turned the Socialists away from their past preoccupation with solely Western writings as the basis of their ideology."[45] Jayaprakash Narayan, an early Marxist and the most prominent of the Praja Socialist leaders, fell increasingly under Gandhian influence. In 1954, skeptical of the promise of industrialization and "progress," Narayan—then regarded as Nehru's heir—withdrew from active politics to dedicate his life to the land-gift movement and the constructive work of Vinoba Bhave. Rapidly losing influence within the P.S.P., he advocated a partyless democracy.

Before his withdrawal, Narayan had entered discussions with Nehru about a closer relationship between the P.S.P. and the Congress. Given the wide areas of agreement between the two parties, socialist leader Asoka Mehta argued that increased cooperation was demanded by the "political compulsions of a backward society."[46] His argument, basically, was that a society of scarce resources such as India cannot afford the luxury of opposition. The national conference of the P.S.P. in 1953 rejected the Mehta thesis in favor of Dr. Rammanohar Lohia's line that the party adopt a position of "equi-distance" from both the Congress and the Communists. Tension between the two wings of the P.S.P. increased when the Congress declared its advocacy of a socialistic pattern of society. To distinguish himself clearly from the Congress, Lohia took a more revolutionary stance. His efforts to organize a militant wing

[45] Myron Weiner, *Party Politics in India* (Princeton, N.J.: Princeton University Press, 1957), p. 30.
[46] The thesis was first advanced in his report to the party in 1953. Quoted in Weiner, *Party Politics in India*, p. 31.

within the P.S.P. soon led to his expulsion and the formation of a new Socialist party.

Even after the departure of the Lohia group, the relationship of the party to the Congress remained the central issue within the P.S.P. Mehta continued to push for closer cooperation with the Congress, and in 1963 he accepted the deputy chairmanship of the Planning Commission. Viewing this as a step calculated to bring Congress-P.S.P. consolidation, the P.S.P. national executive, badly split, voted to expel Mehta from the party. With his followers, Mehta reentered the Congress, and the P.S.P. accepted a bid from Lohia's Socialist Party for merger. In 1964 the Samyukta Socialist party was formed. Within one year, however, disaffected P.S.P. leaders charged the S.S.P. with developing a personality cult around Lohia, with supporting alliances with communal and antidemocratic groups, and with fanaticism in its pro-Hindi language policy.[47] They withdrew to reestablish the P.S.P. The P.S.P. had severe shocks between 1962 and 1967, but it sustained itself and cannot yet be counted out. Their policy pronouncements carry an influence disproportionate to the size of the party.

The Samyukta Socialist Party

With the P.S.P. exodus, the bulk of the rank and file remained with the Samyukta Socialists. The Samyukta Socialist party describes itself as a revolutionary party for radical social change. It is committed to the principle that capitalism and communism are equally irrelevant to building socialism in the Third World. It advocates the decentralization of power in the small units of direct democracy—the village, the town, and the district. The party has a pronounced egalitarian ideology: It would restrict private ownership to property not requiring hired labor, place a ceiling of one thousand rupees on all incomes, strictly limit the ownership of land and redistribute excess lands among poor peasants and landless laborers, and reserve upward of 60 percent of seats in government and education for members of the backward classes. The policy of the S.S.P., while emphasizing the development of regional languages, has generally been associated with the advocacy of Hindi. The party has vigorously opposed the continued use of English, which it regards as an unwelcome reminder of foreign oppression and a badge of national humiliation. Most important, it believes, English is undemocratic in perpetuating and even increasing the social and economic distance between classes.

The S.S.P. is actively committed to the practice of civil disobedience and has used the technique of satyagraha against the Congress Govern-

---

[47] Benjamin N. Schoenfeld, "The Birth of India's Samyukta Socialist Party," *Pacific Affairs*, Vol. 38 (1965–66), p. 266.

ment. On the basis of limited tactical fronts, the S.S.P. has sought to unite the opposition parties—of all positions—to bring an end to Congress rule. "Above all," S.S.P. leader Madhu Limaye has written, "the SSP never forgets that the partial evil that these parties represent is sustained by the greater evil of the Congress Party and the Congress Government itself!"[48] The S.S.P. electoral policy of joint fronts with a minimum program was vindicated in the widespread defeats of the Congress in the 1967 elections. The party has had a heterogeneous character, with cohesion dependent on personal loyalty to Dr. Lohia. His death in October 1967 raised doubts about the party's continued viability, which were underscored by the party's decline in the 1969 midterm elections in Bihar.

The Communist Parties

Since its inception in 1928, the Communist Party of India has been divided in its social character, its base of support, and its ideological stance. These divisions reflect its origins in the regional organizations of the Workers' and Peasants' party. In its early years the C.P.I., closely tied to the Communist Party of Great Britain, was largely under Comintern control and followed Moscow directives with dutiful twists and turns. During the 1930's the party adopted a tactic of "the united front from above" in cooperation with the nationalist movement. Entering the Congress Socialist party, Communists soon secured leadership in the Socialist organization, particularly in the South, where they gained effective control. Expelled in 1939, they took much of the C.S.P. membership in the South with them. The final break with the Congress came with the Nazi invasion of the Soviet Union and the C.P.I.'s call for cooperation with the British in what was deemed an anti-imperialist war. The Congress chose noncooperation, and as Congress leaders languished in jail the C.P.I. infiltrated student, peasant, and labor organizations, expanding its membership from five thousand in 1942 to fifty-three thousand by 1946. Although the C.P.I. effectively gained control of a number of mass organizations, its participation in the war effort, its continued attack on Gandhi and its support for the Muslim League demand for Pakistan tainted the party as antinational and minimized its influence.

Closed out from above, the C.P.I. adopted a tactic of "the united front from below" in alliance with workers and peasants against the Congress leadership. In 1948 P. C. Joshi was replaced as general secretary by B. T. Ranadive, with the advancement of a more militant "left" line. Under his leadership, the C.P.I. embarked on a course of

48 "Why S.S.P.?" in Ramdas G. Bhatkal, ed., *Political Alternatives in India* (Bombay: Popular Prakashan, 1967), p. 281.

revolution—with strikes, sabotage, and urban violence. Following the Russian model, Ranadive emphasized the working class as the instrument of revolution and discounted the peasant uprising in the Telangana region of Hyderabad. The Andhra Communists, however, pushed for the adoption of a Maoist line of revolution from the countryside and obtained a short-term victory for the tactic of rural insurrection with the election of Rajeshwar Rao as general secretary in 1950. The party became increasingly isolated, party membership declined, and in various states the C.P.I. was outlawed.

During this period Nehru was denounced as a "running dog of imperialism" and the Congress, in both its foreign and its domestic policy, as the reactionary captive of capitalist and landlord elements. In the early 1950's, however, the official attitude of the Soviet Union toward the Nehru Government began to change. The C.P.I. was officially advised to abandon its "adventurist" tactics. The policy shift was welcomed by those within the party, notably P. C. Joshi, S. A. Dange, and Ajoy Ghosh, who favored participation in the forthcoming general elections. In 1951 the revisionist line won out, with the selection of Ajoy Ghosh as general secretary of the party. Ghosh, from a centrist position, led the party toward "constitutional communism." The C.P.I. sanctioned Indian foreign policy and extended its full support to all "progressive" policies and measures of the government.[49] Its willingness to engage in parliamentary politics and to seek alliances with parties of the left in a democratic front seemed vindicated by the success of the Kerala Communists in 1957 and the formation of the first democratically elected Communist government under E. M. S. Namboodiripad. The Amritsar thesis, drafted by the party conference in 1958, set forth the nationalist credentials of the C.P.I.:

> The Communist Party of India strives to achieve full Democracy and Socialism by peaceful means. It considers that by developing a powerful mass movement, by winning a majority in Parliament and by backing it with mass sanctions, the working class and its allies can overcome the resistence of the forces of reaction and insure that Parliament becomes an instrument of people's will for effecting fundamental changes in the economic, social, and State structure.[50]

The Amritsar thesis only papered over fundamental tensions within the party between the right and left, between those favoring cooperation with the Congress and the "national bourgeoisie" and those advocating

---

[49] The evolution of this strategy is detailed in Fic, *Peaceful Transition to Communism in India.*

[50] Constitution of the Communist Party of India, adopted at the Extraordinary Party Congress, Amritsar, April 1958 (New Delhi: Communist Party of India, 1958), p. 4.

revolutionary struggle for the defeat of the Congress. Its relationship to the Congress in strategy and tactics posed a dilemma for the C.P.I. It was obliged, on the one hand, to fulfill its ideological commitment to the international Communist movement but, on the other, sought to retain a nationalist identity.[51]

The internal balance within the C.P.I. was soon threatened. In Kerala, sparked by the Education Bill, widespread agitation was launched against the Communist government, bringing Central intervention and the proclamation of President's Rule. The left saw it as patent that the Congress would never allow serious socialist reform, but the fate of the Kerala government only served to define more clearly the polarities emerging on the Sino-Indian question. The Tibet uprising in 1959 and the C.P.I.'s support for Chinese actions had already brought popular reaction against the party in India. The border clashes brought internal conflict into the open. Headed by S. A. Dange, a leading exponent of the right, or nationalist, faction, the national council of the C.P.I. recognized Indian claims to all territories below the McMahon line, the border demarcation. The left regarded this as a betrayal of international proletarian unity. The positions, set in the context of increasing Sino-Soviet conflict, placed the left in what was regarded as the pro-Chinese camp.

In early 1962, as conflict deepened within the C.P.I., Ajoy Ghosh, the balancer, died. The factional settlement—election of Dange to the newly created post of chairman, with Namboodiripad, the centrist, as general secretary—proved fragile. In the wake of the Chinese invasion of Indian territory, as criticism of the C.P.I. mounted, the national council resolved to condemn the Chinese action as "aggression" and to call upon the Indian people to "unite in defense of the motherland."[52] In protest, the leftists resigned from the party secretariat, and as the situation deteriorated, Namboodiripad submitted his resignation as general secretary of the party and as editor of New Age, the official party publication. In response to the widespread arrests of leftist Communist cadres, the C.P.I. sought to reorganize state party units under rightist control. Their actions served only to stimulate the creation of parallel left structures outside the disciplinary organization of the C.P.I.

At the national council meeting in 1964, the left attempted, without success, to oust party chairman Dange. They came armed with a letter, allegedly written by Dange in 1924, in which he had offered to cooperate with the British in exchange for his release from jail. Denouncing the letter as a forgery, the council refused to consider the charges. The left and center, led by Namboodiripad and Jyoti Basu, staged a walkout

---

51 Ralph Retzlaff, "Revisionism and Dogmatism in the Communist Party of India," in Robert A. Scalapino, ed., The Communist Revolution in Asia (Englewood Cliffs, N.J.: Prentice-Hall, 1965), p. 309.
52 Quoted in Retzlaff, "Revisionism and Dogmatism," p. 326.

and appealed to the party to repudiate Dange and the "reformist" line. The split became final when all signatories to the appeal were suspended from the party. The leftists, organized as the Communist Party of India (Marxist), claimed to be the legitimate Communist party of India. The regular C.P.I., closely associated with trade unionists, retained control of official party organs and identified itself with Moscow. It sought to advance the cause of a "national democratic front" with progressive elements of the nationalist bourgeoisie in order to "complete the anti-imperialist, anti-feudal, democratic revolution."[53] The left, favoring alliance with workers and peasants for the defeat of the Congress, was viewed as pro-Peking. Indeed, in 1965 leading left Communists were arrested throughout India and vaguely charged with promoting "an internal revolution to synchronize with a fresh Chinese attack."[54] Although China entered the fray by attacking Dange's revisionism, there was little evidence to link the left Communists with the Chinese as recipients of financial support, as alleged; but in terms of ideological position, the left C.P.I. expressed close affinity with Maoist thought.

Although the Communist party has had an all-India organization, at least theoretically subject to the discipline of "democratic centralism," its structure, like that of the Congress, has been essentially regional in orientation. Significantly, neither Communist party has been able to establish a firm base in the Hindi heartland. This may be related, in part, to the Communists' devotion to the Soviet treatment of the "national problem," which in India stresses the development of regional identity. Tactics have been determined more by the local situation than by directive from the top. In the general elections state party units have frequently adopted variant tactics, for example, supporting "progressive" Congressmen in one state and opposing all Congressmen in another.

In the parliamentary elections the C.P.I., despite the crisis of the Chinese invasion, has gradually increased its support, from 3.30 percent in 1952 to 9.96 percent in 1962. The party split little affected the distribution of the vote, for in 1967 the right, or C.P.I., received 4.80 percent and the left, or C.P.I.(M.), 4.28. However, Communist support in India has not been evenly distributed regionally. Only in West Bengal, Kerala, and Andhra have Communists had a significant base of electoral support, and in Kerala and Andhra this support has been closely tied to particular caste communities (the Ezhavas and Kammas, respectively). Significantly, the C.P.I.(M.) finds its greatest support in these areas of traditional Communist strength. In Kerala, where the two

---

[53] Communist Party of India, "Program of the Communist Party of India," *New Age* (January 10, 1965), p. 10, quoted in Philip G. Altbach, "The Two Indian Communist Parties," *Government and Opposition*, Vol. 2 (February 1967), p. 9.

[54] Home Minister Nanda, quoted in *Hindu Weekly Review* (January 11, 1965), p. 11, cited by Retzlaff, "Revisionism and Dogmatism," p. 335.

parties together polled about 33 percent of the assembly vote in 1967, the left Communists secured nearly three times the support of the right. In West Bengal the left got about twice the vote of the right, with a combined vote of some 23 percent. In each state the two Communist parties participated in the United Front against the Congress and dominated the subsequent coalition governments, with Namboodiripad as chief minister in Kerala. In October 1969, the Marxist-led U.F. government in Kerala was defeated in a no-confidence vote on general charges of corruption, an issue on which ideological coherence was not required. The C.P.I., which had feared the expansion of Marxist support under the United Front, took the lead in organizing a new "mini-front" government, with tacit Congress support. The U.F. government in West Bengal still hung in the balance. In Andhra, although both the left and right each gained about 7 percent of the vote in 1967, the two parties were engaged in bitter dispute, and the election marked the steady decline of Communist support from a high of nearly 30 percent in 1957. Although the strength of the left was concentrated primarily in three states so that it had a base of power, the two parties were close in the number of seats they gained in 1967. In the state assemblies the C.P.I. won a total of 121 seats, the C.P.I.(M.), 127.

Electoral success for the left Communists opened the party to internal conflict, however, as extremists, arguing from an avowedly Maoist position, opposed participation in the coalition governments in favor of armed struggle from the countryside. Soon after the elections in West Bengal, agricultural tenants of Naxalbari in the strategic hill district of Darjeeling began to occupy forcibly the lands of the landlords. Under the leadership of the Kisan Samiti, the Communist peasant organization, thousands of acres were similarly occupied in several districts of West Bengal. As the handful of peasants in Naxalbari sought to secure their position, Radio Peking proclaimed the area a "red district" and lauded the heroic effort to create a "liberated base" from which to wage protracted revolutionary struggle. The Indian Government reacted with alarm to what was viewed as Chinese infiltration in the sensitive border region. The left Communists of the United Front government in West Bengal were embarrassed and confused, and in containing the Naxalbari peasant rebellion, opened tensions within their ranks. In Bengal Communist strength is concentrated in Calcutta, with support from the lower middle class, students, refugees, and workers. Its support in the rural areas has been minimal and the peasant revolt was regarded as adventurist.

However, those supporting the uprising, the "Naxalites," found general favor from the left Communist organization in Andhra and from extremist factions within the C.P.I.(M.) in various states. Naxalites of Kerala in late 1968 attempted to establish a base in the hills of Wynad in Malabar for the formation of a Red army on the Maoist model. The problem of restoring law and order lay with Namboodiripad and what the Chinese viewed as an increasingly revisionist Communist left. Various Naxalite factions came together in 1969 in the formation of a third Communist party, the Communist Party of India (Marxist-Leninist), avowedly Maoist and dedicated to revolution. Although unable to bring all the Naxalite groups into its fold, the new C.P.I. (M.-L.) has taken the lead in calling for immediate armed struggle, the liberation of the countryside, and encirclement of the cities, following the Maoist formula. The C.P.I. (M.-L.) is not large, but as Marcus F. Franda argues, its significance lies in the fact that it provides the only organizational alternative for militant Indian Communists who reject the electoral policies of both the Marxists and the C.P.I.[55]

The Swatantra Party

The Swatantra (Freedom) party was founded in 1959 to save India from "a pointless plunge to the left" and to protect "farm and family" against the inroads of "statism."[56] Among its founders were conservatives, such as C. Rajagopalachari, the guiding force of the party, and former I.C.S. member V. P. Menon, who had been Patel's lieutenant in the integration of states. A more liberal tint was provided by N. G. Ranga, leader of the Congress peasant movement in the 1930's, and M. R. Masani, who had abandoned his earlier socialist leanings to espouse free enterprise. The declared mission of the party is "to restore *dharma* to the country"—not the dharma of Hindu orthodoxy, but of the Indian business community. "In point of fact," Rajagopalachari once said, "my party is the political projection of the Forum of Free Enterprise."[57]

Since its support is derived largely from the business community and the rural establishment, the party has been condemned as reactionary and communal. Its founders were not defenders of orthodoxy or of militant Hindu nationalism, however. Their conservatism reflected not so much tradition as the old Moderate position within the Congress.[58] The liberalism of the party, however, in stressing the threat to freedom from the left has led the party to ignore the dangers to freedom from the right.[59] At the higher levels the party leadership has been moderate,

---

[55] "India's Third Communist Party," *Asian Survey*, forthcoming.

[56] Quoted in P. D. Devanandan and M. M. Thomas, eds., *Problems of Indian Democracy* (Bangalore: The Christian Institute for the Study of Religion and Society, 1962), p. 133.

[57] *Ibid.*, p. 136.

[58] Howard L. Erdman, "India's Swatantra Party," *Pacific Affairs* (Winter 1963–64), p. 399.

[59] Howard L. Erdman, *The Swatantra Party and Indian Conservatism* (Cambridge: Cambridge University Press, 1967), p. 257.

secular, and nationalist, but at the lower levels it has frequently become the captive of reaction. In Rajasthan, Bihar, and Orissa, the party is dependent on princes and landlords. In Rajasthan Swatantra is led by the Maharani of Jaipur and dominated by the Rajputs. In Bihar, Swatantra was virtually coterminous with the Janata party, the personal party of the Raja of Ramgar, and with the defection of the Raja to the Congress, Swatantra was virtually eliminated. In Orissa the Ganatantra Parishad, led by princes, merged with Swatantra to form the mainstay of its support. Only in Gujarat has Swatantra had a broader social base.

Howard L. Erdman describes Swatantra as "a holding company for local dissident groups" who have come together in an effort to provide effective opposition to Congress at the Center.[60] Even with the loss of the Bihar stronghold, Swatantra secured forty-four seats in the 1967 elections to displace the Communists as the second largest party in the Lok Sabha. In Orissa the party emerged as the strongest in the state and took power in coalition with the dissident Jana Congress. In the elections, Swatantra entered into a variety of arrangements with the opposition, as with the D.M.K. in Tamilnadu, and Rajagopalachari was prepared to "ally with the devil himself"[61] in order to defeat the Congress.

Communal and Regional Parties

Hindu Communal Parties

The spectre of communalism has been omnipresent in Indian political life, a threat to unity and to the secular ideal of the constitution. With the memories of partition still bitterly nurtured, Hindu-Muslim tensions easily ignite in rioting. In 1969 Gujarat became the scene of a communal bloodbath, leaving more than five hundred dead and thousands homeless. Muslim communalism contributed to the partition of India in 1947, but today it is communalism in the name of the Hindu majority that poses the major challenge to the secular state. Rooted in the nineteenth-century Hindu revivalism of the Arya Samaj and the extremism of Tilak, Hindu communalism today is most prominently represented by four groups: the Hindu Mahasabha, the Ram Rajya Parishad, the Rashtriya Swayamsevak Sangh, and the Bharatiya Jana Sangh.

THE HINDU MAHASABHA

The Hindu Mahasabha was founded in reaction to the Muslim League, but in its early years the organization was obscured by the

[60] *Ibid.*, p. 288.
[61] *Link*, July 9, 1961, quoted in Robert L. Hardgrave, Jr., *The Dravidian Movement* (Bombay: Popular Prakashan, 1965), p. 72.

Congress party, with which most of its members were associated. The Lucknow Pact of 1924 and the ascendancy of the Moderates within the Congress alienated many of the Hindu Extremists, however, and under the leadership of V. D. Savarkar, an admirer of Tilak and like him a Chitpavan Brahmin from Maharashtra, the Mahasabha parted with the Congress in a call to "Hinduize all politics and militarize Hinduism."[62] Reform fused with revivalism in opposition to untouchability and caste inequality. To overcome the fragmentation of sect, caste, and language, the Mahasabha launched the *sanghatan* movement for the unification, integration, and consolidation of Hindu rashtra, the Hindu nation. The movement sought to reclaim those who had left the Hindu fold and to reassert the fundamental "Hinduness" of the Indian people. The Hindu Mahasabha has regarded the creation of Pakistan as the "vivisection" of Mother India and has sought reunification, by force if necessary. Toward its goal of "Hindu Raj in Bharat," the Mahasabha platform includes a hard stand toward Pakistan, compulsory military training, a total ban on cow slaughter, repeal of all "anti-Hindu legislation," and a vague policy of "Hindu socialism."[63]

THE RAM RAJYA PARISHAD

The Ram Rajya Parishad, founded in 1948, is the most orthodox of the Hindu communal parties. The strength of the party, which is supported by conservative landlords, has been almost entirely limited to Rajasthan. The party seeks to resurrect the Divine Kingdom of Rama and return the people to rule by dharma.[64]

THE RASHTRIYA SWAYAMSEVAK SANGH

The Rashtriya Swayamsevak Sangh was founded as a paramilitary organization in 1925 by Dr. Keshav Hedgewar. He was succeeded on his death in 1940 by M. S. Golwalkar, "Guruji," under whom the R.S.S. grew rapidly. The R.S.S. claims to be a movement directed toward achieving the cultural and spiritual regeneration of the Hindu nation through a disciplined vanguard who represent the ideal model of Hindu society. The movement has drawn its support principally from urban regions of North India, where it has attracted wide support among students and the lower middle classes. R.S.S. volunteers, uniformed in brown shirts, engage in an intensive program of ideological discussion, physical training, and military discipline.[65] In January 1948 Gandhi

[62] Donald E. Smith, *India as a Secular State* (Princeton, N.J.: Princeton University Press, 1963), pp. 455–64.
[63] *Ibid.*
[64] *Ibid.*, p. 464.
[65] *Ibid.*, pp. 465–68. See also J. A. Curran, Jr., *Militant Hinduism in Indian Politics: A Study of the R.S.S.* (New York: Institute of Public Relations, 1951); Richard D. Lambert, "Hindu Communal Groups in Indian Politics," in Park and Tinker, eds., *Leadership and Political Institutions*, pp. 211–24.

was assassinated by a Hindu fanatic who had been associated with both the Mahasabha and the R.S.S. In the face of an explosive public reaction, the Hindu Mahasabha, under the leadership of Dr. S. P. Mookerjee, who had succeeded Savarkar as president in 1943, suspended political activity. The R.S.S. was banned by the Government. Only with the agreement of the R.S.S. to renounce political activity and to publish a constitution was the ban lifted more than one year later.

THE BHARATIYA JANA SANGH

At the time of Gandhi's assassination Mookerjee was a member of Nehru's Cabinet. In December 1948 he resigned from the Mahasabha when his proposal to open membership to non-Hindus was rejected. In early 1950 he resigned from the Cabinet, a leader in search of a party. The *Organizer*, a semiofficial publication of the R.S.S., called for a new political party, with Mookerjee clearly in view, and in 1951 Mookerjee announced the formation of the Bharatiya Jana Sangh, the people's party. The object of the party is the rebuilding of Bharat as a modern, democratic society in accordance with religious precepts. Four "fundamentals" guide the party: one country, one nation, one culture, and the rule of law.[66]

The program of the Jana Sangh is an eclectic mix of tradition and modernity. The party manifesto sets forth a wide range of policy positions, but the Sangh carries a decidedly communal flavor. The Jana Sangh denies being communal, however, and emphasizes its open membership. The president of the Jana Sangh in West Bengal is, in fact, a Muslim, and the Sangh unit in Tamilnadu was organized by a Christian. The ideology is of Bharatiya, *Indian*, culture, not of Hindu raj. The Sangh, however, for all its "non-sectarian" claims, seeks to promote national unity by "nationalizing all non-Hindus by inculcating in them the ideal of Bharatiya Culture."[67] It would guarantee equal rights and opportunities to all citizens, yet would not recognize religious minorities. Secularism, for the Jana Sangh, is simply a disguised policy of Muslim appeasement. The Sangh does not recognize the partition of India and is militantly anti-Pakistan. It seeks a united India under a unitary state, with Hindi as the national language. Hindu dominance is symbolized by the party's stand for cow protection and for the promotion of Ayurvedic, or traditional, medicine.

Since it was organized in 1951, the Jana Sangh has been closely associated with the R.S.S. Indeed, Nehru described the party as its "ille-

---

[66] Craig Baxter, "The Jana Sangh: A Brief Political History," in Donald E. Smith, ed., *South Asian Politics and Religion* (Princeton, N.J.: Princeton University Press, 1966), p. 81.
[67] Quoted in Smith, *India as a Secular State*, p. 471.

gitimate child." The *Organiser* has served as the English language voice of both the Jana Sangh and the R.S.S. The R.S.S. has served as the organizational base for the party, and its influence within the Jana Sangh increased under the leadership of Dindayal Upadhyaya.

The Sangh has at various times sought to weld an electoral alliance with the Mahasabha and the Ram Rajya Parishad. Their failure to co-operate, although affecting the electoral success of each, has served to draw support to the Jana Sangh from the other two communal parties, and with each election the Mahasabha and the Parishad have increasingly lost support. The Jana Sangh in 1962 and 1967 entered into a number of "local adjustments" with other opposition parties. In 1967 the Sangh, which made substantial gains in the Hindi areas, entered coalition governments in the states of Bihar, Madhya Pradesh, Uttar Pradesh, Haryana, and the Punjab (where in united opposition to the Congress it cooperated with the Akali Dal). The Jana Sangh, once considered a party of urban middle-class Hindus, has made increasing inroads into the rural areas of North India, and in each election its strength both at the Center and in the states has grown.

Serious discussions have been carried on over possible alliance with Swatantra. The two parties share an essentially identical economic policy, but elements in both parties have opposed cooperation. Swatantra's secular position and its stand for reconciliation with Pakistan and the Jana Sangh's demand for Hindi as the national language are mutually unpalatable.[68] The split in the Congress, however, raises new possibilities for Jana Sangh—Swatantra cooperation and the formation of a right-wing alliance with old Syndicate forces of the Congress.

The Dravida Munnetra Kazhagam

The efforts to transcend narrow and parochial identification in the nation-building process in India continue to be frustrated by the "fissiparous tendencies" of regionalism—the demand for States Reorganization, for Punjabi Suba, and for an independent Naga state. Among the strains on India's unity, one of the most dramatic has been the Tamil secessionist movement and its manifestation today in the demand for increased state autonomy by the Dravida Munnetra Kazhagam.

The D.M.K. is the heir of the Dravidian movement, with roots in the anti-Brahmin conflict in Madras in the early years of the century. After the Montagu-Chelmsford Reforms, the Justice party was organized in Madras to secure an uplift of the non-Brahmin community and to oppose the nationalist movement, which would, in its view, replace the neutral administration of the British with a Brahmin oligarchy. The

[68] Baxter, "The Jana Sangh," pp. 99–100.

Justice party held power in Madras until 1934, when it was routed in a Congress victory. Weakened and tainted by its support of the British, the party found a new dynamism in the leadership of E. V. Ramaswamy Naicker, founder of the "self-respect movement," which aimed to purge South India of Brahmin tyranny and the religion by which the Dravidian people were held in submission. In the first of his anti-Hindi campaigns, Naicker launched agitation against the Congress government's introduction of Hindi in Madras schools. He then announced that his goal was the creation of a separate Dravidian state, Dravidasthan, and to that purpose the party was reorganized as a quasi-military organization, the Dravida Kazhagam, or Dravidian Federation.

In reaction to the élitist character of the D.K., C. N. Annadurai, a young journalist and film writer, in 1949 led a breakaway faction to form the Dravida Munnetra Kazhagam, the Dravidian Progressive Federation. Whereas the D.K., continuing as a reform movement, had never contested elections, the D.M.K. combined the techniques of agitation with electoral activity. The party, although still waving the banner of Dravidasthan, became increasingly oriented to pragmatic economic issues. During the Chinese invasion, the D.M.K. rallied to the national cause, and on adoption of the antisecessionist amendment to the constitution in 1963, the party formally dropped its demand for an independent Tamilnadu. Although the D.M.K. has failed to gain a foothold outside Tamilnadu (the Tamil-speaking area of old Madras State), the party has expanded its social base within the state, appealing to non-Brahmin and Brahmin alike. Awakening Tamil nationalist sentiment, the D.M.K. demands greater state autonomy and an end to northern domination. Its platform emphasizes the ideals of a casteless and classless society (although the party leadership is so dominated by members of the Mudaliar caste that the party is frequently referred to as the Dravida Mudaliar Kazhagam). Its economic program reflects a radical populism, calling for the creation of a socialist economy, with nationalization of banks and transport, for example, and a vigorous policy of land reform and redistribution.

With each election the D.M.K. has extended its base of strength from the urban centers deeper into rural areas. The D.M.K. and its army of student volunteers responded to the issues of rising prices and the imposition of Hindi on an unwilling South with demonstrations and propaganda against the Congress Government, and a number of Tamil film stars added their glamor to the rising party. In 1962 the D.M.K. emerged as the strongest opposition party ever to challenge the entrenched Congress in Tamilnadu, capturing 50 seats in the legislative assembly and 7 in the Lok Sabha. In 1967, through electoral arrangements with Swatantra and the left and right Communist parties, the D.M.K. crushed the Congress in a landslide victory. The Congress suffered defeats throughout India, but the D.M.K. was the only opposition party to secure an actual majority of seats and to form a ministry without a coalition. The D.M.K. won 138 out of a total of 231 seats in the assembly, reducing the Congress to only 49 seats. The D.M.K. also gained 25 seats in the Lok Sabha to become the fourth largest party at the Center.[69]

Annadurai, founder and leader of the D.M.K., died in 1969. The leadership of the party and government was taken by M. Karunanidhi. "Anna" had already established a working relationship with the Congress ministry in New Delhi, and the D.M.K. extended support to Mrs. Gandhi in her struggle with the Syndicate, not without considerable favor in return, which strengthened the position of the D.M.K. over the Tamilnad Congress led by Kamaraj.

The Akali Dal

The Akali Dal is both regional and communal. It is confined to the Punjab and open only to members of the Sikh community, of which it claims to be the sole representative. The Akali Dal was first organized as a reform group to bring the *gurdwaras* (the Sikh shrines) under the control of the orthodox Sikh community. Following a policy of direct action, the Akalis succeeded in 1925 in bringing the gurdwaras under the authority of a committee elected by universal adult franchise within the community. Control of the committee, with jurisdiction over hundreds of gurdwaras and their endowments and with great patronage powers, considerably strengthened the position of the Akali Dal in the Punjab. Master Tara Singh, leader of the dominant Akali faction until 1965, declared the necessity of a Sikh state to protect the gurdwaras and defend the Sikh religion. At the time of partition, the Akalis had sought an independent Sikhistan, but in the agitation of the 1950's for linguistic states, the Akali demand was translated to that of a Punjabi-speaking state of Punjabi Suba.

In a bilingual settlement, the Akalis made their truce with the Government and merged with the Congress at the time of the 1957 elections. In 1960, however, Master Tara Singh launched militant demonstrations for Punjabi Suba and filled the jails with Akali volunteers. Factionalism within the Akali Dal deepened with its failure to gain its demand, and a rival Akali party organized by Sant Fateh Singh won control in the gurdwara elections of 1965. Sant Fateh Singh then issued an ultimatum that the Government accept the Akali demand or he would fast for fifteen days and if still alive would immolate himself. At this point war broke out with Pakistan; Sant withdrew his threat and called upon the Sikhs to rise in defense of India. On the cessation of the war, the Congress announced its acceptance of Punjabi Suba.

[69] See Hardgrave, *The Dravidian Movement*, and "The Politics of Tamil Nationalism," *Pacific Affairs*, Vol. 37 (Winter 1964–65), pp. 396–411.

For all its influence, the Akali Dal has never had wide electoral appeal, even among the Sikhs. The Akali obtained 11.9 percent of the total vote in the Punjab in 1962. In the Punjabi-speaking region, where the Sikhs numbered 55 percent of the population, it secured only 20 percent of the vote, or no more than 40 percent of the Sikh vote.[70] In the 1967 elections in Punjabi Suba, the two wings of the Akali Dal together received approximately 25 percent of the vote (with twenty-four seats secured by the Sant group and two by the Tara Singh group). In a united front with Congress dissidents, the Jana Sangh, and the Communists, the Akali Dal led the formation of a coalition government.

Other Parties

There are a vast number of other parties in India—based on caste, language, religion, and fine points of ideology; some are solely regional; others have all-India status, if not wide support. Among the more important are the reactivated Muslim League, limited primarily to the South, and the Republican party (formerly the Scheduled Castes Federation), founded by Dr. Ambedkar, leader of the untouchables.

The Party System and Political Development in India

The emergence of increasingly vigorous opposition parties in electoral competition with the Congress has been a significant catalyst of the "participation explosion." The possibilities for victory, dramatized in the 1967 elections and heightened by Congress disunity, have accelerated party efforts to mobilize new bases of support and to aggregate a range of varied interests. The opposition, no longer on the periphery, provides a meaningful alternative to Congress rule in many states, but it has yet to achieve cohesion at the Center. Once weak and relegated to the status of a permanent minority, opposition parties have become more responsive and have assumed greater responsibility. Participation in government has served to strengthen commitment to the system, to the constitutional rules of the game. The assumption of power in Kerala and West Bengal has "domesticated" the Indian Communist parties, strengthening their willingness to work within the framework of a democratic constitution—though in the case of the Marxists, the strategy is to use the Constitution in order to destroy it. In Tamilnadu, as it gained increased support, the Dravida Munnetra Kazhagam was transformed from a secessionist movement, nurtured on vague dreams of a

[70] Baldev Raj Nayar, in Myron Weiner, ed., *State Politics in India* (Princeton, N.J.: Princeton University Press, 1967), p. 481. See also Nayar, "Sikh Separatism in the Punjab," in Smith, ed., *South Asian Politics and Religion*, pp. 150–75.

glorious past and an impossible hope for the future, to a party of political maturity and parliamentary discipline. As it was drawn into the political system, interests became more specific and were formulated as pragmatic political demands.

India's parties, Congress and non-Congress, have been instruments for the stimulation of political consciousness and expanded participation. As agents of induction into the political system, the parties have given organization and structure to participation, in a dual process of vertical and horizontal integration. Parties provide the institutional means of initiating, sustaining, and accelerating change and of absorbing the impact of that change.[71] The Congress defeats at the hand of the opposition and the Congress split have seriously challenged the political *status quo*, but the elections revealed an enhanced institutional capacity of the party system to accommodate and respond to rapidly increasing participation.

The system of one-party dominance has come to an end, however, and if the political horizon affords a prospect of unstable coalition government, both in the states and at the Center, it brings with this threat also the possibility of government genuinely more responsive to the people.

[71] Huntington, *Political Order in Changing Societies*, p. 404.

RECOMMENDED READING

Baxter, Craig, *The Jana Sangh: A Biography of an Indian Political Party.* Philadelphia: University of Pennsylvania Press, 1969.
    A study of the origins and history of the quasi-communal Hindu party.

Brass, Paul R., *Factional Politics in an Indian State: The Congress Party in Uttar Pradesh.* Berkeley: University of California Press, 1966.
    An analysis of party organization at the local and district levels and of the impact of internal factionalism on party effectiveness.

Burger, Angela S., *Opposition in a Dominant Party System.* Berkeley, University of California Press, 1969.
    An examination of the Jana Sangh, the Praja Socialist party, and Socialist party in Uttar Pradesh.

Erdman, Howard L., *The Swatantra Party and Indian Conservatism.* Cambridge: Cambridge University Press, 1967.
    A study of the origin, social base, doctrines, and political organization of the Swatantra party.

Franda, Marcus F., "India's Third Communist Party." *Asian Survey* (December 1969.)
    A perceptive analysis of the Indian Communist parties, focusing on the Naxalite movement.

Hardgrave, Robert L., Jr., *The Dravidian Movement*. Bombay: Popular Prakashan, 1965.
>An analysis of the politics of Tamil nationalism, from the non-Brahmin movement to the rise of the Dravida Munnetra Kazhagam.

Kochanek, Stanley A., *The Congress Party of India*. Princeton, N.J.: Princeton University Press, 1968.
>Focuses on the development of the party at the national level in the years since independence, the changing role of the Congress president and the Working Committee, and their relationship to the Prime Minister and the Government.

Kothari, Rajni, ed., *Party Systems and Election Studies*. Occasional Papers of the Center for Developing Societies, No. 1. Bombay: Allied Publishers, 1967.
>A collection of essays by some of India's most astute political scientists. Of particular importance are the essays on the system of one-party dominance.

Nayar, Baldev Raj, *Minority Politics in the Punjab*. Princeton, N.J.: Princeton University Press, 1966.
>A detailed study of the Akali Dal and the Sikh demand for Punjabi Suba.

Overstreet, Gene D., and Windmiller, Marshall, *Communism in India*. Berkeley: University of California Press, 1959.
>Still the most complete study of the Communist movement in India, its history, organization, and leadership.

Ram, Mohan, *Indian Communism: Split Within a Split*. Delhi: Vikas, 1969.
>An examination of the development of Maoist perspective in the Indian Communist movement.

Retzlaff, Ralph, "Revisionism and Dogmatism in the Communist Party of India," in Robert A. Scalapino, ed., *The Communist Revolution in Asia*, 2nd ed. Englewood Cliffs, N.J.: Prentice-Hall, 1969.
>An up-to-date account of the changing character of India's Communist party.

Weiner, Myron, *Party Building in a New Nation*. Chicago: University of Chicago Press, 1967.
>An analysis of the Indian National Congress through case studies of the party in five districts, with a focus on the problems of adaptation and development.

————, *Party Politics in India*. Princeton, N.J.: Princeton University Press, 1957.
>An examination of the relationship between parties through the cases of the Socialists, the Hindu communalists, and the Marxist left parties.

VII

ELECTIONS AND POLITICAL BEHAVIOR

IN 1967 THE PEOPLE OF INDIA WENT TO THE POLLS FOR THE FOURTH time. The campaign was conducted "in an atmosphere of frustration, despondency, uncertainty, and recurrent—almost continual—agitation."[1] Rising prices, food scarcities, near famine in Bihar, strikes, and mass agitations had contributed to a situation of such seeming gravity that some observers were exceedingly pessimistic about India's future as a democracy.[2] The election results were dramatic: The Congress failed to secure majorities in eight states, and its majority at the Center was reduced to a narrow margin of 54 percent. But in spite of the political upheaval that followed it, the election may have reflected growing political maturity rather than the decline of democracy. Indeed, it was proclaimed variously as India's "first true General Elections" and as a "second revolution." It marked the emergence of a new political era in India—more participant, less stable.

[1] Norman D. Palmer, "India's Fourth General Elections," *Asian Survey*, Vol. 7 (May 1967), p. 277.
[2] Neville Maxwell, "India's Disintegrating Democracy," London *Times* (January 27, 1967), quoted in Palmer, "India's Fourth General Elections," pp. 277–78.

The End of One-Party Dominance

The election radically changed the political map of India. In Tamilnadu the Dravida Munnetra Kazhagam won 138 out of 234 assembly seats. Congress secured only 49. In Kerala the Congress won only 9 of the 133 seats, not even enough to form a recognized opposition party. The Communist-led United Front victory was decisive, bringing Namboodiripad to power again, eight years after the imposition of President's Rule had ended his first government. In Orissa Swatantra emerged as the largest party, with 49 of 140 seats, and formed a ministry with its allies. Congress defeats in other states were less overwhelming. United Front governments were formed in the Punjab, Bihar, and West Bengal. The Congress entered into shaky coalitions in Haryana, Uttar Pradesh, and Madhya Pradesh. In Rajasthan the Congress succeeded in forming a government only after an inauspicious period of President's Rule that was imposed immediately after the election.

The voters brought down from power not only the Congress party but some of its most prominent leaders. Congress president Kamaraj was defeated in his own home town by a D.M.K. student leader. Congress bosses Atulya Ghosh of Bengal and S. K. Patil of Bombay were defeated. Nine Union ministers, four chief ministers, and numerous state ministers were defeated. The losses were not wholly confined to Congress. Acharya Kripalani, Krishna Menon, and N. G. Ranga, all long on the Indian political scene, were also defeated. Most subsequently found their way back to the Lok Sabha in by-elections.

The elections were interpreted both as a swing to the right and as a swing to the left. In fact, however, the pattern of Congress defeats was highly idiosyncratic, related to the peculiarities of each state, with no consistency in the direction of opposition sentiments. In the Lok Sabha Swatantra gained twenty seats to become the largest opposition group, with forty-four members. It emerged as the largest single party in Orissa and as the main opposition in Andhra, Gujarat, and Rajasthan. The Jana Sangh, which made gains throughout North India, increased its strength in the Lok Sabha from fourteen to thirty-five seats, captured control of the Delhi Municipal Corporation, and became the main non-Congress party in three states, Haryana, Madhya Pradesh, and Uttar Pradesh. The Samyukta Socialist party doubled its strength and emerged as the major non-Congress party in Bihar. The Praja Socialist party, however, declined in both the number of seats secured and in the votes polled. The combined vote of the two Communist parties remained close to that of 1962, and their seats in both the Lok Sabha and in the state assemblies were substantially increased. The C.P.I.(M.) became the largest party in Kerala and the major non-Congress party in West Bengal.

TABLE 7–1

THE DISTRIBUTION OF CANDIDATES, SEATS, AND VOTES IN LOK SABHA ELECTIONS, 1952–67

Parties	Number of candidates	Number of seats won	% of seats	% of votes
1952				
Congress	472	364	74.4	45.00
C.P.I.	49	16	3.3	3.30
Socialist Party	256	12	2.5	10.60
Kisan Mazdoor Praja Party	145	9	1.8	5.80
Hindu Mahasabha	31	4	0.8	0.95
Jana Sangh	93	3	0.6	3.10
Ram Rajya Parishad	55	3	0.6	2.03
Republican Party	27	2	0.4	2.36
Other parties	215	35	7.2	11.10
Independents	521	41	8.4	15.80
Total		489		
1957				
Congress	490	371	75.1	47.78
C.P.I.	108	27	5.4	8.92
Praja Socialist Party (S.P. and K.M.P.P.)	189	19	3.8	10.41
Jana Sangh	130	4	0.8	5.93
Republican Party	19	4	0.8	1.50
Hindu Mahasabha	19	1	0.2	0.86
Ram Rajya Parishad	15	—	—	0.38
Other parties	73	29	5.9	4.81
Independents	475	39	7.9	19.39
Total		494		
1962				
Congress	488	361	73.1	46.02
C.P.I.	137	29	5.9	9.96
Swatantra	172	18	3.6	6.80
Jana Sangh	198	14	2.8	6.44
Praja Socialist Party	166	12	2.4	6.84
D.M.K. (Tamilnadu only)	18	7	1.4	2.02
Socialist Party	107	6	1.2	2.49
Republican Party	69	3	0.6	2.78
Ram Rajya Parishad	35	2	0.4	0.55
Hindu Mahasabha	32	1	0.2	0.44
Other parties	64	14	2.9	4.31
Independents	497	27	5.5	12.27
Total		494		

TABLE 7–1 (*Continued*)

Parties	Number of candidates	Number of seats won	% of seats	% of votes
1967				
Congress	516	283	54.42	40.73
Swatantra	179	44	8.46	8.68
Jana Sangh	250	35	6.73	9.41
D.M.K. (Tamilnadu only)	25	25	4.80	3.90
C.P.I.	109	23	4.42	5.19
Samyukta Socialist Party	122	23	4.42	4.92
C.P.I.(M.)	59	19	3.65	4.21
Praja Socialist Party	109	13	2.50	3.06
Republican Party	70	1	0.19	2.48
Other parties	65	19	3.65	3.67
Independents	865	35	6.73	13.75
Total		520		

SOURCE: Adapted from W. H. Morris-Jones, *Government and Politics in India* (London: Hutchinson, 1966), pp. 163–66, and from the Indian Election Commission, *Report on the Fourth General Elections in India*, Vol. 1 (New Delhi: Government Press, 1968), pp. 94–95.

TABLE 7–2

THE DISTRIBUTION OF CANDIDATES, SEATS, AND VOTES
IN STATE ASSEMBLY ELECTIONS, 1952–67

Parties	Number of candidates	Number of seats won	% of seats	% of votes
1952				
Congress	3,153	2,246	68.4	42.20
Socialist Party	1,799	125	3.8	9.70
C.P.I.	465	106	3.2	4.38
Kisan Mazdoor Praja Party	1,005	77	2.3	5.11
Jana Sangh	717	35	1.1	2.76
Ram Rajya Parishad	314	31	0.9	1.21
Hindu Mahasabha	194	14	0.4	0.82
Republican Party	171	3	0.1	1.68
Other parties and independents	7,492	635	19.3	32.14
Total		3,283		
1957				
Congress	3,027	2,012	64.9	44.97
Praja Socialist (S.P. and K.M.P.P.)	1,154	208	6.7	9.75

TABLE 7-2 (Continued)

Parties	Number of candidates	Number of seats won	% of seats	% of votes
C.P.I.	812	176	5.7	9.36
Jana Sangh	584	46	1.5	3.60
Ram Rajya Parishad	146	22	0.7	0.69
Republican Party	99	21	0.7	1.31
Hindu Mahasabha	87	6	0.2	0.50
Other parties and independents	4,863	611	19.7	29.81
Total		3,102		

1962

Congress	3,062	1,984	60.2	43.53
C.P.I.	975	197	6.0	10.42
Praja Socialist Party	1,149	179	5.4	7.69
Swatantra	1,012	170	5.2	6.49
Jana Sangh	1,135	116	3.5	5.40
Socialist Party	632	64	1.9	2.38
D.M.K. (Tamilnadu only)*	142	50	—	—
Ram Rajya Parishad	99	13	0.4	0.29
Republican Party	99	11	0.3	0.56
Hindu Mahasabha	75	8	0.2	0.24
Other parties and independents	5,313	555	16.8	23.00
Total		3,297		

1967

Congress	3,443	1,694	48.59	39.96
Jana Sangh	1,607	268	7.70	8.78
Swatantra	978	257	7.37	6.65
Samyukta Socialist Party	813	180	5.16	5.19
D.M.K. (Tamilnadu only)*	174	138	3.96	4.34
C.P.I.(M.)	511	128	3.67	4.60
C.P.I.	625	121	3.47	4.13
Praja Socialist Party	768	106	3.04	3.40
Republican Party	378	23	0.66	1.53
Other parties	430	195	5.59	4.75
Independents	6,774	376	10.79	16.67
Total		3,486		

* In Tamilnadu in 1962 the D.M.K. gained 24.3 percent of the assembly seats and 27 percent of the vote. In 1967 it secured 59.4 percent of the seats and 44.66 percent of the vote.
SOURCE: Adapted from W. H. Morris-Jones, *Government and Politics in India* (London: Hutchinson, 1966), pp. 163–66, and from the Indian Election Commission, *Report on the Fourth General Elections in India*, Vol. 1 (New Delhi: Government Press, 1968), pp. 94–95.

The various united fronts of the 1967 elections were at least as disparate in ideological complexion as the Congress itself, if not more so. In his analysis of coalition politics following the 1967 elections in North India, Paul R. Brass argues that "inter-party ideological divisions are less decisive in the formation and breakup of governments than intraparty divisions." It thus becomes possible for "independents or party defectors to hold the balance and dictate terms to the established parties . . . ."[3] In Bihar, Uttar Pradesh, and the Punjab, the initial non-Congress governments were broadly eclectic. Ranging across the entire political spectrum, the coalition in each included all non-Congress parties, if not in the government itself, at least in its legislative alliance.[4] Although major ideological cleavages between the parties persist, the parties have shown a willingness to ignore or to compromise matters of principle. Issues not so easily resolved are those involving power—issues related to intraparty factionalism, the relationship of groups within the parties, and the position of such groups in the governments. The formation and collapse of the non-Congress governments depended primarily on such issues. Defections and multiple floor-crossings introduced a pattern of flux and instability in which floating independents and party defectors held power far greater than their numbers alone ordinarily would command.

The coalition governments of North India quickly proved unstable. In Haryana the Congress gained a narrow majority only to have its government brought down through defection almost immediately after it was formed. The United Front ministry formed from Congress defections lasted only eight months before its own support was eroded through floor-crossings to the opposition. President's Rule was imposed, and in midterm elections, held in May 1968, the Congress was returned to power. The process was repeated in state after state.

In West Bengal the situation was complicated by the powerful position of the C.P.I.(M.) in the ruling coalition. The United Front held power until November 1967. With the defection of seventeen M.L.A.'s from the Front, the governor, ready to act against the leftist coalition, announced its loss of a majority and its displacement by a new "law and order" government under the Progressive Democratic Front, backed by the Congress. Amid protests against the highhanded action, the political situation rapidly deteriorated. In February 1968 a riot broke out in the legislative chamber in opposition to the governor. Unable to

---

[3] "Coalition Politics in North India," *American Political Science Review*, Vol. 62 (December 1968), p. 1174.

[4] *Ibid.*, p. 1178. Walter Weisburg, in a study of coalition formation in three states, emphasizes the threat of President's Rule and new elections as an impetus to coalition formation. Dissertation, in progress, Department of Government, University of Texas.

continue, the P.D.F. government resigned, and Bengal came under President's Rule.

With half of North India under President's Rule, new elections were coordinated for what was to be a crucial test of the Congress's ability to recoup its strength. The assembly elections held in February 1969 in West Bengal, the Punjab, Uttar Pradesh, and Bihar seemed only to confirm the pattern of the earlier general election. The people's verdict of 1967 was renewed emphatically. The trend toward regional parties and bases of support was bringing an end to the Congress system of one-party dominance in India. The United Front of leftist parties in Bengal was returned to power with an absolute majority. The two Communist parties made decisive gains, and both Swatantra and the Jana Sangh lost the few seats they had had in the previous assembly. The Congress was reduced to 55 of the 280 assembly seats. The Akali Dal, nearly doubling its seats, was returned as the largest party in the Punjab and led the formation of a government in collaboration with other non-Congress parties. In only two states of the four did the Congress emerge as the leading party. In Uttar Pradesh the Congress rallied to secure a near majority and form a ministry. In Bihar it retained its position as the largest party, though without a majority. The Jana Sangh increased its position slightly, and the Samyukta Socialist party was set back. The Congress, with the support of minor parties and independents, formed a coalition ministry. After four months in the familiar process of defection, the ministry was defeated. A non-Congress coalition ruled nine days before it too was defeated and President's Rule imposed.

The Congress split inevitably must be fought out at each level of the party organization. Congress governments in the states may be threatened with defeat or, as at the Center, forced to rely on opposition members for continued power. Without outside support, the government of C. B. Gupta in Uttar Pradesh is vulnerable to defeat at the hands of the Prime Minister's group, but the Syndicate might be able to retaliate against the pro-Indira Gandhi governments in Rajasthan, Madhya Pradesh, and Haryana. Though the Congress in each state is divided by factional disputes, all factions in the states of Andhra, Assam, and Jammu and Kashmir pledged support to the Prime Minister. In Maharashtra, the Congress government is securely in Mrs. Gandhi's camp. The Congress government in Mysore, however, is firmly in Syndicate hands. The Syndicate's position is less secure in Gujarat.

In the states where the Congress is not in power, the Prime Minister's position varies; she commands general support in Orissa and the Punjab (although here the Government's decision on Chandigarh will be critical) while she is opposed in Tamilnadu. The Congress organizations in West Bengal, Kerala, and Bihar are deeply divided. With a rally of popular support behind the Prime Minister, the Syndicate may have little power even in its own bailiwick. Syndicate members, such as Kamaraj, Ghosh, and Patil, have lost much of their political base. They no longer command the political capital to challenge Mrs. Gandhi effectively. A political machine out of power lacks patronage: It lacks the political leverage to extract support and offer reward. The opposition Congress may succeed in holding the organization in a few states, but its viability can only be revealed in the elections.

Elections

Elections in India have generally been orderly, with only isolated instances of rioting or violence. The occasional disorders are often the product of electoral propaganda—and sometimes they are even staged. The campaigns are filled with charges and counter-charges of "arranged" assaults, kidnappings, and even murders, though few such allegations are ever brought to court. Stories abound, however, of candidates who have stepped down because they were intimidated or because they were "bought off." Posters and symbols are often defaced, and tensions, aggravated by rumor, often reach the breaking point.[5] The 1967 campaigns were marked by somewhat greater unrest than earlier elections, notably by the serious beating of a leader of the Samyukta Socialist party and the injury of the Prime Minister, Indira Gandhi, who was hit by a rock at a public meeting in Bhubaneswar. A number of rallies were disrupted, fasts-unto-death were threatened, and demonstrations and processions occasionally got out of hand. The most dramatic disturbance took place in New Delhi in November 1966, when several thousand people, led by Hindu holy men, saffron-robed *rishis* and naked, ash-covered *sadhus*, marched to the Parliament building in support of legislation against cow slaughter. In the confusion, rowdies overturned and burned cars and buses and attacked the residence of Congress president Kamaraj only minutes after his hasty escape. Given the size of the Indian election, however, the incidence of such disturbances is remarkably low.[6]

The Voting Procedure

The Indian constitution grants all Indian citizens twenty-one years old or older the right to vote. In 1967 more than 250 million people were eligible to vote, making that year's election the world's largest. From the members of the Central Election Commission down to the local polling officers, about one and one-half million people were involved in conducting the election. There were some 260,000 polling stations and

[5] See S. P. Verma and C. P. Bhambhri, *Elections and Political Consciousness in India* (Meerut: Meenakshi Prakashan, 1967), pp. 87–93.
[6] Palmer, "India's Fourth General Elections," pp. 278–79.

more than 1,300,000 ballot boxes.[7] The size of the electorate and convenience were major considerations in determining the number and location of the stations. They were spaced so that "ordinarily" no person should have had to travel more than three miles to cast his vote. The sheer magnitude of the elections and the inadequacy of transportation and communication facilities have made extended voting periods necessary. The first general elections were held in the winter of 1951–52 over a four-month period. The time was reduced to a span of nineteen days in 1957, ten days in 1962, and seven days in 1967.

In the first two general elections, each voter was given ballot papers for assembly and parliamentary seats. There was a ballot box for each candidate in each contest, and the voter placed the paper in the box marked by the symbol of the candidate he supported. (Some voters reportedly worshipped the ballot box after casting their vote.) The system was confusing and involved a vast number of ballot boxes. A new procedure that provides for marked ballots and a single box in public view was adopted in 1962 and has been used since then. Voters queue at the station, and a polling officer checks each voter's identity slip against his name on the electoral roll. The voter's finger is then marked with indelible ink, and he receives two ballots, pink for the assembly, white for the Lok Sabha. He marks both ballots secretly with a rubber stamp on the symbol of the candidate for whom he wishes to vote, folds the ballots, and drops them into the box. Although the procedure is involved, the number of invalid votes has been relatively small, averaging 3 to 4 percent of the total cast. The whole procedure is scrutinized by polling agents representing each candidate. Their presence and assistance also serve to identify voters and prevent impersonations.

Constituencies and Seats

The States Reorganization Act passed in 1956 provided for the establishment of the Delimitation Commission, consisting of the chief election commissioner and two active or retired judges of the Supreme Court or a state high court. Their responsibility is to delimit the constituencies for each election. These have varied somewhat with each election, but with the exception of the major changes caused by States Reorganization, there has been sufficient continuity to permit comparative analysis. The Lok Sabha constituencies have been drawn in successive elections to contain from 750,000 to 1,000,000 people. Within each parliamentary constituency are a number of state assembly constituencies, varying in size from state to state, but having an overall average of some 150,000 people. As a result of population growth, the total number of constituencies for the 1967 elections was increased to 521 for the Lok Sabha and to 3,383 for the state assemblies.

[7] *Ibid.*, p. 279.

The constitution prohibits separate electorates, which were for so long an object of political controversy. However, it does provide for reserved seats in both the Lok Sabha and assemblies for scheduled castes and tribes. In 1967 there were 114 reserved seats in the Lok Sabha and a total of 765 reserved seats in the assemblies—approximately 20 percent of the seats, somewhat less than the percentage of scheduled castes and tribes in the total population. The reserved seats guarantee representation. Although members of the scheduled castes and tribes may run for general seats, they do so infrequently and victories are rare.

During the first two elections a system of double-member (and in some cases three-member) constituencies was used in areas where scheduled castes and tribes were numerous. Constituencies were drawn twice the normal size and were allowed to return two members. Each voter was given two ballots, but he was not permitted to cast both for the same candidate. In double-member constituencies each party put up two candidates, one of whom was a member of the scheduled caste. The candidate receiving the highest number of votes was declared winner of the "general" seat. Among the remaining candidates, the scheduled caste member receiving the highest number of votes was declared winner of the "reserved seat." In constituencies with an actual majority of scheduled castes, this led to schemes to elect untouchables to both seats regardless of party label: Instead of casting his ballot for the Congress candidates for both general and reserved seats, for example, a voter might support the Congress candidate for the reserved seat and the Scheduled Castes Federation candidate for the general seat. In 1957 this tactic succeeded in four Lok Sabha constituencies and in thirteen assembly constituencies.[8] In 1962 the double-member constituencies were abolished in favor of simple reserved constituencies in which all voters make their selection among candidates from the scheduled classes.

The Selection of Candidates

Among the conflicts in Indian political life, perhaps none has been more intense or significant than the selection of candidates within the Congress party. The selection process has in fact become increasingly critical, since the election of the Prime Minister has come to depend on the balance of factional strength in the Lok Sabha. As conflicting interests become more vocal, the Congress is forced to reconcile its pledge to select the "best" candidates with the competing personal and parochial claims of those upon whom its support depends. Ramashray Roy, in analyzing this process in the states of Bihar and Rajasthan, argues that the selection process is "a crucial test of the party's flexibility and adapt-

[8] Phillips Talbot, "The Second General Elections: Some Impressions," American Universities Field Staff, INDIA PT-5-'57, p. 8.

ability in coping with the pressures and counter-pressures that impinge upon it from both within and without."[9]

FORMAL CRITERIA OF THE CONGRESS

The formal criteria established by the Congress for selecting candidates emphasize (1) the applicant's record of party loyalty; (2) his commitment to the Congress program; (3) his activity in "constructive work" as well as his legislative experience; and (4) reflecting the Congress's concern to broaden its base of support, his representation of groups the Congress may wish to attract.[10] But there has been little agreement in the Congress on the mechanism of selection. Rather, there has been a tug-of-war between the national leadership, which has favored centralization of decision-making, and the lower strata of the party organization, which have pushed for more power. Consequently, different procedures have been adopted for each election. Those party members supporting centralization argue the importance of freeing the selection process from local and parochial considerations, while those at the bottom claim that they are in a better position to judge the merits of a winning candidate. In 1952 the district Congress committees played the key role in the selection of candidates, but in 1957 they were relegated to an advisory position and the pradesh Congress committees were responsible for making recommendations to the Central Parliamentary Board, which is responsible for the final approval of all Congress candidates. In 1962 the district organizations were given more importance, but the 1967 procedure placed the pradesh committees in decisive control again.[11]

FACTIONAL PRESSURES

The Congress ticket is highly coveted, and factional confrontation and intense competition are characteristic of the struggle to win it. In 1962 there were in Bihar, for example, an average of 6.5 applications for every ticket. The various claims put forward often force sharp deviation in prescribed selection procedures. Individual attempts to bend procedural arrangements for personal advantage are likely to be defeated by higher authority, but group efforts, sustained by factional rivalry within the party, are likely to succeed.[12] There is always the fear, however, that the dominant faction at the lower levels may attempt to exploit its hold on

9 "Selection of Congress Candidates, Part I," *Economic and Political Weekly*, Vol. 1 (December 31, 1966), p. 835.
10 *Ibid.*, p. 837.
11 *Ibid.*, pp. 838–39, and Stanley A. Kochanek, "Political Recruitment in the Indian National Congress: The Fourth General Elections," *Asian Survey*, Vol. 7 (May 1967), p. 298.
12 Ramashray Roy, "Selection of Congress Candidates, Part II," *Economic and Political Weekly*, Vol. 2 (January 7, 1967), p. 21.

the organization by securing all tickets for itself, thus driving out the minority. Under Nehru's consensus-oriented leadership, such conflicts were resolved by central intervention. But with the increasing autonomy of the state parties after Nehru's death, the mechanisms of conflict resolution were threatened, particularly since the central leadership itself was divided. At the demand of state leaders, the selection process for the 1967 Congress tickets was controlled at the level of the pradesh committee, effectively placing the power to draw up the list of Congress candidates in the hands of the chief minister and the dominant faction.[13] Isolated from power by the refusal of the dominant faction to accommodate their claims and unable to secure central intervention in their behalf, as they might have done under Nehru, minority factions in various states withdrew from the Congress. Widespread defections led to the formation of rival Jana Congress parties.

At the local level party activists are more concerned with winning than with adherence to the formal criteria of selection and may thus be drawn to the man most likely to command the greatest base of support—even though his party loyalty, constructive work, or commitment to the Congress program might be minimal. Further, the local organization is more sensitive to the social base of the constituency and thus more willing to take caste and community into consideration in selecting their candidate. They also feel that voters prefer a local candidate and distrust an outsider—no matter how distinguished a Congress record he may have.[14] Reflecting this view, in contrast to earlier elections candidates now are almost always local men.

If the Congress is to retain its position of dominance, it must be able to accommodate the various group pressures, both state and local, in its selection of candidates. Ramashray Roy identifies four kinds of claims advanced in the selection process: personal, regional, socioeconomic, and institutional. Personal demands are those made by individual Congressmen who press for recognition and the reward of a Congress ticket for their sacrifice, service, experience, and competence. Regional claims are those that derive from feelings of localism, such as the demand that the candidate belong to the constituency. Various socioeconomic groups may also seek to advance their interests by claiming the right to representation among Congress candidates. Institutional demands for representation are made by the various organs of the Congress, such as the Youth Congress and the Indian National Trade Union Congress. The failure of the Congress to respond to these conflicting demands might well mean that even before the election important social sectors are lost to the opposition. However, factional competition within the Congress has served to articulate and aggregate these diverse group demands and to provide them with access to political power and a stake in the po-

[13] Stanley A. Kochanek, *The Congress Party in India* (Princeton, N.J.: Princeton University Press, 1968), p. 298.
[14] Roy, "Selection of Congress Candidates, Part II," pp. 22–23.

litical process.[15] Candidate selection thus is a vital recruitment and mobilization process.

In addition to competition between state and local groups and between factions, there is intense competition between the "old guard" and young political aspirants. In order to open channels of access, there has been an attempt to ensure some degree of turnover by requiring that one-third of the Congress tickets go to candidates who have not run before. Although the Congress has frequently been attacked as an aging party of old men, "the veterans of the freedom struggle are on the wane and their place is increasingly being taken by newcomers who perhaps join politics not because it demands sacrifice of them but because it opens new avenues for the realization of power and/or status."[16] The drama of the 1969 Congress split reflected something of this generational conflict.

The distribution of Congress tickets also reflects the party's increasing congruence with society. In Bihar, although higher education is still essential for positions of prestige within the party, some 40 percent of the Congress candidates have had very little schooling. The fact that nearly half are landowning agriculturalists reflects the dependence of the party on the rural sector. But the land is still controlled primarily by the upper castes, and they remain dominant within the Congress party. The lower castes, increasingly politically conscious and well organized, are far better represented, however, than are the scheduled castes or the Muslims.

The dominant elements of Congress thus are still drawn from the dominant elements of society.

> This means that traditionally entrenched social as well as economic sectors of the society have greater access to positions of power, not only in the party but also in the government, with the result that radical policies of social transformation are bound to be delayed if not sabotaged. The dominance of the vested interests in the Congress, therefore, prevents it from carrying out measures of reforms which may adversely affect the interests of the upper castes.[17]

UNIFICATION OF THE OPPOSITION

While intraparty strife led in 1967 to a decline in the Congress vote in some states, in others it was rather the ability of the opposition to unite that brought down the system of one-party dominance. In earlier elections Congress had been able to capitalize on the splintered opposi-

[15] Ramashray Roy, "Selection of Congress Candidates, Part III," *Economic and Political Weekly*, Vol. 2 (January 14, 1967), pp. 61–62, 69.
[16] Ramashray Roy, "Selection of Congress Candidates, Part IV," *Economic and Political Weekly*, Vol. 2 (February 11, 1967), p. 371.
[17] *Ibid.*, p. 375.

tion. Indeed, even in 1967, 184 Congress seats were won by less than 50 percent of the votes—and 80 of these by less than 40 percent.[18] The Congress was vulnerable, and the opposition parties sought to advance their position. The Congress has generally contested all seats, whereas the opposition parties, all-India as well as regional, have followed a policy of selective confrontation. This contest policy of the opposition parties, the result of their limited organization and resources, is a critical element of their election strategy and has influenced the election outcome. If a party's resources are limited, the more seats it contests, the more difficulty it may have in winning anywhere. Consequently, the opposition parties wait until the Congress has announced its final lists of candidates and then take the Congress candidates and constituency strength as their reference points in choosing which seats to contest.

In single member–simple majority constituencies, the candidate with the largest vote wins. A candidate may thus gain the seat with a minority vote. Such a system benefitted the Congress, with its more extensive organization, but it also motivated opposition to unite. In the 1967 elections this "multiplier" effect worked against the Congress. In terms of the total assembly seats in 1967, the Congress fell 5 percent in the votes it received, but 14 percent in the seats it secured. Only in Madhya Pradesh did the Congress retain its position. The Congress decline was most dramatic in Tamilnadu, where it secured a larger percentage of votes than any other party, 41.04 percent, but was reduced from some 67 percent of the assembly seats to 21 percent. In negotiating an electoral arrangement, the various opposition parties in Tamilnadu were so determined to unseat the Congress government that they agreed to step down in favor of the D.M.K., the most serious challenge to the Congress and the most effectively organized opposition in the state. It was calculated by both the Swatantra party and the Communist party that the D.M.K. candidate alone, rather than one of their own, would be able to capture a broad base of anti-Congress support in a marginal constituency. A Communist candidate would have driven the right into the arms of the Congress; a Swatantra candidate would have been unacceptable to the left.

There were, however, a number of multi-cornered contests between the Congress and the opposition parties, and there is little question that they greatly benefitted the Congress. In 1962 there were thirteen parties in Tamilnadu, each with its own candidates, all facing each other in a scramble that left the Congress victorious in 139 of the 206 assembly seats. With Congress popularity declining in the face of the anti-Hindi agitations and the food crisis, the opposition parties succeeded in forming an alliance with the D.M.K. in central position. Under the guiding hand of C. Rajagopalachari, the alliance included, in addition to the D.M.K., Swatantra, the C.P.I.(M.), the S.S.P., the Muslim League,

[18] Gopal Krishna, "The Problem," in the special issue of *Seminar* on the Congress party, No. 121 (September 1969), p. 14.

and several minor parties. Under the agreement the D.M.K. was to contest 173 of 234 assembly seats and 25 of 37 parliamentary seats. The balance was to be divided among the other parties of the alliance. The number of candidates for the Tamilnadu seats showed no appreciable decline, however, and the number of straight contests was no greater than in 1962. In fact, however, almost all contests were between the Congress and the alliance led by the D.M.K. Nearly all other candidates —independents and candidates of minor parties—did so poorly that they lost their deposits.[19] To appear on the ballot, a nomination for a seat from a parliamentary constituency must be accompanied by a deposit of five hundred rupees, for an assembly or council seat by a deposit of two hundred fifty rupees. (Members of scheduled castes and tribes need deposit only half these amounts.) Unless the candidate receives at least one-sixth of the total vote he forfeits his deposit.

There have been innumerable attempts to forge mergers and alliances among the opposition parties, at the national as well as at the state level, and with the Congress split, these attempts may well become more pronounced. One effort, begun after the 1967 elections, was that of the various rebel Congress groups in North India to achieve unity in the formation of the Bharatiya Kranti Dal. Their attempt was feeble and shortlived. The Bangla Congress of West Bengal withdrew almost immediately, and shortly thereafter the party lost strength almost everywhere except the western region of Uttar Pradesh, where it continued to command the support of rich peasants. The B.K.D. did play a critical role in the 1969 presidential elections, however, in providing V. V. Giri with the second-preference votes needed to secure victory.

THE SOCIAL BASE OF THE CONSTITUENCY

In the selection of candidates each of the major parties, including the Communist party, is sensitive to the social base of the constituency. When one community is dominant within a constituency—in the traditional terms of landed wealth, ritual status, and political power, or, increasingly, in terms of the modern calculus of numbers—each party is likely to draw its candidate from that community. It has been argued that this practice neutralizes caste as a political factor, but the fact remains that castes do not have equal access to power.

Dominant castes are themselves arenas of political competition between factions, each of which may try to aggregate the support of other castes. More frequently, a faction will seek vertical support, cutting through caste lines. Thus, the divisions within the dominant caste are mirrored in divisions within each of the other castes that follow traditional patterns of economic dependence and patron-client relationships.

<hr>

[19] See Chandra Mudaliar, "Madras Verdict," *Political Science Review* (University of Rajasthan), special number combining Vol. 6, Nos. 3 and 4; Vol. 7, Nos. 1 and 2 (1967–68), pp. 281–302.

Frequently the candidates, while all from the same community, do not have equal claim to support from within their own caste. When the castes are self-conscious and solidary in their political behavior, one candidate of the dominant caste may often be clearly identified as the "community man," and other castes will polarize in opposition around the other candidate, even though he is from that same community.

In constituencies in which two or more communities are in relative balance, candidates may be selected from numerically insignificant castes in order to depoliticize the caste factor. Where there are a number of small castes, none of which commands disproportionate influence, the candidate may be selected without regard to his caste. In any case, determination of the party candidacy must always take the caste complexion of the constituency into account, and state-wide there may be a conscious attempt to put together a balanced ticket, with each of the major communities represented.

Frequently "dummy candidates," running as independents, are put up to split votes and to draw support away from an opponent. Usually these are more a nuisance than a threat, but in a close election the loss of even a few votes may mean the difference between victory and defeat. An amusing example involved the parliamentary contest in Jaipur in 1962. The major contender was the Maharani Gayatri Devi on the Swatantra ticket. When the nominations were filed, it was discovered that another Gayatri Devi, an illiterate woman from a scheduled tribe, was also in the running—probably, it was suspected, at the instigation of others.[20] She polled only a few thousand votes.

The Election Campaign

PARTY FUNDS AND CAMPAIGN FINANCING

Political parties in India derive their funds from a variety of sources: membership dues, contributions, public meetings, and so on. The Congress party is the best financed. Its paid membership (in 1964, 4,637,208 primary members and 65,494 active members) provides a substantial portion of its financial backing, but additional contributions must be secured. These come regularly from wealthy supporters and are solicited in fund-raising campaigns. The birthday of Congress leader Kamaraj, for instance, has provided the Tamilnad Congress with a yearly occasion for bringing money into the party coffers. Contributions are frequently wrested from industry and business, often through considerable pressure. In Tamilnadu bus owners, dependent on the government for licenses, were reportedly "taxed" one thousand rupees per bus, and mill owners were "taxed" by the spindle. It is said that certain wealthy businessmen

[20] Verma and Bhambhri, *Elections and Political Consciousness in India*, pp. 69–72.

and industrialists are quietly urged to contribute a portion of their "black money" (income not reported for tax purposes) to the Congress party.

Whatever the multitude of sources tapped by the Congress, receipts are staggering. In the celebration week of Kamaraj's sixty-third birthday in July 1965, the main festivals were held in the town of Trichinopoly in Tamilnadu. Sixty-three arches were constructed at a cost of two thousand rupees each, and a procession under the arches was led by sixty-three cars and included sixty-three bullock carts. In other towns colorful processions were followed by public meetings, poetry competitions, essay contests, distribution of food to the poor, and special *pujas*, or worship services, in the temples. Each of the celebrations culminated in a meeting at which the local Congress leader presented Kamaraj with a "birthday purse" for the Congress campaign fund. Each district was to contribute 63,000 rupees, but in competition to outdo one another, the twelve districts contributed over 1,700,000 rupees ($350,000) during the birthday tour.[21]

The Congress's long control of the Center and the states, at least until 1967, gave the party a tremendous advantage. Dependent for licenses on the "permit raj," businesses contributed richly to the Congress. However, many have also made sizable contributions to Swatantra, a party with which they might have more ideological affinity. Some, taking no chance with a volatile electorate, have contributed to each of the major parties, right and left. The opposition, however, has generally had far less access to financial support than the Congress.

Each of the parties divides membership dues between the center and lower organizational units. The Congress party's constitution specifies that the central organization is to receive one-eighth of the income from dues; the rest is distributed among the state units. Other parties have similar arrangements, but ones involving considerably smaller amounts. Income from dues fluctuates considerably, since party membership is largest immediately before elections—often the result of mass recruitment or bogus membership arranged by factions to strengthen their bargaining position in the competition for party tickets. The candidates themselves may be expected to make sizable contributions to the party election fund. Indeed, tickets are occasionally awarded for a major commitment of financial support. This practice varies considerably from party to party and from seat to seat—for there are clearly a number of candidates from the Congress as well as from other parties without any major source of private income. Levies are also made on the salaries of Parliament and assembly members. Congress M.P.'s contribute forty rupees per month (10 percent of their parliamentary income) to the

[21] J. Anthony Lukas, "Political Python of India," *New York Times Magazine* (February 20, 1966), p. 54.

party. The average Communist M.P. contributes one hundred rupees each month to his party.[22]

Each of the parties derives some income from publishing. Most successful is the Communist Party of India, which prints several newspapers and operates a publishing house and a chain of bookstores. In addition, the sale of Soviet books and magazines, provided by the U.S.S.R. at minimal cost, brings the Communists considerable profit. The financial capacity of the Communist party has always been a source of speculation and rumor. The right faction is allegedly financed by the Soviet Union, and the C.P.I.(M.) was once accused of receiving Chinese support. Reports also circulate that the United States has backed specific candidates of various parties through the secret use of Central Intelligence Agency funds. Sources of funds are by no means clear for any party. Swatantra receives substantial contributions from business interests and recently perhaps more money from princes and former zamindars. The Jana Sangh also relies in part on zamindari funds, but the bulk of its contributions probably comes in relatively small sums from shopkeepers, refugees, and government clerks.

The costs of mounting a campaign are high and have increased with each election. In a closely competitive state assembly contest, each candidate may easily spend more than one hundred thousand rupees— considerably beyond the legal limit set by the Indian Election Commission. The laws governing campaign expenses allow up to twenty-five thousand rupees for a parliamentary seat and up to nine thousand rupees, depending on the region, for an assembly seat. The amount of expenses must be filed, but

> no expense, however large the account may be, which is incurred by a party organization in furthering the prospects of a candidate supported by it is required to be entered in the account of the election expenses of the candidate so long as he can make out that such expense was not authorized by him or by his election agent.[23]

For the 1962 elections Congress organizers claim to have spent about three million rupees. An opposition leader says it was probably closer to fifty million.[24]

MOBILIZING VOTERS

With each election, Indian political campaigns have become more expensive and intense, a mixture of festival and struggle, penetrating even

---

[22] A. H. and G. Somjee, "India," *Journal of Politics*, special issue on comparative studies in political finance, Vol. 25 (November 1963), p. 692. See also A. H. Somjee, "Party Finance," *Seminar*, No. 74 (October 1965).

[23] Indian Election Commission, *Report on the Second General Elections: 1957*, Vol. 1 (New Delhi: Government Press, 1959), p. 183.

[24] A. H. and G. Somjee, "India," p. 700.

the most isolated villages. Each candidate, backed by party funds and contributions, builds a team of party volunteers and paid election workers for the campaign. Insofar as possible, local offices are set up throughout the constituency, and transportation, by jeep whenever possible, is arranged. Weeks before the election, posters, painted slogans, and party symbols appear everywhere, competing for available wall space. There is a flood of printed handouts, and children parade through the streets with badges and party flags. Neighborhood party strongholds in villages and in cities prominently display flags, often vying with each other to raise the party flag highest. Jeeps and horse-drawn *tongas*, or carts, bedecked with party flags and the ubiquitous symbol, carry loudspeakers that saturate the air with a jumble of amplified slogans.

Each of the parties has an exclusive symbol by which it is identified. Because of widespread illiteracy and because the symbol, not the name of the party, appears on the ballot next to the name of the candidate, emphasis on symbols is a major part of the campaign. The symbol is the critical link in the mind of the voter between the candidate and the party, and for this reason, in the Congress split, the issue of which side gets the traditional Congress bullocks is not a trivial one. Figure 7–1 shows the official party symbols allotted by the Election Commission and used in all the states. The symbols are supposed to be neutral but each party strives to attach to them positive or negative connotations. Congress candidates, for example, may claim that their symbol, the pair of bullocks, represents the identity of the party with the rural peasant base of the nation.[25]

The government's All-India Radio has not been used by the parties because they cannot agree among themselves on the allotment of time offered to them. Few campaign advertisements appear in the press, probably because of India's low literacy level, although the papers provide detailed election coverage. In reviewing the 1967 elections, Norman D. Palmer commented that "it is doubtful that such complete election coverage has ever been given by the press of any country in the history of democratic elections."[26] While India's principal English and vernacular dailies are free to take an independent, even critical stance, they tend generally to be pro-Government and pro-Congress. Some of the major vernacular newspapers do support opposition parties, however. In addition, each party has its own weeklies in both English and local languages, as have many factions.

Parties often organize mass processions, with decorated floats, elephants, and a throng of party cadres as a means of publicizing their campaign. Torchlight parades evoke memories of early American political campaigns. Parties also make use of traditional folk dramas, particularly for satirical purposes. Some parties, such as the D.M.K. in Tamilnadu, have successfully used motion pictures to advance their cause. Mass

25 Verma and Bhambhri, *Elections and Political Consciousness*, pp. 82–83.
26 "India's Fourth General Elections," p. 281.

FIGURE 7-1

SYMBOLS OF POLITICAL PARTIES

SYMBOL	PARTY
1. Two yoked bullocks	Congress
2. Sickle and ears of corn	Communist Party of India
3. Hut	Praja Socialist Party
4. Lamp	Jana Sangh
5. Star	Swatantra
6. Banyan tree	Samyukta Socialist Party
7. Hammer, sickle, and star	Communist Party of India—Marxist
8. Elephant	Republican Party

public meetings bring a mixture of politics and entertainment, blending spellbinding orations with renditions of popular film songs. In addition to the luster provided by film stars, national political figures may also make appearances with the local candidates. Depending on the drawing power of the main speaker and on the galaxy of stars present, these meetings may attract several hundred thousand people. Street-corner meetings and spot appearances by a candidate bring the election even closer to the voters, but with each succeeding election emphasis on door-to-door canvassing has increased.[27]

PARTY MANIFESTOS

Each of the parties prepares a manifesto, a formal electoral platform, which may be a statement of minimum ideological agreement or a pledge of aspirations. The manifesto can hardly be expected to have

[27] See Verma and Bhambhri, *Elections and Political Consciousness*, pp. 83–85.

more importance in India, with its mass illiteracy, than does the party platform in the United States. In both nations few voters are aware of the formal party positions on most issues; fewer still ever read these documents. The fact that Indian parties devote such concern to the manifesto, however, may have great significance for legislative behavior if not for popular voting behavior.

The party manifestos may reflect the changing internal character of the party, the rise and fall of various factions, shifts in ideological stance, and efforts to secure new and broadened bases of support. In the first two elections, the Congress manifesto, like the Congress campaign, emphasized the party as the embodiment of the freedom movement. The Congress stood before the people on the record of its struggle and achievement, and individual Congressmen sought to establish their credentials of sacrifice by citing the time they had spent in British jails. By 1962, however, more than half of the electorate had come to political maturity after the struggle and sacrifice of the nationalist movement. These appeals were lost upon them. To the young the Congress was a party of privilege, wealth, and power, not of martyrdom. Responding to this change in the electorate, the Congress, no longer able to trade on history alone, tried to demontrate that it could satisfy popular demands. The manifesto sought to do this, but it could do so only in terms of real issues.

ISSUES

There have been few national issues in India. In North India, Pakistan has been an issue of emotional concern for many, but it does not stir the South. Cow slaughter has aroused the rancor of the orthodox, but its impact on the general public is fleeting. The issue of food scarcity has had considerable impact, but it is more a regional than a national concern, related to the particular problems of drought, rationing, and distribution peculiar to individual states. Inflation and rising prices have aroused national concern. Corruption has been decried from all sides. Regional nationalism has perhaps provided the most emotive issues. In 1957 the demand for the bifurcation of Bombay, reflected in the formation of separate Maharashtra and Gujarat parties and registered in a heavy anti-Congress vote, brought a serious challenge to Congress. In 1967 anti-Hindi, pro-Tamil feeling in Tamilnadu was an important ingredient in the victory of the D.M.K.

However, although these larger issues capture the headlines and the concern of party leaders and coffeehouse intellectuals, they are not likely to get out the vote. Even an issue so intense as language elicits little enthusiasm beyond the highly vocal student-intellectual community. National, even regional, issues seem remote and arouse little sense of efficacy in most of the electorate. These issues reflect real frustrations, however. Perhaps the *Times of India* is right in suggesting that "there are no all-India issues as such—there are only all-India grievances."[28] To reach the villager or the average urbanite, the campaign must be personalized, made immediate through translation into local issues that affect him and that he feels he can to some extent control. He may know or care little for the problems of food distribution or for the economics of inflation; but he does know that he does not have enough to eat and that he can buy less and less with the rupees he earns.

VOTE-BUYING

In the course of the election campaign, party workers attempt to contact each household in behalf of their candidate. In personal contact arguments might be advanced that could never be made publicly— specific appeals to caste loyalty, for example. These electoral efforts are frequently accompanied by payment. "Money politics" is an important lubricant of the Indian political machine. In many constituencies voters have come to expect payment of money by all candidates. It is clear, however, that a man cannot buy his election by bribing the electorate; a candidate spending a disproportionate amount frequently loses. In the first elections, payments were primarily group-directed. A candidate made a sizable payment to a village or caste leader in return for his promise to deliver a bloc of votes. Such payment sometimes was used for the group's benefit, but more often it simply enriched the leader alone. More recently, as traditional blocs of support fragment, individual contacts and payments are replacing group payments.

Vote-buying is probably less prevalent in cities than in villages, but in urban constituencies cases are reported—particularly among poorer classes—of a few rupees being enclosed in an election leaflet. Many politicians speak of "the price of a vote," complaining that it has risen with each election, but there is no definite pattern of voter response to offers of payment for support. There seem, however, to be four forms of reaction. Some voters will accept money from no candidate. Others will accept payment from all candidates and feel bound to none. Some barter their vote to the highest bidder, negotiating with each candidate to see who will pay the most. Once the bargain is struck, they feel bound to support the candidate. There are others who will accept money only from the candidate to whom they are already committed—a reflection of traditional patron-client relationships.[29] Instances have been reported of money being taken from one candidate and given to another. Because of the Congress's access to greater financial resources, voters are more

---

[28] February 14, 1967, quoted in Palmer, "India's Fourth General Elections," p. 289.
[29] Robert L. Hardgrave, Jr., *The Nadars of Tamilnad: The Political Culture of a Community in Change* (Berkeley: University of California Press, 1969), p. 214n.

likely to expect payments from Congress candidates, but few parties are exempt. Perhaps only the Communists have successfully avoided this trap.

In the first elections the privilege of voting may have seemed insignificant to many voters; in the course of time, payment for votes has made plain the importance of voting, but as a result payments have less and less effect on the way voters use their power. F. G. Bailey has described the pervasive cynicism and mistrust among voters in an Orissa hill village. Having the experience of two elections behind them, they received the politician's offer of payment for support with the same skepticism with which they received his ordinary protestations of devotion to the public weal.

> Neither the would-be corrupters nor their potential beneficiaries had any faith in one another's probity, and since the ballot was secret there was no check upon individual voters. The voters did not think that they would get the money; the candidates believed that voters accept money from both sides and vote the way they would anyway, without a bribe.[30]

No doubt widespread vote-buying has contributed to attitudes of cynicism, but ironically, vote-buying has a democratic effect, for the parties become agents of a periodic income redistribution. More important, however, is the fact that money politics impresses the people with the importance of a single vote and serves to draw nonparticipants to the polls. In much the same way the gifts of the American political machines early in this century politicized new immigrants to the United States and served to integrate them into the society and the political system. As individuals become increasingly involved politically and as voting practice thus becomes institutionalized, payment declines in importance.

APPEALS TO SPECIFIC GROUPS

The adept candidate has done his demographic homework. He has at his fingertips information on the patterns of social cleavage and the numbers and relative strength of each caste within his constituency. Before he ever arrives in a village, he has attempted by whatever means possible to determine its caste and factional complexion, the degree of his support, and the specific felt needs of the villagers. Since voters may readily pledge to vote for every candidate, it may be necessary to get an independent assessment. Candidates therefore may enlist undercover

[30] F. G. Bailey, *Politics and Social Change: Orissa in 1959* (Berkeley: University of California Press, 1963), p. 33.

workers in villages and neighborhoods to probe voter feelings. Some even infiltrate the organization of other parties.[31]

On his village tours a candidate may leave his jeep some distance from the village and enter the village on foot, accompanied by an impressive group of party workers. Having previously ascertained what the villagers want most, he may well promise them this alone if he is elected, emphasizing his credentials of integrity by *not* offering them everything but, conveniently, just what they want. After a short public speech he may make personal visits to villagers at all levels, particularly those in pivotal or decisive positions. The appearance may then be followed, perhaps some days later, by individual contacts by party workers.

The political candidate must make mass appeals, but, as in the United States, much of his attention is directed toward specific groups. If there is a relatively low turnout at the polls or a large number of candidates, victory may hinge on only a small number of votes. Bailey writes that "the structure of traditional society may become the mould within which representative politics operate at constituency level. Old loyalties and allegiances may continue within the new framework of representative politics."[32] Candidates thus may attempt to capture the support of traditional groups that can be guaranteed as a "vote bank" to deliver a bloc of votes on instruction by a leader. The framework of modern politics does not simply foster the continuation of traditional behavior, however. It structures new forms of behavior, and the traditional patron-client ties of the vote bank are weakening as a result. In most cases traditional sentiments are all that remains of the old structures of authority. Unless bloc leaders can reinforce these sentiments by securing for their groups the benefits they demand, traditional blocs are not likely to survive. In all but the most isolated villages, vote banks can no longer be relied upon. Despite pledges of united support, castes and communities are increasingly likely to fragment their support. A candidate for municipal election in central India described the change in his own constituency thus:

> In 1954, people would vote for the man they promised to support. Sometimes they decided this through a council of the sub-caste, sometimes they were brought in through workers, or through the tempo at public meetings. Now people only vote after they have each been reached and persuaded, and they vote because of their own benefit, or because of the person who talks to them; so they can be changed up to the last minute. Maybe

[31] A. C. Mayer, "Municipal Elections: A Central Indian Case Study," in C. H. Philips, ed., *Politics and Society in India* (London: George Allen & Unwin, 1963), p. 124.
[32] *Politics and Social Change*, p. 113.

in a few years they will vote because of Municipal policies. You
see, we are progressing all the time, and our people are learning
about elections.[33]

Election law clearly declares any appeal based on religion, race, caste,
community, or language to be illegal. Religious communities, however,
have historically been the object of political appeal. It was the Muslim
League, advancing its claim to be the sole representative of the Muslim
people, that successfully challenged the secular Congress in securing
partition of India and the formation of the Islamic state of Pakistan.
The Muslims of India today are self-conscious and frequently respond
to political appeals as a group. In constituencies where their numbers
are significant, they may constitute a major base of local power to be
courted by all parties. In Kerala and to a lesser extent in Tamilnadu, a
revived Muslim League continues to claim their political loyalty.
Christians, although by no means united politically or religiously, are in
certain areas sufficiently numerous to exercise a powerful political force.
In Kerala, where they number about one-third of the population, they
have been the main support of the Congress, and the pulpit has frequently served as a rostrum for political exhortation. The gurdwaras of
the Punjab have served as bases for the political activity of the Akali
Dal. Eighty percent of India's people are Hindu, however, and although
even the Jana Sangh cautiously phrases its public appeals in secular
terms, Hindu communalism is a potent factor in Indian politics. Cow
protection and the Hindu Code Bill, reforming Hindu marriage and
inheritance practices, are issues that stir the orthodox; and the nostalgia
for Bharat, Hindu India, is a dynamic element of nationalist feeling
readily exploited by the traditional right.

But caste has perhaps been an even more prominent feature of the
contemporary Indian political landscape than religion. In the process of
modernization, with the development of communications and the
spread of education and literacy, castes have emerged as solidary political units through the formation of associations. The introduction
of caste and community into the political system has been decried as
a reversion to tribalism. Nevertheless, politicians and political scientists
alike speak of the "Reddy vote" or the "Jat bloc," just as in the United
States people often talk of the black, Irish, or Italian vote.[34]

The process by which an atomized and divided community gains
consciousness and unity, entering the political system as a major actor,
is a familiar one in the broader process of political behavior. The unity
of such blocs is situational and temporal, however, varying from con-

[33] Quoted in Mayer, "Municipal Elections," p. 125.
[34] For a discussion of the similarities of caste and ethnicity, see Robert L. Hardgrave,
Jr., "Caste: Fission and Fusion," *Economic and Political Weekly*, special number
(July 1968), pp. 1065–70.

stituency to constituency and from time to time. Indeed, the very success of the community's bid for power, as among the Nadars, may become the vehicle for internal social and economic differentiation and the dispersion of political support. Caste has by no means ceased to be an important factor in determining political behavior, but it is only one of many variables that affect the individual voter's decision. The political party may choose its candidates from the dominant caste of a particular constituency, but it does no more than the American city boss who seeks to aggregate the support of ethnic communities by offering candidacies to their leaders. Few politicians can afford to court a single caste, for in most constituencies no single caste so predominates as to command a majority. Although they may seek to gain the support of a caste by appealing to its particular interest in a given situation, they must do so without alienating other communities and driving them into united opposition. The appellation "caste man" would severely limit the political horizon of an aspiring office-seeker.[35]

The Indian Electorate

Expanding Participation and the Impact of Panchayati Raj

Given the level of literacy in India, political consciousness is remarkably high. Since independence levels of political awareness and of participation have risen among all segments of the population. The relationship between urbanization and participation is unclear. With the notable exceptions of Kashmir and Kerala, most states in which the population is highly participant are also highly urbanized. Rural voting in these states, however, is also higher than in other states, perhaps reflecting the impact of the city as a locus of social change. A breakdown of the 1957 vote in urban and rural assembly constituencies indicates exactly the same turnout for both urban and rural males—45.4 percent. For women, however, the difference was marked: 52.4 percent of the urban women voted, compared to 37 percent of the rural women.[36]

Participation by women has increased with each election. During the first election many refused to give their proper names and therefore were not registered. By 1962 two-thirds as many women as men voted, and by 1967 the proportion had risen to three-fourths. The effect of the increase in the number of votes cast by women is probably negligible, however. Perhaps in Kerala, where women (particularly Christians) have received more education and have traditionally had more independence than

[35] Robert L. Hardgrave, Jr., "Varieties of Political Behavior Among the Nadars of Tamilnad," *Asian Survey*, Vol. 6 (November 1966), pp. 620–21, and *The Nadars of Tamilnad*, pp. 202–23.

[36] Myron Weiner, *State Politics in India* (Princeton, N.J.: Princeton University Press, 1968), pp. 33–34.

in other states, women may have given disproportionate support to the Congress in opposition to the C.P.I. Generally, however, voting among women follows the pattern of one constituency in which "women were not only led to the polling booth by the male members of the family, but in almost all cases voting behaviour was determined by their advice, which was eagerly sought, given, and followed."[37]

A number of women are prominent in Indian politics, notably Indira Gandhi, the Prime Minister, and the Maharani of Jaipur. The Congress has tried to encourage women to enter politics by reserving about 15 percent of its tickets for them.

Although political awareness and participation have increased throughout India, there is evidence on any number of scales that political mobilization is taking place faster in rural areas than in urban areas. The most dramatic increases have been noted among rural poor and illiterate populations, whose levels of awareness and participation remain, however, very low indeed. Expansion of participation in rural areas is closely related to the impact of panchayati raj in politicizing the village. Élite factions, which once needed only the support of the dominant castes, must now seek a wider base of support to legitimize their traditional position. A critical determinant of the rural turnout is the degree to which local conflicts are identified with struggles at the constituency level. Factions become the vehicle of political mobilization and voting turnout. Almost every village is torn by factionalism and almost inevitably village conflicts are drawn into the wider political arena. Party struggles thus become an opportunity for each village faction to further its interests and solidify its position within the village.

Factional struggle is by no means new. Land has traditionally been a source of intense conflict; various families in the dominant caste have fought among themselves to enlarge their holdings. Factional conflict has also served to divide castes as vertical relationships of dependence have cut through village society in the formation of client groups. Such factions, although not permanent, have often endured for several generations. The establishment of panchayati raj and the availability of government development money have intensified conflict in the competition for new resources.

Each village faction may try to associate itself with the winning assembly candidate both to command reward for support and to legitimize its local dominance. The Congress, with its own factional division, has often been able to command the support of an entire village through the alignment of village factions with various Congress groups, often simply on the basis of polarization. That is to say, one village faction sides with a particular faction within the Congress, so the opposing village faction aligns with the opposing Congress group. A village faction,

[37] J. C. Anand, "Panchayat Elections in the Punjab: A Case Study," *Political Science Review* (University of Rajasthan), Vol. 2 (March 1963), p. 34.

however, may well extend its support to an opposition party candidate just because the dominant faction of the village supports the Congress. Voting may thus reflect issues and conflicts peculiar to a village alone and virtually unrelated to the issues of the larger constituency.[38]

Levels of Political Awareness

For most of India there is no "public opinion." Although beginning to expand, the identity horizon of most villagers rarely extends beyond the narrow range of personal encounter; their knowledge and concerns remain highly parochial. Local elections are the most likely to arouse enthusiasm, and even assembly elections are contested on highly local issues. Appeals are calculated in parochial terms, but probably no more so than in any other democratic country.

Levels of political literacy have risen rapidly in India as a result of the penetration of mass communications and the broadening of political competition. There have been few all-India public-opinion surveys. Those of the Indian Institute of Public Opinion provide a useful index of change, although the samples have been biased in favor of urban, literate, and upper-income groups, and men have been overrepresented. The I.I.P.O. studies find a higher level of political interest in urban than in rural areas for all groups except illiterates, who, in both urban and rural areas, have very low levels of political awareness. These surveys do, however, confirm increases in political interest and participation in all sectors of society.

In early surveys the limited political horizon of most Indians was evidenced in the widespread inability to identify even such well-known national leaders as Nehru. Today there are few Indians in such isolation. Mass media have reached the villages and expanded the average villager's threshold of political identity. Indians have become increasingly aware of the world beyond the village, increasingly conscious of their vote. Opinions are multiplying; if surveys continue to register a large number of "don't knows," the statistics should not be taken to mean that Indians simply have no orientations or sentiments about the matters at issue. Although not articulate, they have real interests of which they are aware.

The attitude of Indian villagers toward politicians is ambivalent. "Peasant communities," Bailey writes, "are proverbially hard and centered upon themselves; within the boundary there is some degree of trust, some rule of morality; beyond the boundary they expect to be cheated or bullied, as they would themselves deal with a stranger. Rela-

---

[38] See Myron Weiner, "Village and Party Factionalism in Andhra: Ponnur Constituency," in Myron Weiner and Rajni Kothari, eds., *Indian Voting Behaviour* (Calcutta: Mukhopadhyay, 1963), pp. 177–202.

tionships with outsiders have not yet acquired 'legitimacy.' "[39] The villagers' acceptance of the new framework of government does not rest upon its efficiency alone, but also "on moral judgments about the persons associated with the new institutions."[40] The contrast between the reality of political life in India and Indians' idealized image of the democratic process has served to breed a general cynicism. Interest-group activity and responsiveness to group demands are considered immoral. The qualities the legislator *ought* to possess are sacrifice, unselfishness, service, and impartiality. But these are unlikely attributes of a successful candidate—perhaps they are more those of a philosopher-king than a democratic politician. Yet the voters themselves, with little conception of the public interest, demand selflessness of their leaders, while at the same time they project their own code of morality upon all but a very few politicians. Anyone in political life, they believe, must be working for his own betterment: No one would offer himself as a candidate unless he were out to make money for himself.[41]

Although there is a general belief that assembly members ought to be disinterested, Indian voters are primarily concerned with the distribution of benefits. "The voters look to their MLA not for his record and performance as a legislator, but expect him to be their representative, a man who can stand up for them against the local administrators and win favours for them in the distribution of development money or other favours."[42] The voters expect the M.L.A. to be the broker between the mass and the élite.

Many voters have supported the Congress, no doubt as a form of traditional loyalty to the government: Not to do so would be disloyal. Others feel that it is in their personal interest to do so. Many groups consider it to their advantage to vote for "the government," no matter who it is. Some believe that the government distinguishes between its supporters and opponents and that they will suffer if they oppose it—or, at least, be deprived of its benefits. These attitudes reflect, in part, a failure to distinguish between the ruling party and administrative services. In the first elections it may have involved as well "an incomplete acceptance of the idea that Governments may be thrown out by means of an election."[43] However, these attitudes also reflect the considerable advantage of the ruling party. Patronage is a powerful political instrument with which to command support. The links between the government and the Congress party organization have also provided channels of influence and response. Like the Democratic party in the United States, the Congress enjoys association with a variety of services it has

[39] *Politics and Social Change*, p. 65.
[40] *Ibid.*, p. 68.
[41] *Ibid.*, pp. 35–36.
[42] *Ibid.*, p. 84.
[43] *Ibid.*, pp. 23–24. See also Mayer, "Municipal Elections," pp. 128–29.

established as the party in power. Access to these government services and welfare and development benefits is most often through the intervention of a Congress leader.

Opposition victory might well break this flow of benefits through the party, seriously affecting the ability of the Congress organization to deliver the votes. The political machine operates on the patronage and benefits it can exchange for support. It is fueled, in Bailey's words, "not by moral fervour, but by calculations of profit and advantage."[44] Machine support is contingent; yet it may be the agent not simply of mobilization and integration but, with time, of a party loyalty that transcends the immediate reward. Loyalty to the Congress as government, long association with the party as the embodiment of the nationalist movement, and the charismatic force of Gandhi and Nehru have served to institutionalize the Congress and to sustain party identity among considerable numbers of voters, who contribute a stable base of political support. Even in the widespread defeats of the 1967 elections, the actual percentage of Congress votes declined only a few points. Bailey found that in Orissa Congress support did not rest on personal interests and parochial issues alone. "Voting for the Congress had become a habit, that same fundamentally irrational—one might call it 'moral'—identification with a party which characterizes party support in the older democracies."[45] The 1969 split confronts the voter with two Congress parties. For most people personality means more than ideology, and, aside from a few local and state leaders, Indira Gandhi, third-generation Congress leader, is the dominant personality.

Voting Turnout and Trends

The Montagu-Chelmsford Reforms of 1919 provided for limited franchise based on property qualifications, the specific criteria varying among the provinces. The total electorate for the various provincial legislative councils was about 5,350,000. Easing the franchise qualifications, the Government of India Act of 1935 extended suffrage to include some 30 million people. After independence, the constitution abolished all property qualifications and, in what Rajendra Prasad called "an act of faith," established universal adult suffrage. The electorate has grown from 173 million in 1952 to 193 million in 1957, 216 million in 1962, and 250 million in 1967.

While the size of the electorate has expanded with population growth, there has also been a steady increase in the percentage of voting turnout; 45.7 percent[46] in 1951–52, 47.74 percent in 1957, 56.29 percent in 1962, and 61.33 percent in 1967. (The United States turnout

---

[44] *Politics and Social Change*, p. 141.
[45] *Ibid.*, p. 85.
[46] Valid votes only; other figures represent the total number of votes cast.

in 1968 was only 61 percent). Rates of participation vary considerably among the states, from a high of 76.57 percent turnout in Tamilnadu in 1967 to a low of 44.05 percent in Orissa in the same year. In every state, however, participation has increased. Paul R. Brass finds that rates of participation among the states correspond closely with levels of modernization, as registered in terms of per capita income, urbanization, literacy, and mass communications.[47] Significantly, he does not find an association between high levels of social mobilization and the Congress's decline. The three weakest Congress states in 1967 (Orissa, Uttar Pradesh, and Bihar) are among the lowest on the modernization scale. Brass traces Congress weakness in these states to a decline in organizational coherence. Intense and unresolved factionalism led to increasing defections that then undermined the base of party support.

The number of candidates in a race is a significant factor in determining the outcome of the contest, but the decisive factor is still the number of votes each candidate receives. In 1967 there was an average of nearly five candidates for every parliamentary and assembly seat, but voters tended to ignore all but two or three "serious" candidates. The trend toward fewer independent candidates was reversed in 1967: There were 5,793 independents in the assembly elections that year as compared with 3,888 in 1962. Their number no doubt reflected defections from the Congress. Only 298 won seats, however, and the vast majority forfeited their deposits. In fact, deposits were lost by seven out of eight independent candidates for the Lok Sabha and by five out of every six independent assembly candidates. These defeats register the fact that the electorate has become more party-conscious.

In 1967 some 18,500 candidates stood for Lok Sabha and assembly seats—about 1,000 more than in 1952. In the first general elections approximately one-third of the candidates were independents. There were fourteen national parties and fifty-nine state parties. Of the 17,500 candidates in 1951–52, more than half lost their deposits because they did not secure the needed minimum vote. The largest number of these were independents. The number of forfeitures for independents has increased with each election. While this may reflect "the number of individuals, unable to judge their capacity to translate personal influence into electoral votes,"[48] it also reveals a more rational electorate, unwilling to waste its votes on a variety of minor aspirants. Those states with the highest levels of participation and consciousness, mobilized by party competition, are those in which voters are most party-oriented, with the fewest number of returned independents.

As Table 7–3 shows, the percentage of the Congress vote, despite the 1967 reverses, has remained remarkably stable. It has varied within only

[47] "Political Participation, Institutionalization and Stability in India," *Government and Opposition*, Vol. 4 (Winter 1969), p. 27.
[48] Weiner, *State Politics in India*, p. 41.

TABLE 7-3

THE CONGRESS VOTE IN STATE ASSEMBLY ELECTIONS, 1952–67

	1952		1957[d]		1962[e]		1967	
	% of vote	% of seats	% of vote	% of seats	% of vote	% of seats	% of vote	% of seats
Andhra Pradesh[a]	29.7	28.1	41.72	62.13	47.25	57.00	45.32	56.79
Assam	43.8	72.3	52.35	65.94	48.25	75.23	43.60	55.55
Bihar	41.4	72.7	41.90	66.04	41.35	58.18	33.08	40.25
Gujarat	54.9	86.3	48.66	59.09	50.84	73.38	45.74	55.35
Haryana	34.8	65.0	47.51	77.92	43.72	58.44	41.33	59.25
Kerala	34.3	32.8	37.84	34.12	34.42[b]	50.00	35.43	6.76
Madhya Pradesh	48.1	77.4	49.83	80.56	38.54	48.26	40.69	56.41
Tamilnadu	40.0	50.4	45.34	73.65	46.14	67.48	41.04	21.36
Maharashtra	45.2	82.1	48.66	59.09	51.22	81.44	47.03	74.81
Mysore	51.5	84.2	52.08	72.59	50.22	65.38	48.62	57.40
Orissa	38.8	47.8	38.21	40.00	43.28[c]	58.57	30.66	22.14
Punjab	34.8	65.0	47.51	77.92	43.72	58.44	36.56	45.19
Rajasthan	39.7	50.0	45.20	67.61	40.02	49.43	41.42	48.36
Uttar Pradesh	47.9	90.6	42.42	66.51	36.33	57.91	32.20	46.82
West Bengal	38.9	63.2	46.14	60.32	47.29	61.90	47.13	45.35
India	42.2	68.4	45.49	65.14	44.38	61.61	39.96	47.50

[a] The 1957 figures for Andhra Pradesh are a composite made up of the results from the midterm election in Andhra in 1955 and in Telengana in 1957.
[b] This figure is for midterm elections held in 1960.
[c] This figure is for midterm elections held in June 1960.
[d] The figures in these columns under Gujarat and Maharashtra are for undivided Bombay and under Punjab and Haryana for the old Punjab state.
[e] The figures for Haryana and Punjab are for the old Punjab state.
Source: The 1952 figures are derived from Myron Weiner, ed., *State Politics in India* (Princeton, N.J.: Princeton University Press, 1968), p. 46. All other figures have been taken from the reports on the general elections published by the Election Commission.

SOURCE: Paul R. Brass, "Political Participation, Institutionalization and Stability in India," *Government and Opposition*, Vol. 4 (Winter 1969), p. 25.

six percentage points, from a high of 45.49 percent in 1957 to a low of 39.96 in 1967; in only a few states has the Congress ever gained an actual majority of the votes. But although Congress has been able to retain a core of support, it has lost significant sectors of the electorate. Congress support seems to show a decline among minorities—Sikhs, Christians, and Muslims—and among various urban middle-class groups, such as students, teachers, and government servants.[49] Most significant,

[49] Brass, "Political Participation," p. 38.

however, are substantial losses from among three groups: those under thirty-five years of age, illiterates, and those with incomes below two hundred rupees per month. The Congress formerly enjoyed a well-balanced base of support, in terms of literacy, age, and occupation, but it has increasingly lost touch with youth and with the lower rungs of the social order.[50]

> The Indian electorate, believed inert and incapable of dramatic choice, is showing signs of a revolutionary change. The young, the less educated, and particularly the illiterates, the minorities, and, most unpredictable of all, the lowest income groups are all rewriting their basic loyalties. To the candidate this is, perhaps, a struggle for power. To a political scientist it is . . . the beginning of a break with the past.[51]

Political Mobilization and India's Future

The Congress was the architect of political mobilization, but when participation expanded it was no longer able to accommodate it fully. The party organization, although the most extensive in scope, has not successfully provided channels of access to newly participant groups. Because its machine structure made it politically dependent on the middle-level peasantry and petty landlords, the Congress remained basically unresponsive to those at the bottom, those without land or power. Increasingly isolated from an awakening majority, the Congress organization, captive to narrow interests, was challenged by the Prime Minister in 1969, precipitating crisis and ultimately division.

Tamilnadu has experienced the most rapid rates of political mobilization. Between 1957 and 1967, with the rise of the D.M.K., participation increased 28.29 percent to make Tamilnadu the state with the highest voting turnout. This expansion was accompanied by rapid increases in industrialization and communications. The Congress was dramatically defeated (although with an actual decline of only 5 percent in the vote), but expanding participation did not produce political decay. The D.M.K. came to power with an absolute majority, the only non-Congress party to do so, and consolidated its position once in control.

Brass, in comparing Tamilnadu and Uttar Pradesh, concludes that

> there is not the slightest evidence . . . that social mobilization and political participation [following Huntington] "are directly responsible for the deterioration of political institutions" in the

---

[50] E. P. W. da Costa, "The Indian General Elections 1967" (New Delhi: Indian Institute of Public Opinion, 1967), pp. 2–3.
[51] *Ibid.*, p. 23.

Indian context. In fact, the evidence from India is entirely to
the contrary, namely, that low levels of social mobilization and
political participation are associated with political decay . . . .[52]

Expanding participation thus provides the impetus for developing higher
levels of institutionalization. The Congress defeats among highly mobilized populations can be interpreted as political decay only if stability
in itself is the highest value. The *status quo* in India has indeed been
radically disrupted; yet the emergent system may be capable of attaining
a higher level of development.

Whether the system has the will to respond to the increasing demands upon it is of course another question. The enhanced capacity of
the party system to both generate and absorb change in expanding participation has held the critical balance in India's political development.
The parties, in organizing and structuring participation, may provide
access to demands, but they cannot wholly satisfy them. The viability
of the political system depends on both the will and the capacity of the
government to respond to these demands. Despite the "fissiparous
tendencies" of regionalism and the states' demands for greater autonomy, India's national identity seems increasingly secure. The institutions of government in the years since independence have gained
increasing legitimacy. The constitutional framework has been strengthened through its continued operation.

The institutions of government in India, notably the bureaucracy,
were grounded in the structure of the British raj. They were designed
for administration and for the maintenance of stability; their purpose
was to contain demands, not to respond to them. The fundamental
problem of transition was to adapt these instruments of repressive
order to the needs of social change and democratic response. But rapidly expanding participation and escalating demands quickly outran the
capacity of the highly institutionalized structures that India's new
leadership had inherited. Control of the government and the administration, particularly in the states where the mass and the élite met in
closest contact, rested largely in the hands of those who sought to resist
change, to reinforce the vested interests of the *status quo,* and who
lacked the will to respond to the demands stimulated by increasing political consciousness.

As the will to effect a fundamental transformation of society has
declined, so, in the face of scarcity, have capacities to meet rising demands. Poverty remains the basic fact of India's existence: Scarcity
conditions her political life. The party system can order participation
only so long as the governmental institutions at the Center and in the
states can reasonably meet the aspirations of India's newly conscious,
newly participant mass. The comparative order of Indian political life

[52] "Political Participation," p. 48.

may conceal an unrest that lies just beneath the surface. "Leaders function at the top," Nehru once wrote, "but they are driven in particular directions by the anonymous and unthinking will of an awakening people, who seem to be outgrowing their past."[53]

[53] Jawaharlal Nehru, *The Discovery of India* (London: Meridian Books, 1960), p. 518.

RECOMMENDED READING

Bailey, F. G., *Politics and Social Change: Orissa in 1959*. Berkeley: University of California Press, 1963.
   Analyzing various levels of political life in a single state, Bailey provides one of the most illuminating studies of political life in India.

Brass, Paul R., "Coalition Politics in North India." *American Political Science Review*, Vol. 62 (December 1968).
   A penetrating analysis of the events following the 1967 elections.

————, "Political Participation, Institutionalization and Stability in India." *Government and Opposition*, Vol. 4 (Winter 1969).
   A comparative analysis of Tamilnadu and the North Indian states, concluding that high levels of participation do not necessarily produce political decay.

Brecher, Michael, *Political Leadership in India: An Analysis of Elite Attitudes*. New York: Praeger, 1969.
   An examination of élite perceptions of the events surrounding the 1967 election.

Fox, Richard G., *From Zamindar to Ballot Box*. Ithaca, N.Y.: Cornell University Press, 1969.
   A study of social and political change in an Uttar Pradesh market town.

Kashyap, Subhash C., *The Politics of Defection*. Delhi: National Publishing House, 1969.
   A detailed study of defection and floor-crossing in Indian legislatures.

Philips, C. H., ed., *Politics and Society in India*. London: George Allen & Unwin, 1963.
   Papers explore the interaction between society and politics.

* Rosen, George, *Democracy and Economic Change in India*, new ed. Berkeley: University of California Press, 1967.
   An analysis of the impact of economic change on India as a whole and on specific groups within Indian society.

Sirsikar, V. M., *Political Behaviour in India*. Bombay: Manaktalas, 1965.
   A case study of four constituencies of Poona in the 1962 elections.

Stern, Robert W., *The Process of Opposition in India: Two Studies of How Policy Shapes Politics*. Chicago: University of Chicago Press, 1970.
   An examination of opposition stimulated by specific Government policies.

* Available in a paperback edition.

Verma, S. P. and Bhambhri, C. P., *Elections and Political Consciousness in India*. Meerut: Meenakshi Prakashan, 1967.
    A comparative analysis of political behavior in two Rajasthan constituencies, urban and rural, with a treatment of election strategy and campaign techniques.

Weiner, Myron, and Kothari, Rajni, eds., *Indian Voting Behaviour*. Calcutta: Mukhopodhyay, 1963.
    A collection of constituency studies of the 1962 elections that originally appeared in the *Economic Weekly*.

RESEARCH GUIDE*

General Bibliographies

Guide to Indian Periodical Literature.
A major new reference source in the social sciences for India. Published monthly since 1964. (Gurgaon, Punjab)

Index India.
This periodical index, published quarterly by the University of Rajasthan, is an extremely valuable source for research in contemporary politics.

Indian National Bibliography.
Quarterly and annual. Two sections—"Books and Articles" and "Government Publications"—each with an index. Exhaustive listings of all items published in India in all languages. Useful for students who are engaged in fairly specialized research or who read an Indian language.

Indian News Index.
Quarterly guide to English newspapers in India.

International Guide to Periodical Literature.
An important guide to scholarly articles. Useful for book reviews.

* Adapted from a research guide originally prepared by Lloyd I. and Susanne H. Rudolph, the University of Chicago. Their permission is gratefully acknowledged.

Journal of Asian Studies.
Since 1956, this scholarly quarterly has published a fifth bibliographical number. A most *useful* guide to the literature.

Mahar, J. Michael, *India: A Critical Bibliography.* Tucson: University of Arizona Press, 1964.
Outstanding annotation. Strongest on history, philosophy, and religion. Unfortunately Mahar lists books only.

Patterson, Maureen L. P., and Inden, Ronald B., eds., *Introduction to the Civilization of India; South Asia, an Introductory Bibliography.* Chicago: University of Chicago Press, 1963.
The most comprehensive and up-to-date bibliography. A good place to start. Includes a section on general and specialized bibliographies.

Public Affairs Information Service, *Bulletin.*
An invaluable guide to the literature of public policy around the world. Lists books, articles of a scholarly and a more popular nature, and publications of the United States and foreign governments, international agencies, and private research groups. Indexing and cross-indexing are particularly valuable.

Special Bibliographies

Alexandrowicz, C. H., ed., *A Bibliography of Indian Law.* Madras: Oxford University Press, 1958, 69 pp.

Case, Margaret H., *South Asian History, 1750–1950.* Princeton, N.J.: Princeton University Press, 1967.

Cohn, Bernard S., *The Development and Impact of British Administration in India: A Bibliographic Essay.* New Delhi: Indian Institute of Public Administration, 1961, 88 pp.

Damle, Y. B., *Caste—A Review of the Literature.* Cambridge, Mass.: M.I.T., Center for International Studies, 1961.
Includes a thirty-three-page essay on theoretical issues, a twenty-five-page bibliography, and a sixty-five-page section containing "Abstracts of Important Works on Caste."

Leonard, T. J., "Federalism in India," in William S. Livingston, ed., *Federalism in the Commonwealth: A Bibliographical Commentary.* London: Cassell, 1963.
An excellent bibliographic essay, ranging far beyond federalism itself to include Indian politics and government generally.

Matthews, William, *British Autobiographies: An Annotated Bibliography of British Autobiographies Published or Written Before 1951.* Berkeley: University of California Press, 1955, 376 pp.
Indexed by subject; thus works that deal with India can readily be located.

Morris, Morris David, and Stein, Berton, "The Economic History of India: A Bibliographical Essay." *Journal of Economic History,* Vol. 21 (June 1961), pp. 179–207.
An excellent guide. Includes a discussion of needed research concerning theory and approaches.

Muin ud-din Ahmad Khan. "A Bibliographic Introduction to Modern Islamic Development in India and Pakistan 1700–1955." Appendix to *Journal of the Asiatic Society of Pakistan*, Vol. VI, 1959, 17 pp. (Dacca)

Select Bibliography on Electoral Behavior in India. Jaipur: University of Rajasthan, 1966.

Select Bibliography on Indian Government and Politics. Jaipur: University of Rajasthan, 1965.

Sharma, Jagdish S., *Indian National Congress: A Descriptive Bibliography of India's Struggle for Freedom.* Delhi: S. Chand, 1959, 816 pp.

————, *Jawaharlal Nehru: A Descriptive Bibliography.* Delhi: S. Chand, 1955, 421 pp.

————, *Mahatma Gandhi: A Descriptive Bibliography.* Delhi: S. Chand, 1955, 565 pp.

————, *Vinoba and Bhoodan, A Selective Descriptive Bibliography.* New Delhi: Indian National Congress, 1956, 92 pp.

Spencer, Dorothy M., *Indian Fiction in English: An Annotated Bibliography.* Philadelphia: University of Pennsylvania Press, 1960, 98 pp.

Reference and Sources

All-India Reporter.
  The official reports of high court and Supreme Court cases.

Asian Almanac.
  Weekly abstract of Asian affairs. (Singapore)

Asian Recorder.
  A very useful archive of public events based on a collation and reproduction of the English press in Asia. Published in India, its coverage of India is extensive and detailed. The index is well done.

Census of India.
  1891, 1901, 1911, 1921, 1931, 1941, 1951, 1961.

India, A Reference Annual. New Delhi: Ministry of Information and Broadcasting.
  Convenient summaries of all aspects of government. For research purposes see the bibliographies of each chapter collected at the end of each annual volume. They contain an excellent inventory of major government reports.

Indian Annual Register: An Annual Digest of Public Affairs of India. 1919–1947.
  The major source for political events in the inter-war years. A contemporary archive.

Indian Information.
  A fortnightly record of the activities and official announcements of the Government of India. (New Delhi)

Indian News Index.
  Quarterly index of Indian newspapers.

Indian Recorder and Digest.
  Formerly *Indian Affairs Record.* Published by the Diwan Chand Institute of

National Affairs. Gives synoptic chronologies of events on a monthly basis, including national, state, and party affairs. Includes excellent monthly bibliographies. A most useful research tool.

Kessing's Contemporary Archives.
An extremely useful, objective, and detailed record of national and international events, including extensive selections from speeches and public documents. Its Indian coverage, both domestic and international, is quite good. Excellently indexed. Published in Bristol, England.

Lok Sabha and Rajya Sabha. *Debates* and *Reports* of the Estimates and Public Accounts Committees.

Lok Sabha Secretariat. *Abstracts and Index of Reports and Articles.* Quarterly. (New Delhi)

Monthly Commentary on Indian Economic Conditions.
Published by the Indian Institute of Public Opinion. (New Delhi)

National Diary.
A biweekly record of Indian events, with an index.

Parliamentary Studies.
Published by the Indian Bureau of Parliamentary Studies. (New Delhi)

Public Opinion Survey.
Indian Institute of Public Opinion organ, published monthly.

Quarterly Economic Report.
Published by the Indian Institute of Public Opinion. (New Delhi)

Times of India Directory and Yearbook, Including Who's Who.
Very useful. Published annually since 1914.

Scholarly Journals

The journals listed below regularly publish articles on India.

Asian Economic Review.
Quarterly journal of the Indian Institute of Economics. (Hyderabad, Andhra Pradesh)

Asian Survey.
Successor to *Far Eastern Survey* of the Institute of Pacific Relations. Includes shorter pieces and work by younger scholars. Particularly good on recent developments.

Conspectus.
Quarterly journal of the India International Center. (New Delhi)

Eastern Anthropologist.
A scholarly journal of high standards that often contains articles of first-rate interest and importance. (Lucknow)

Economic Development and Cultural Change.
Published at the University of Chicago, it reflects the concerns for economic development, "new nations," and South Asia prevalent there. Stimulating.

Enquiry: Forum of Research and Discussion.
Lively—shows intellectual life of Delhi University. (Delhi)

India Quarterly.
Published by the Indian Council of World Affairs, it is the best Indian journal in the field of international politics.

Indian Economic and Social History Review.
Published by the Delhi School of Economics, the journal is one of the best in India and regularly carries contributions from Western scholars.

Indian Economic Journal.
Published by the University of Bombay.

Indian Economic Review.
The biannual journal of the Delhi School of Economics.

Indian Historical Quarterly.
(Calcutta)

Indian Journal of Political Science.
Journal of the Indian Political Science Association.

Indian Journal of Public Administration.
Published by the Indian Institute of Public Administration in New Delhi, the journal maintains good standards and carries articles on a broad variety of topics on public policy.

Indian Journal of Social Research; An International Journal.
Published three times a year. (Meerut)

Indian Journal of Social Work.
"A quarterly devoted to the promotion of professional social work, scientific interpretation of social problems and advancement of social research." (Bombay)

Indian Political Science Review.
Quarterly, published by Delhi University.

Indian Press: Quarterly Journal of the Indian and Eastern Newspaper Society.

Indian Sociological Bulletin.

Indian Studies: Past and Present.

International Studies.
Quarterly publication of the Indian School of International Studies. Good standard journal. Extensive bibliographies in the manner of *Foreign Affairs.* (New Delhi)

Journal of African and Asian Studies.
New Indian quarterly.

Journal of Asian Studies.
Formerly the *Far Eastern Quarterly.* Sound and scholarly. Its book review section is excellent and its annual bibliographic number very useful.

Journal of Commonwealth Political Studies.
Published by the Institute of Commonwealth Studies. (London)

Journal of Constitutional and Parliamentary Studies.

Journal of the Indian Anthropological Society.

Journal of Indian History.
    Published three times a year by the University of Kerala. (Trivandrum)

Journal of the Maharaja Sayajirao University of Baroda.
    A social-science journal.

Man in India; A Quarterly Record of Anthropological Science with Special Reference to India.

Modern Asian Studies.
    Quarterly, published by Cambridge University.

Modern Review.
    Monthly. (Calcutta)

Pacific Affairs.
    An "established" but lively scholarly journal.

Parliamentary Studies.
    Published by the Indian Bureau of Parliamentary Studies.

Political Science Review.
    Biannual journal of the Department of Political Science, Jaipur.

Public Opinion Surveys of the Indian Institute of Public Opinion.
    The most important source of survey data on India. Monthly.

Quarterly Journal of Indian Studies in Social Sciences.

South Asian Studies.
    Published by the Department of Political Science, University of Rajasthan. (Jaipur)

Journals of News and Opinion

Avard Newsletter.
    Published six times a year. Jayaprakash Narayan's journal.

Bharat Sevak.
    Monthly organ of the Bharat Sevak Samaj.

Blitz.
    Sensational and exposé oriented, with a strong leftist (pro-Moscow) perspective.

Broadway Times.
    Sensational; pro-Congress Government. News weekly. (Madras)

Capital.
    By its own admission, India's leading financial newspaper devoted to the development of industry and commerce. Weekly.

Citizen.
    Edited by Pran Chopra, one of India's most astute journalists, it covers news events with depth and offers signed articles expressing divergent views. Biweekly. (New Delhi)

Congress Forums.
    Journal of the Congress Forum for Socialist Action.

Current.
Exposé oriented; conservative. Weekly. (Bombay)

Eastern Economist.
Another Birla enterprise, it is not unaware of an English journal of the same name. Its political and economic commentary, reporting, and criticism are quite good and its statistical data most useful.

Economic and Political Weekly.
Probably India's premier journal of analysis and opinion. Indispensable for contemporary politics and economics.

Flame Newsweekly.
Sensational; conservative. (New Delhi)

Forum.
Monthly. (Bombay)

Frontier.
A well-edited weekly magazine reflecting a quasi-Maoist position somewhere to the left of the C.P.I.(M). (Calcutta)

Gandhi Marg; A Quarterly Journal of Gandhian Thought.
(New Delhi)

Himmat.
Weekly voice of Moral Rearmament.

Hindu.
Daily. (Madras)

Hindu Weekly Review.
Published by one of India's oldest and most staid newspapers, the *Hindu*, a national English daily of independent but conservative opinions. Its editorials are thoughtful, informed, and well-researched, its news coverage extensive, and its feature stories probing and comprehensive. (Publication was discontinued following a strike in 1969.)

Hindustan Times.
Daily. (Delhi)

India Weekly: Journal of Politics, Commerce and Industry.
Moderate; independent. (New Delhi)

Indian and Foreign Review.
An independent government publication. Semimonthly. (New Delhi)

Indian Libertarian; An Independent Journal of Public Affairs.
Conservative toward Goldwaterism. (Bombay)

Indian Worker.
Journal of the Indian National Trade Union Congress (I.N.T.U.C.), affiliated with the Congress party. Weekly.

Kashmir Affairs.
A bimonthly study of trends and events in Jammu and Kashmir. Galraj Puri, its editor, is very able and perceptive.

Link.
Published in Delhi since 1959, *Link* models itself on *Time* but presents the "news" with a left rather than right bias. It publishes "inside dope" and digs

out stories not otherwise available but should always be checked out against more staid sources. Particularly valuable for its treatment of politics in the states.

Mainstream.
Leftist. Relatively good quality. (New Delhi)

March of the Nation.
Exposé oriented from conservative perspective. Like *Current,* an answer to *Blitz.* (Bombay)

Now.
Weekly journal of opinion.

Overseas Hindustan Times.
Published weekly by the *Hindustan Times,* a North Indian English daily owned by the Birlas but managed on a quite independent basis. Its strong feature is coverage of state politics.

Quest.
Started in 1955, it essays to be an Indian version of *Encounter* and is backed by the same organization, the Congress for Cultural Freedom. Some of the best Indian thought and criticism can be found in it.

Radical Humanist.
Weekly, founded by M. N. Roy. (Calcutta)

Sarvodaya.
(Thanjavur, Tamilnadu)

Seminar.
A monthly edited by Romesh Thapar, a regular contributor to *Economic and Political Weekly,* where his views can be sampled. *Seminar* examines one topic per issue. It tries to get a good range of opinion on it and includes most useful bibliographies on each occasion.

Shankar's Weekly.
India's established political *Punch.*

Siraat, The Fortnightly of Indian Minorities.
A journal of Muslim opinion.

Statesman (daily).
(Calcutta)

Statesman (weekly).
Published by the Bengal and North Indian English daily of the same name; an old-timer in the Indian journalistic world. Its editorials are thoughtful and elegant.

Thought.
An informed journal of independent but conservative opinion. Covers literature as well as politics.

Times of India.
Daily. (New Delhi)

Party Periodicals

(A.I.C.C.) Economic Review.
Published by the All-India Congress Committee of the Indian National Con-

gress, it provides a lively and useful forum for the discussion of policy issues even though a party publication.

Call.
Published on behalf of the Central Committee of the Revolutionary Socialist party. (Delhi)

Congress Bulletin.
Issued by the Indian National Congress.

Janata.
Weekly journal of the Praja Socialist party.

Liberation.
The official publication of the Naxalite C.P.I.(M.-L.) Monthly. (Calcutta)

New Age (weekly).
Journal of the Communist Party of India. Primarily news.

New Age (monthly).
Political monthly of the Communist Party of India. Longer, more analytic, and more theoretical articles than in the weekly *New Age.*

Organiser.
Weekly journal of the Jana Sangh. Tries to include a broad range of conservative opinion.

People's Democracy.
The official publication of the C.P.I.(M). Weekly. (Calcutta)

Socialist Congressmen; A Journal of Congress Socialist Opinion.
Semimonthly. (New Delhi)

Swarajya.
The unofficial weekly journal of the Swatantra party. (Madras)

Swatantra Newsletter.
Official monthly of the party.

INDEX